The Caribbean Front in World War II: the Untold Story of U-boats, Spies, and Economic Warfare

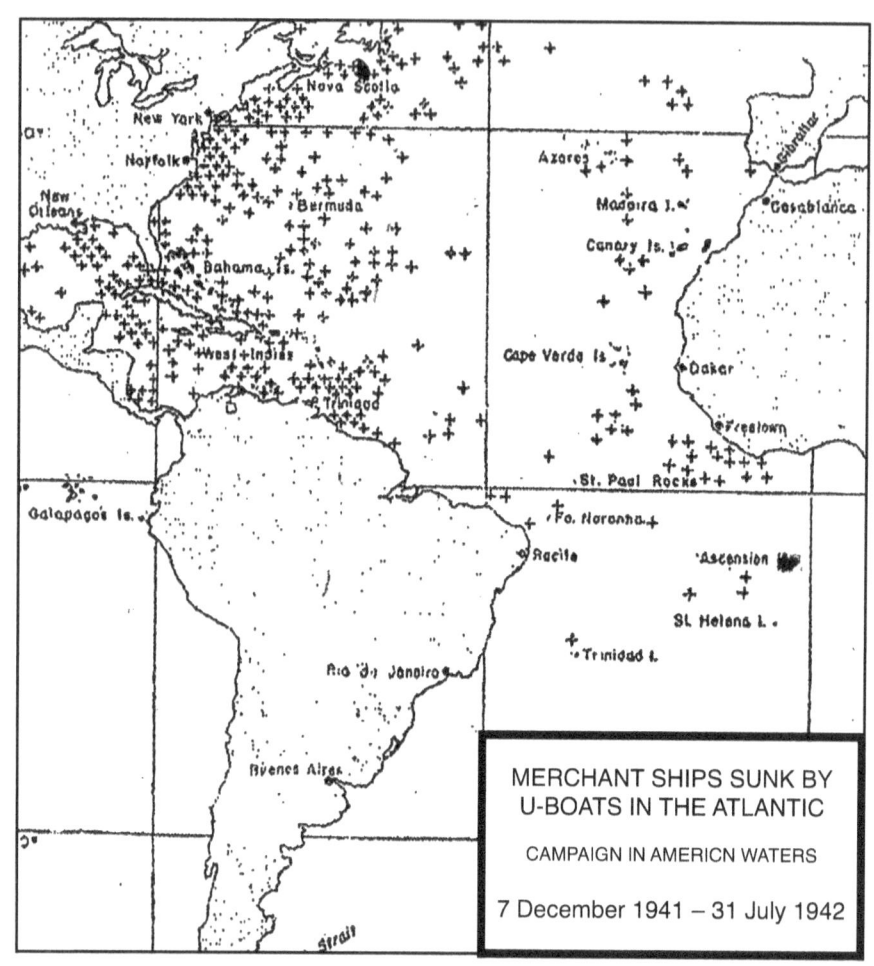

Source: Samuel Eliot Morrison, *History of the United States Naval Operations in World War II*. Volume I. The Battle of the Atlantic 1939-1945.

The Caribbean Front in World War II

THE UNTOLD STORY OF U-BOATS, SPIES, AND ECONOMIC WARFARE

José L. Bolívar Fresneda

Markus Wiener Publishers
Princeton

Page i photo: German U-boat U-442 in front of burning tanker from convoy TM in January 1943 that lost 8 of 9 tankers. Convoy was traveling from Aruba to North Africa. Catalog #: NH 111257 Copyright Owner: Naval History and Heritage Command. Original Creator: Photo taken from U-575 by Kptlt. Heydemann. Original Medium: BW Photo. https://www.history.navy.mil/content/history/nhhc/ our-collections/photography/numerical-list-of-images/nhhc-series/nh-series/NH-111000/NH-111257.html. Retrieved October 4, 2020.

Copyright © 2021 by José L. Bolívar

All rights reserved. No part of this book may be reproduced or transmitted in any form or by any means, whether electronic or mechanical—including photocopying or recording—or through any information storage or retrieval system, without permission of the copyright owners.

For information write to:
Markus Wiener Publishers
231 Nassau Street, Princeton, NJ 08542
www.markuswiener.com

Library of Congress Cataloging-in-Publication Data

Names: Bolívar, José L., author.
Title: The Caribbean Front in World War II: The Untold Story of U-boats,
   Spies, and Economic Warfare / by José L. Bolívar.
Other titles: Untold story of U-boats, Spies, and Economic Warfare
Description: Princeton: Markus Wiener Publishers, 2021
   Includes bibliographical references and index.
Identifiers: LCCN 2020033201 | ISBN 9781558769557 (paperback)
   ISBN 97sSubjects: LCSH: World War, 1939-1945—Caribbean Area. |
   World War, 1939-1945—Economic aspects—Caribbean Area. |
   World War, 1939-1945—Martinique. | World War, 1939-1945—Campaigns
   —Atlantic Ocean. | World War, 1939-1945—Naval operations—Submarine. |
   Caribbean Area—Foreign relations.
Classification: LCC D768.18 .B65 2021 | DDC 940.53/729—dc23
LC record available at https://lccn.loc.gov/2020033201

*I dedicate this book to my uncle and cousin
who served with distinction in the United States Navy.*

Lt. Robert Fresneda (1959–1962)
Officer of the deck. Diving officer.
USS Escape, diver-class rescue salvage ship.
Commissioned in 1942.
Guantánamo Naval Base, Cuba; Isla Grande Naval Base, San Juan

Lt. Patrick Fresneda (1988–1996)
Reactor Controls Assistant. Communications Assistant.
USS Tennessee, nuclear submarine
Kings Bay, Ga.

Officers and crew of the *USS Escape* at Guantánamo Naval Base, Cuba, 1959. Lt. Robert Fresneda is in the front row, fifth from right. (Private archive of the Fresneda family)

USS Escape entering San Juan Bay. The lookout tower of El Morro can be observed on the left-hand side. Circa 1950. (Personal archive of the Fresneda family)

TABLE OF CONTENTS

List of Tables ix
Acknowledgments x

Introduction 1

Chapter I
Preparedness and a Surprise Attack 5

Chapter II
Lopsided Affair (February–June 1942) 37

Chapter III
Beginning of the End (July 1942–July 1944) 79

Chapter IV
Gibraltar of the Caribbean 121

Chapter V
War Economy 145

Chapter VI
The Silent war with Britain, the United States
and Martinique 167

Epilogue 227
Notes 233
Bibliography 259
Index 269
About the Author 273

Map of the Caribbean. Digital ID: http://hdl.loc.gov/loc.gmd/g4390.ct001544. Washington, D.C.: Central Intelligence Agency, 1990. Medium: 1 map: col.; 19 x 17 cm. Call Number/Physical Location G4390 1990. U5 Repository Library of Congress Geography and Map Division Washington, D.C. 20540-4650 USA dcu. Library of Congress Control Number: 2005631604. Language: English. Online format: Image. Description: Shows West Indies, eastern Central America, northern South America, and southern Florida. "801553 (544517) 8-90." Available also through the Library of Congress Web site as a raster image. LCCN Permalink: https://lccn.loc.gov/2005631604. Additional Metadata Formats: MARCXML Record.

LIST OF TABLES

Table 1
Shipping losses in the Caribbean, 1942 38

Table 2
U-boats sunk in the Caribbean 120

Table 3
U.S. military expropriations in Puerto Rico, 1939–43 138–9

Table 4
Origins of rum consumed in the United States, 1937–47 160

Table 5
Government of Puerto Rico revenues from rum, 1941–47 161

Aerial view of the Caribe Hilton Hotel with the Normandie Hotel in the background. The Normandie was the first luxury hotel in Puerto Rico and the residence of the French Vichy Admiral Georges Robert and his entourage as guests of the US Navy in 1943 (see pages 223-225). Note the 18th-century Spanish fortification in front of the Caribe Hilton. It was instrumental in the defense of Puerto Rico during the English invasion of 1797. Circa 1950. (Collection Swartgendruber, Archivo Histórico Fundación Luis Muñoz Marín)

ACKNOWLEDGMENTS

The Caribe Hilton Hotel is one of the iconic tourism attractions of Puerto Rico. Its history, architecture and location make it one of the most popular hotels on the island. One of its frequent visitors is Markus Wiener. During each visit, Markus makes it a point to call on the many friends he has made over the years on this beautiful island.

In one such visit, Markus and I sat in the hotel lounge which overlooked the old historic Normandie Hotel, now abandoned, and talked about possible future projects. It was here that the idea of writing a book about submarine warfare in the Caribbean originated.

Once the COVID-19 pandemic reached the shores of Puerto Rico in mid-March 2020, the Governor dictated a *de facto* economic closure and curfew (a "toque de queda" in Puerto Rican lingo) whereby every citizen, with few exceptions, had to be home by 7:00 P.M. This shutdown offered historians like me a once-in-a lifetime-opportunity to research and write with little or no distractions.

I would, therefore, like to thank Markus Wiener for the opportunity to publish this manuscript. During this time, my friend César J. Ayala, professor at UCLA, offered his council and shared with me his valuable and insightful archive. César and I had previously worked on a book titled *Battleship Vieques*, also published by Markus Weiner, and a good companion reference for this book. Jorge Rodríguez Beruff, a friend, mentor, former Dean of General Studies at the University of Puerto Rico, and co-author of a number of publications instrumental in researching this book is also one who I owe deep gratitude.

A book is never complete without the careful eye of an editor. I was truly fortunate that Craig Leisher accepted this challenge.

He worked his magic on my manuscript, made major cuts to sections that were probably repetitive, and highlighted sections that were not. Cheryl Mirkin, the graphic artist, transformed the readers' experience by adding an artistic element to this book.

Finally, I would like to acknowledge and thank the unconditional support of my family. To my parents, José A. Bolívar Pérez and Sally Marie Fresneda Reilly, I owe my love of history and the pursuit of knowledge. From my son Alejandro José Bolívar Cervoni and my daughter Carolina Sofia Bolívar Cervoni, I learned that life is filled with unexpected turns, yet each has its own special fascination that one must treasure. To my loving wife, María de Lourdes Cervoni Ruiz, who is no longer able to cherish these moments or communicate her joy, I thank her for the years we shared together.

INTRODUCTION

The terrible toll that the German U-boats inflicted on the Caribbean has not been as thoroughly analyzed and documented as other theaters of the Second World War. Yet it was in the Caribbean where, from January 1942 to July 1943, 20 percent of all the allied shipping was sunk as a result of the one-sided naval battles that occurred there.[1] Why would the Germans be interested in the Caribbean when they were already fighting a two-front war that drained so much of their resources? What strategy did they employ that made them so successful? What impact did the enormous sinking of freighters, tankers, and merchant ships that were critical items to these islands' economies have on their inhabitants? What changes to their social and economic structures were brought about as a result of the war? How did the war impact the colonial status of many of these islands?

In the 1940s, most of the oil production required to sustain the East Coast of the United States came via the Caribbean. The islands of Aruba and Curaçao each had one of the largest oil refineries in the world, and their geographical closeness to Venezuelan oil production provided the ideal situation for reducing transportation costs and ensuring adequate supplies. Bauxite, a critical ore used in the manufacture of aluminum for airplanes and other war-related products, was mined in British Guiana and Surinam and transported through the Caribbean to the southern ports of the United States.

On December 11, 1941, Germany and Italy declared war on the United States. By January 1942, U-boats were sinking ships off the East Coast of the United States. Then they expanded to the Caribbean. The exact number of ships sunk in the Caribbean is still in dispute. According to historians David J. Bercuson and Holger H.

Herwig, 397 ships were sunk between January 1942 and July 1943.[2] Stetson Conn, Rose C. Engelman, and Byron Fairchild's number is a little lower at 371 until December 1943[3], but it is still a lot of ships and lives that were lost.

The Army's unpreparedness for the submarine assault — particularly during the fateful year of 1942 — was not entirely due to a shortage of the long-range bombers required to seek out and destroy the U-boats, though this was certainly a factor. Part of the blame lay with "the reluctance of air officers to employ their bombers in this fashion."[4] The Navy was also to blame as it was reluctant to employ escorts to convoys as Britain had done rather successfully since the beginning of the war. Once the United States started employing convoys between the mainland and the Caribbean, the number of ships sunk decreased dramatically.

To protect the flow of oil and bauxite and the Panama Canal, the United States invested billions of dollars building bases, landing strips, roads, and the infrastructures required to support a military contingent in the Caribbean. Guantanamo, acquired in 1903 after Cuba's independence from Spain, was expanded. In Puerto Rico, the U.S. Navy built a naval base in San Juan and a larger one in Ceiba. A submarine base was expanded in St. Thomas, U.S. Virgin Islands. With the Destroyers-for-Bases Agreement, the United States acquired a 99-year lease on all the British bases located in the Caribbean. Local inhabitants were not included in these negotiations which resulted in heated clashes with the American military. In addition, the application of the segregationist policies of the United States military on the islands' inhabitants, many of whom were non-white, brought additional tensions to the surface.

The submarine blockage in 1942 caused a shortage of food in the Caribbean, and it was in the French colony of Martinique where the food shortages were most acute. After the fall of France in June 1940, a Vichy-controlled government was installed in the Caribbean colonies of France: Martinique, Guadeloupe and French Guiana. The 1940 Armistice gave Germany firm control of France, but the French fleet and the French colonies were beyond Germany's grasp.

A significant portion of the French Navy, along with $384 million in gold bullion, a sizeable contingent of marines, and a Vichy governor were inside the Monroe Doctrine boundaries. For Hitler, it was important that the French fleet be immobilized and not fall into British hands; for the British, it was the opposite: that the fleet not be seized by the Germans. The Americans went so far as saying that should the French surrender the fleet, it would permanently lose their friendship and goodwill.

On Martinique, the French governor Admiral Georges Robert had at his disposal 106 new airplanes, battleships, destroyers, tankers, submarines and marines — a formidable force. Between 1940 and the end of 1942, the United States permitted the importation of food and other critical items to Martinique in exchange for keeping the French Navy ships and men immobilized. This gentlemen's agreement lasted until 1943, when tired of it, the United States tightened the screws and Vichy Admiral Robert was forced to flee.

It has been many years since World War II and the U-boat campaign ended. Yet few studies have been published on submarine warfare in the Caribbean. This was partly due to U.S. censorship during the war. Another reason was that battles in the Atlantic, Pacific, Africa, and the Soviet Union more visible, as ships, airplanes, tanks, and other military equipment were more easily recognizable than a quickly vanishing oil spill from a sunken submarine.

In recent years, Jorge Rodríguez Beruff, a renowned historian and former Dean of General Studies at the University of Puerto Rico, and myself have published two edited volumes in Spanish on the effect the Second World War had on Puerto Rico and the Caribbean. *Puerto Rico en la Segunda Guerra Mundial: Baluarte del Caribe*, published in 2012, is a compendium of 19 articles written by historians detailing how the war impacted Puerto Rico. *Puerto Rico en la Segunda Guerra Mundial: El Escenario Regional*, published in 2015, adds 19 articles of which 5 cover the English colonies, Cuba, Haiti, the Dominican Republic, and Martinique. In 2015, we also published *Island at War: Puerto Rico in the Crucible of the Second World War*, a collection of 10 articles, written in English, which covers Puerto Rico's role in the war. However, yet to be published is an English version of the submarine warfare in the Caribbean that details both the history of the attacker (the U-boats) and the defenders. Most books, such as *The Long Night of the Tankers*, focus on the German point of view and the military aspects of the conflict. This applies to the book *The U-Boat War in the Caribbean* as well. We hope that this publication bridges this gap. The history of the misery that the U-boat blockage imposed on the islands of the Caribbean is too little known. Here we concentrate on a few significant battles at sea and the effect the war had in the Caribbean, with specific emphasis on Puerto Rico and Martinique. Puerto Rico was known as the Gibraltar of the Caribbean due to the enormity of the military investments, and Martinique's Vichy-controlled government was a potentially hostile power within the Caribbean that had a substantial military force at its disposal.

CHAPTER I

Preparedness and a Surprise Attack

On May 14, 1942, Rexford G. Tugwell, Governor of Puerto Rico, had left Puerto Rico for a meeting of the Naval Air Transport in Guantanamo, Cuba. On his return flight, he boarded an amphibious Grumman Goose aircraft. Tugwell was seated in the copilot's seat and was not expecting an encounter with a German U-boat. As recounted in his memories:

> Almost a once the sea began to show the wreckage that, the pilot told me, was all that remained of a general cargo ship which had been torpedoed the day before. And soon we saw another litter of debris on the glittering surface below. We had just finished shouting to each other about its extent — the ship must have been blown open to have spewed out so much of her freight — when I saw something dead ahead cutting the sea. It looked just for an instant like a long rowboat traveling fast enough to make a wake. Then it came to me stunningly that I was staring at a conning tower. I jerked at the pilot's arm and pointed. He swore, reached for the overhead throttle with his right hand, and pushed hard on his wheel with the left. Instantly we were slanting down toward the submarine at a pace the JRF [Grumman Goose] were not supposed to be built for but evidently were.

A view from the copilot's seat permitted Governor Rexford G. Tugwell to spot a similarly surfaced U-boat in the Caribbean. This photo shows German submarine U-36. Deutsche U Boot Museum, Cuxhaven.

It was all very swift, like the taking of a photograph. The men in the conning tower saw us at the same instance that we saw them, and almost by the time we had aimed our nose at them their nose aimed at the ocean floor. There was a brisk breeze which wrinkled the sea and her disappearance was so complete that once she had gone under there was no sign of her existence, I could have believed that I had imagined it all…if the experienced pilot had not seen it too. We saw nothing more, and when we got to the spot where it had disappeared, we had no depth bombs to drop, this not being even a patrol plane.[1]

The naval and air forces of the Empire of Japan attacked the U.S. naval base at Pearl Harbor on December 7, 1941, and a few days later, on December 11, Germany and Italy declared war on the United States. War came soon to the American shores. Five Type

IX U-boats working under the code name Operation Paukenschlag (Drumbeat) attacked the shipping lanes of the East Coast of the United States during January and February 1942. They sank 25 ships totaling 156,939 tons.[2] On January 15, 1942, five experienced U-boat captains met with German Admiral Karl Doenitz to plan similar attacks in the Caribbean area. This would result in the initial stages of Operation Neuland (New Land), a naval strategy that paralleled Operation Drumbeat. What made the attacks in the Caribbean indispensable for the success of the German war effort? It was vital to curtail the significant flow of oil and bauxite which the United States and Great Britain imported from the Caribbean.[3]

In 1942, roughly 95 percent of the oil required to sustain the East Coast of the United States — 59 million gallons per day — came from the Caribbean. "No pipelines connected the oil-producing regions of Texas, Louisiana, and Oklahoma with the United States East Coast as far west as the Appalachian Mountains. Thus, all of New York, New Jersey, New England, and most of Pennsylvania and Virginia were supplied by tankers"[4] with oil originating in Venezuela. Caribbean oil was therefore a vital commodity for the war effort, and from information Admiral Doenitz gathered from the Hamburg-Amerika Line captains, it was also very vulnerable.[5]

Between the start of U-boat operations in January 1942 and their eventual collapse in July 1943, U-boats sunk 397 ships and more than 2 million tons in the Caribbean.[6] According to an article in the *Washington Post* on July 5, 1943, "it is a great pity that the public has been kept so completely in the dark"[7] regarding the U-boat warfare and the successes that the Allies were having in hunting them.

> The public knows enough about the warfare, for instance, to have a fair general picture of what it means to fight Germany with bombing planes. The public learned about the North African campaigns [Operation Torch] through admirable work by corres-

pondents as well as through official releases. The story of Guadalcanal has been published. So has the Pacific naval warfare. Everyone is aware that "security" has prevented the release of all the details of these actions. Methods and weapons have never been described. But at least the public has learned the things presumably known to the enemy.

By contrast, submarine warfare has from the beginning been treated with a hush-hush that has made its defeat and its victories seem illogical and inexplicable to the citizen in the street. How is it possible that things were going so badly in January and so well in April? Why the official gloom at one time, followed so soon by the official glow of success?

We have, of course, been told about the destroyer-escort vessels, about aircraft-carriers converted from merchant ships, about very long-range aircraft on mid-Atlantic patrol. We've heard about radar and sound detection, about the antisubmarine organization that covers the whole Atlantic, directed from control centers ashore. We know that apart from all organizations, the war against the U-boat has been fighting men at sea.

Now that the Atlantic campaign is going well, it would be good to tie all these things together enough to let John Citizen know just how big a fight how his Navy has been in — and how it was won.[8]

Sabotage, disinformation, and war preparations

When the Second World War began on the first of September 1939, the United States was officially neutral. The outbreak of the European war had placed three principal burdens on the American Government. First, neutrality had to be maintained and respected in order to keep the country out of the war. Second, the manpower of the armed forces had to be increased and the infrastructure updated. Third, the American economy must be protected from the shocks emanating from an upset world economy.[9] Since the sinking of the

Lusitania on May 7, 1915, a catalyst that catapulted the United States into World War I, there was concern among government officials that history might repeat itself. As a result, they ordered all American ships to navigate with their lights turned on and to paint the American flag on both sides of the vessel and the decks. The ships would not be armed or have the protection of traveling in convoys. Sabotage and espionage became an "immediate government concern."[10]

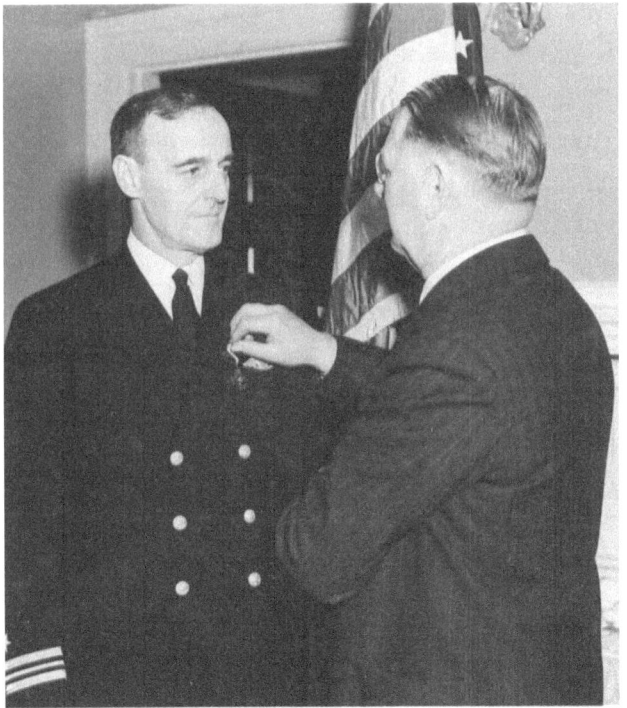

Presentation of the Navy Cross to Lieutenant Commander Joseph A. Gainard by the Secretary of the Navy William F. Knox for his outstanding service while serving about the steamer *City of Flint* when it was seized by the Germans. Circa December 1940. Catalogue #: NH 114220. Naval History and Heritage Command. BW Photo. https://www.history.navy.mil/content/history/nhhc/our-collections/photography/numerical-list-of-images/nhhc-series/nh-series/NH-114000/NH-114220.html. Retrieved October 4, 2020.

Yet despite American neutrality, in October 1939, the Germans captured the *City of Flint*, an American freighter en route to Southampton, and rerouted it to Murmansk, a port city on the far northwest part of Russia. "Undoubtedly it was carrying a certain amount of contraband, although it had no munitions of war."[11] Russia released the ship to Germany though it took some time to confirm that the crew was unharmed. This incident occurred despite the ship having the American flag painted on its side with the American flag flying. The Germans then took possession of the *City of Flint* which made its way to Norway thereupon the Norwegian Government took the German crew off the ship and interned them, over the bitter protests of the German Government. On November 7, the restored American crew and the ship made their way to Glasgow.[12] The United States, despite its official neutrality stance, was finding it harder to ignore the war.

The threat of espionage and hidden supply venues for the U-boats became a major concern for both the United States and Great Britain. On October 3, 1939, it was reported that the Dominican Coast Guard Cutter No. 3 was sunk "presumably" as a result of an "accidental collision" with a French cruiser whose identity was not revealed. Manuel Alsina, Cutter No. 3's captain, and his crew of five were killed in this incident, which occurred off the northeast extremity of Samana Peninsula in the Dominican Republic. At the time, two cruisers — also not identified — from the French West Indies base in Martinique were scouring Dominican waters "following repeated reports that German submarines were supplied clandestinely by small, fast craft similar to the sunken cutter."[13] The United States believed that British and French authorities had been advised that secret rendezvous had been going on between the Dominican Coast Guard cutters and unidentified German submarines. The cutters were presumably obtaining supplies from a small

Dominican freighter, the *San Rafael*, formerly the Grace Line freighter *Mayan*.

According to "private sources," the Dominican Coast Guard Cutter No. 3 "was caught in the act of refueling German submarines off the Dominican Republic by the French cruiser patrolling those waters on September 22. In firing at the submarine, the cruiser "accidentally" sank the Coast Guard Cutter. These unofficial reports claim that there were land bases set up in the Dominican Republic to repair German submarines in addition to refueling them at sea. It was suspected that some of the "larger boats belonging to the Dominican Government were being used as 'mother ships' for meeting submarines on the high seas."[14]

More than a week before the invasion of Poland on September 1, the *New York Times* had reported "that four large German submarines were on their way to the Caribbean" in a daring venture to seize the French island of Martinique in order to secure a base so that the German submarines could raid the North Atlantic commercial routes with ease. The French and British were aware of this plan and had for some time strengthened both the land and naval defenses of the island.[15]

Rafael Trujillo, the despotic dictator of the Dominican Republic, had for some time flirted with the Axis Powers. In 1938, he permitted the German battleship *SMS Schlesien* and its escort oil tanker to visit Samana Bay. The United States responded by sending the destroyer *USS Mugford*, which steamed from the naval base at Guantanamo Bay. Despite what might have seemed to be a tense situation, Dominican officials defused it by treating both American and German officers to dinner at the City Clubhouse. The next day, the German captain responded by inviting the Americans and the British and German councils to lunch aboard the *Schlesien*. However, these were not the only overtures Trujillo made to the Germans.

In 1936, he invited the German Horn Line steamship company to initiate regular service from Germany to Santo Domingo, with stops in San Juan and Jamaica. Two years later he allowed the establishment of the Dominican-German Scientific Institute with a staff of German scientists. The Americans suspected that its real purpose was to set up a Nazi colony. In the meantime, he placed his daughter Flor de Oro and her husband Porfirio Rubirosa, a protégé of Trujillo, in the newly inaugurated Dominican Ministry in Berlin.

Trujillo, however, also courted the United States. After the visit of the *USS Texas* in February 1939, he professed his readiness for military cooperation with the United States. He voiced to the members of the House of Representatives visiting the island that the harbor and other facilities in the Dominican Republic would be at the disposal of the United States. He furthermore stated to the American press his desire to build air and naval bases in the Dominican Republic that could be leased to the U.S. Armed Forces. Trujillo was, therefore, waffling between his support for the Axis powers and the United States, either of which would come with a steep price tag.[16]

On October 4, the day after the incident with the Dominican cutter was reported in the press, President Roosevelt "issued a stern warning against smuggling aid to U-boats."[17] Asked about reports that rum-runners and "unscrupulous skippers of freights" were ferrying oil, food and drinking water to German submarines off the Dominican coast, the President answered "that if anybody was doing that sort of thing, they'd better not."[18] The following month Trujillo signed a treaty with the United States in which he agreed to permit the U.S. Navy to patrol within the territorial waters of the Dominican Republic.[19]

Prior to Roosevelt's arm twisting, Trujillo had the British worried. In London, Rear Admiral Murray Sueter asked the government what action it was taking to prevent rumrunners from supplying German submarines with fuel oil and water. More to the point, Sueter asked "if mother ships are being used by the Dominican Government to refuel German submarines operating in the Caribbean Sea" to which Geoffrey Shakespeare, Parliamentary Secretary to the Admiralty, replied that he was satisfied that the Dominican Government was fulfilling its duties, thereby dismissing any suggestion of wrongdoing by the Dominican Government. When asked by the press if German submarines were operating off the American Atlantic coast, Shakespeare refused to answer. In the meantime, the British were detaining American cargo ships bound for Germany as dictated by the British Contraband Control Service.[20]

On October 14, the French Legation at Santo Domingo "issued a denial that a French destroyer had encountered or sunk any unit of the Dominican Government."[21] Government officials in London, Washington, and Paris were convinced that Nazi submarines were in fact operating in the Caribbean and being supplied from the Dominican Republic. Clearly, despite Rafael Trujillo's denial, he was not believed.[22] However, the Dominican Republic was not the only nation suspected of aiding German submarines.

A few days before the start of hostilities in Europe, the United States had put a squadron of its warships to sea under strict orders "to observe and keep surveillance of any belligerent submarine, surface vessel or aircraft" that might pose a threat to it. It was not to engage any German vessel they might encounter. The main concern of both neutral United States and the warring parties was the 82 German ships in American waters and 34 anchored in Caribbean ports when war was declared on September 1, 1939. Rumors had been spreading in the news media that the Germans planned to attack Allied shipping with U-boats supplied from dummy freighters. "The presence of so many tankers and freighters lent credence to these rumors, even more so after a number of them began behaving rather suspiciously."[23] Roosevelt instructed the Navy to be vigilant on the movements of these ships but only as observers. He was especially concerned that the United States would be dragged into the war as Britain might attempt to seize these ships inside U.S. territorial waters, thereby violating its sovereignty and inciting others to do the same.[24] As described later, the U-boats were actually supplied with fuel and provisions from German submarines specially designed for this purpose and not for combat. The rumors that the German ships would be used to supply the U-boats turned out to be just that, rumors.

There were also concerns among the American military personnel that the U-boats might be operating off the coast of Mexico. According to these sources, though all attempts to authenticate the presence of German submarines in Mexican waters had failed, there was sufficient circumstantial evidence that one or more submarines were "ready to begin operations against shipping in the Caribbean as soon as the appropriate instructions were received from Berlin."[25] As a result, the Mexican Government had been closely monitoring all port activities, particularly the 82,000-ton German liner *Columbus*[26] as well as other German ships and nations "sympathetic with her" waiting for supplies in Mexican ports.

In the case of the *Columbus*, the largest German ship in Mexican waters, it had been observed that she left the anchorage protection of the port of Veracruz for the bay of Anton Lizardo, known as a location for carrying out illegal activities. The ship was riding "low in the water," meaning that she had taken aboard large quantities of stores and oil. Foodstuffs and other stores were being loaded in quantities disproportionate to the need of its crew of 620. Though the ships sending antenna was dismantled, it could still receive "wireless instructions from the German Admiralty."[27] Even more alarming was the fact that the captain confiscated all private radio sets and did not allow journalists to come aboard his ship which might point to the fact that he wished that his crew not read what might be considered subversive or propaganda materials not in line with Germany's vision of events. Also, "money was circulating freely ashore which might indicate bribery and corruption on a fairly extensive scale."[28]

Even more "extraordinary" were unconfirmed reports in the case involving the German tanker *Emmy Friedrich*, anchored in the port of Tampico, Mexico. She was not only loading oil but also live cows and hogs. As these could not be "slaughtered for lack of refrigeration facilities," it was likely that they would be delivered to a German submarine somewhere in the Caribbean.[29] Despite the information contained in this "official" report, it was not possible to positively determine whether German submarines were receiving fuel and supplies in Mexico.[30]

As a result of confidential reports being circulated in Washington regarding U-boat activities in the Caribbean, the United States dispatched a destroyer to Haiti, as "it was rumored that Nazi submarines have entered the port of Tiburon, on the southwest coast of Haiti, and obtained supplies from native merchants."[31] This "supposed violation of Haitian neutrality brought the instant dismissal of the German agent of a gasoline company at Cap-Haïtein," as it was rumored that he had supplied German submarines with fuel. American marines also took up positions at various points along the coast in order to prevent "any contact with German agents in Haiti and those who may be hovering in Nazi U-boats in Haitian waters as this country was suspected of being "dominated by German commercial and financial interest."[32]

British sources on January 26, 1940, claimed that three German U-boats were "prowling" in the vicinity of Port of Spain, Trinidad, where a huge Standard Oil facility that refined Venezuelan oil was located. According to these sources, the submarines were ordered to sink all British and French ships they might encounter, as they were probably carrying grain and oil to England. The threat of German submarines in this area became a major concern to the military planners in Britain. Authorities believed that German ships that recently sailed from South American ports would secretly rendezvous with these submarines in order to resupply them with fuel and foodstuff. Sources added that German residents in Curaçao were aware that U-boats would likely show up soon in order to disrupt Allied shipping. Meanwhile, British warships had been patrolling along the east coast of South America in search of the German ship *Altmark*, the prison vessel that accompanied the German cruiser *Admiral Graf Spee*, scuttled off the coast of Uruguay on December 17, 1939, after battling British naval forces.[33]

War strategies in the Caribbean

George Fielding Eliot, a military intelligence reserve officer who published broadly on military matters, wrote a widely circulated and influential book on military strategies in 1938. In *The Ramparts We Watch: A Study of the Problems of America's National Defense*, he recommended a "hemispheric security" based on a balanced expansion of naval and military forces. He placed a greater emphasis on the Navy's role and sharply criticized the expansion of airpower. Regarding the Caribbean, Eliot argued that the Panama Canal was of vital importance. He stressed the need for naval control over the entire region and the necessity of additional bases. He added that control of the Caribbean was considered essential for the defense of Brazil and that the bases in Panamá, Cuba, Puerto Rico, and the Virgin Islands should be developed and strengthened. Eliot also called for the acquisition of additional bases and mentioned the following as possible sites: Jamaica, Curaçao, Trinidad, Barbados and St. Lucia — all European possessions.[34]

In November 1938, the Joint (Army-Navy) Board instructed the Joint Planning Committee to revise its war plans as President Franklin D. Roosevelt had an inkling that the United States should be better prepared should war come to its shores. The Japanese were creating havoc in Korea and China, and Hitler had already made his desires known regarding his vision of a Greater Germany. Given these circumstances, President Roosevelt traveled to the Caribbean in February 1939 to inspect the Fleet Maneuvers, codenamed Fleet Problem XX, with Admiral William D. Leahy, his friend and Chief of Naval Operation. There he proposed that Leahy take over the governorship of Puerto Rico. As governor, he would oversee the construction of military bases and related infrastructure projects never before seen on the island.[35] In preparation for war, Roosevelt directed a squadron of naval vessels to visit Curaçao and Aruba, home of the Royal Dutch Shell and Standard Oil of New Jersey refineries.[36]

Aruba and Curaçao formed part of the Netherlands Antilles colonies. They were composed of two groups of islands: the Curaçao group and the Leeward group. The Curaçao group includes the islands of Curaçao, Aruba, Bonaire and several smaller adjacent islands while the Leeward section is composed of St. Martin (half Dutch and half French), St. Eustatius, and Saba. Curaçao has a land area of 170 square miles, Aruba of 70 square miles, and Bonaire of 100 square miles. The islands are in the southern part of the Caribbean within view of the Venezuelan coast.[37]

In 1499, the Spaniard Alonso de Ojeda "discovered" the islands of Bonaire, Curaçao, and possibly Aruba, which he found inhabited by the peaceful Arawak Indians. On April 6, 1634, the directors of the Dutch West Indies Company approved a plan of conquest of the island of Curaçao. An expedition led by Johan van Walbeek and Pierre Le Grand, which consisted of 180 sailors and 225 soldiers, conquered Curaçao on July 29, 1634. The 22 Spanish that surrendered were free to leave with the majority of the Indians, around 40, to Spanish Venezuela.[38] The Dutch occupied Aruba in 1636 in order to protect the salt supply they obtained from South America as well as to ensure a naval base in the Caribbean. This proved critical for their navy as they had been fighting Spain for their independence in what is known as the Eighty Years' War (1568-1648). The Dutch victory led to the formation of the United Provinces of the Netherlands (the Dutch Republic).[39] During the Napoleonic War, the British invaded and took control of Aruba, though the Netherlands retook it in 1816. Aruba officially became part of the Netherlands Antilles in 1845.[40]

By early 1939, war loomed both in Europe and the Pacific. The United States, concerned about the defense of the Panama Canal and the entire Caribbean region, started a program of land acquisition and construction of bases in the Panama Canal Zone and throughout the Caribbean. Bases in Cuba, Haiti, and Puerto Rico were either expanded or built from scratch. The Guantanamo naval base in Cuba began with a lease from the Cuban government on July 2, 1903. The annual rent negotiated with the Cuban government was $2,000, and the term of the lease was 99 years. The base consisted of 36,000 acres, of which 13,400 were land and the remainder water and salt flats. The initial development in the bay area consisted of an air station. With the advent of the Second World War, and due to the importance and value of this base, construction activity increased in 1942. By 1944, the base had a ship-repair facility, a fuel and supply depot, an infrastructure capable of sustaining 2,000 military personnel, and two airfields. Extensive dredging was undertaken to deepen certain areas of the bay to permit the mooring of deep-draft vessels.

Naval Operating Base, Guantanamo Bay, Cuba. Post exchange, headquarters and barracks of the U.S. Marine Corps compound. February 1943. Note shipping in distance. Catalog #: 80-G-K-944. Copyright Owner: National Archives. 1939-1945. Color Photograph. https://www.history.navy.mil/content/history/nhhc/search.html?q=Guantanamo&start=105. Retrieved October 4, 2020.

In the Panama Canal Zone, defensive plans were drawn and new installations authorized. Work began for a new supply depot at Balboa in Panamá as well as an enlargement of the two inland radio stations at Gatun and Summit. A new naval operating base was built in Balboa. Construction work included: a bombproof command center, additional housing and warehouses, docks, railways, ammunition depots, and a submarine base. A new 200-bed naval hospital was built on a 40-acre tract of high land. By the end of 1943, the total ship repair facilities available in the Panama Canal Zone were estimated to be equal to those at Pearl Harbor when the Japanese attacked.[41]

Destroyers-for-Bases exchange

In July 1940, Britain lost 11 destroyers over a 10-day period, and replacements were quickly needed. As Great Britain's ability to pay for supplies was nearing its end, Lord Lothian, the British ambassador to the United States, persuaded a reluctant and newly elected British Prime Minister Winston Churchill to lay the financial facts openly before President Roosevelt. Out of this approach came Roosevelt's call for the Destroyers-for-Bases exchange, which was agreed upon on September 2, 1940.[42] This agreement stipulated that the United States would provide Britain with 50 old destroyers. In exchange, Britain would lease to the United States for a period of 99 years bases in the Bahamas, Bermuda, Antigua, Jamaica, Saint Lucia, Trinidad, and British Guiana. The Navy Department received authorization on January 3, 1941 to enter Bermuda, Trinidad and British Guiana; on January 13 to enter Antigua and St. Lucia; and on January 27 to enter Great Exuma in the Bahamas. The Jamaican government authorized entry into Little Goat Island on January 16, 1942. Final lease agreements for all bases were concluded on March 27, 1941.[43] The United States invested over $180 million in modernizing and upgrading these facilities.[44] This resulted in a major controversy in Congress regarding the neutrality of the United States in this "European conflict."

The strategically important island of Trinidad protects the vulnerable approach to the Panama Canal and the South American trade routes. It lies off Venezuela and is approximately 35 miles by 55 miles in size. The site for the United States naval base was in the northwest tip of the island. It was acquired under two separate lease agreements, the first with the British Crown and the second with private owners. On April 22, 1941, the Crown leased 7,940 acres and included the small islands in the Gulf of Paris for an agreed period of 99 years. During December 1942, the Navy acquired the remaining 3,800 acres. Of the four bays and two valleys acquired, Chaguaramas and Tucker became the focus of naval activity.

Construction began in March 1941, though almost from its inception, the scope of the project was enlarged. This reflected the changing world events. Dredging operations began in August 1941 and over a two-and-a-half-year period, 13 million cubic yards of material were removed in order to provide navigable channels to the piers, seaplane base, and fleet anchorage in Carenage Bay. Two million yards of this were placed in swamps to eliminate mosquito breeding areas. The construction projects included a 150-bed hospital, two 250,000-gallon underground gasoline tanks, a supply depot, a radio station, a degaussing range, 57 miles of roads, and ship-repair facilities. Meanwhile, the Army was building two major airfields — Waller Field and Carlsen Field — which were also to be used by the Navy as bases for carrier planes and transport service.

Both the U.S. Army and Navy recognized the strategic value of Bermuda, as it commanded the approach to the Mid-Atlantic coastline. The Bureau of Yards and Docks awarded a fixed-fee contract in February 1941 for the construction of an air station for seaplanes, fuel and supply depots, a submarine base, and an anti-aircraft training school in Bermuda. The base was designed to support a 1,500-plane program which contemplated that Bermuda would be a major naval air station.

A naval air station was built in Jamaica to provide base facilities for two squadrons of seaplanes whose mission was to patrol the approaches to the Caribbean via the Windward Passage. The air station was located on Little Goat Island, on the south side of Jamaica, about 30 miles from the city of Kingston. Little Goat Island with approximately 150 acres was leased from the Crown. A total of 2.8 million cubic yards of dredging was required to make way for the seaplane runway and the channel approaches to the piers. The air station was commissioned on April 4, 1941.

The naval air station on St. Lucia was built by Arundel Corporation. The base was built on a 221-acre site on Gros Islet Bay at the extreme northwest tip of the island. The base was equipped to support a patrol squadron of seaplanes. The building included barracks for 200 men and quarters for 25 officers, a ten-bed dispensary, a power plant and ten 5,000-gallon steel tanks for gasoline storage, three magazines, a cold-storage plant, and two industrial buildings. Rainfall collected on a 60,000 square foot concrete catchment furnished the freshwater supply.

In Antigua, the Navy selected the Crabbs Peninsula and the adjoining waters of Parham Sound, on the northern shore of the island, as the site for a naval air station. The facilities built were an exact duplication of those in St. Lucia. Arundel Corporation was the main contractor. Work started in February 1941.

The naval air station on Great Exuma island in the Bahamas was built to support a squadron of seaplanes used to patrol the southeastern coast of the United States and the numerous passages through the Bahamas leading to the Florida straits and the Caribbean. The base was a compact development on 324 acres on the southeast tip of the island. Construction began during December 1941, and the station was commissioned on May 15, 1942. The principal facilities comprised a seaplane ramp and a 180-foot pier, barracks, a ten-bed dispensary, an administration building, storehouses, a chapel, a bakery, a powerhouse, and several industrial buildings. The construction project was done by the Arundel Corporation.

The naval air station in British Guiana, located on a 1,400-acre site 40 miles up the Essequibo River, was initially equipped with the minimum necessary essentials to support the operation of a patrol squadron of seaplanes and blimps. Construction was supplemented with the addition of a 12-bed hospital, more barracks, and a new water supply system whereby water from the Essequibo River was treated. The Army constructed a 2,000-foot runway at Atkinson Field, 25 miles from Georgetown, British Guiana. The Army airbase consisted of two mooring circles for blimps with connecting taxiways, a shop, and an administration building. Construction started in March 1943 and was completed in September of the same year.[45]

Lend-Lease

On January 10, 1941, the Lend-Lease bill (H.R. 1776) was introduced by Majority Leader John W. McCormack of Massachusetts in the House of Representatives and Alben Barkley in the Senate. The bill's isolationist opponents called H.R. 1776 "a dictator bill" designed to destroy the Republic [of the United States]. Senator Robert Taft of Ohio stated that: "Lending war equipment is a good deal like lending chewing gum. You don't want it back."[46]

On March 8, the full Senate approved the bill and three days later, the House of Representatives did the same. This bill repealed the "cash only" provision of the Neutrality Act, and let Britain pay on credit. Congress approved $7 billion to fund the first shipment of war materials; at the time, the largest single appropriation in American history. The Lend-Lease Act allowed the United States to lend or lease war supplies to any nation deemed vital to the defense of the United States. The irony of this "loan" soon became apparent. In the three months before the passage of this bill, Britain had lost 142 vessels carrying about 800,000 tons of shipping to the U-boats. Roosevelt responded to this threat by agreeing with the Danish government to establish a base in Greenland. The United States was then able to expand its security zone and have the Navy patrol all convoys traveling inside it, giving the British Navy a respite.[47]

Oil and bauxite

On May 10, 1940, Germany invaded the Netherlands, Belgium, and Luxemburg ending the "phony war." This invasion had immediate repercussions in the Caribbean and specifically, the Dutch West Indies. On June 11, British and French forces landed in Dutch Aruba and Curaçao to take control of the refineries owned by Standard Oil of New Jersey and Royal Dutch Shell, a British-Dutch multinational, located on these islands.[48] In 1916, during the First World War, the Royal Dutch Shell Oil Company founded a large refinery on Curaçao. In 1925, the Standard Oil Company of New Jersey founded a refinery on Aruba.[49]

> The Standard Oil complex at Aruba could refine 250,000 barrels of crude a day, and store over 11 million barrels of crude and other products. The oil produced and refined in this region, including a large portion of high-grade airplane fuel produced in Trinidad for the Royal Air Force, was essential for the Allied war effort. Also, in the region were located the extremely valuable bauxite mines of British Guiana and Surinam, vital for the U.S. aluminum production and Roosevelt's ambitious plans of producing thousands of war planes.[50]

Meanwhile, on June 4, the Allied evacuation of Dunkirk was completed, and on June 22, the German-French armistice was signed at Compiegne.[51] At this time, the terms of the armistice had not been announced to the public. However, in a stern message to the French government, Winston Churchill pronounced that this armistice would not release France from its obligation to fight alongside the British, adding that he was extremely disappointed that France had sued for a separate peace.[52]

Tensions mount in the Caribbean

The 1940 German conquest of France and the Netherlands brought to light the plight of the Caribbean colonies of these nations. Would the Germans have access to the Caribbean possessions of the conquered countries, more specifically, Aruba and Curaçao, Martinique, Guadeloupe, St. Marteen, St. Barts, and French Guiana? After meeting with President Roosevelt, William D. Leahy, by then the Governor of Puerto Rico, declared to the *New York Times* that Puerto Rico would become "the Gibraltar of the Caribbean." This was a clear warning to Germany against any incursion in the Caribbean. Leahy added that "when defense works intended to make Puerto Rico the Gibraltar of the Caribbean are completed, it will be impossible for any overseas power to send an expeditionary force to the southern coast of the United States, Central America, or the northern coast of South America."[53]

It was in this context that Leicester Hemingway and Anthony Jenkinson, two journalists working for the *New York Times*, ventured a trip along the western Caribbean and Central America in a search for hidden fueling bases for the German U-boats. At the end of their trip, they wrote a six-part series that was published in the *New York Times* and the *Atlanta Constitution*. Hemingway (1915-1982) was the younger brother of the famed writer Ernest Hemingway.[54] According to this unofficial report, Hemingway and Jenkinson claimed there were Nazi refueling depots for submarines and armed raiders on remote islands in the western Caribbean. They also claimed to have made these discoveries while traversing these places on their 12-ton schooner *Blue Stream*. To make matters more exciting for their readers, the authors claimed that during these incursions they were shot at, offered bribes, and repeatedly searched. According to their version of events, Cozumel, a 24-mile-long island off the coast of

Quintana Roo, Mexico, the Corn Islands, leased to the United States by the Nicaraguan Government, and Old Providence and St. Andrews, possessions of the Republic of Colombia all had refueling stations. They also "learned" of plans to build airfields or to enlarge existing ones "where no planes, commerce or tourist were to be found."[55] When they landed at Corn Island, the journalists met with Sub-Lieutenant Kruger, commandant of the garrison of 10 Nicaraguan National Guard who told them that his father was German, that he had been taught to love the fatherland and that Hitler would someday rule the world.[56] All this made for exciting and somewhat fearful reading to a public that was constantly bombarded with news of the war in Europe.[57]

Tensions mounted in Puerto Rico. On May 4, 1941, the Italian ship *Colorado* was confiscated by the U.S. Navy and brought to San Juan. Its crew was arrested when they tried to sabotage the ship and then jailed at *La Princesa* in Old San Juan. The 23 crew members were set to stand trial at the Federal Court House in San Juan. The trial was presided over by Judge Robert A. Cooper who had a long history with Puerto Rico. He was appointed on January 8, 1934 as a federal judge by President Roosevelt. On June 9, 1937, during a turbulent time in the history of this island, there ensued an attempt on his life for his role as a representative of the Federal Government. Fifteen shots were fired at him as he was driving to his home, though he was not harmed.[58] This incident would have a profound impact on those he perceived as plotting against the government of the United States. The defense team of both the crew members and the Italian Captain Giugni consisted of James R. Beverly, former Governor of Puerto Rico, and the prestigious New York law firm of Loomis & Williams. Despite this impressive defense team, Judge Cooper sentenced Captain Giugni to five years in a federal penitentiary and the crew members to three. They were then sent to Fort Missoula, Montana to serve out their sentence.[59]

Caribbean Defense Command

The United States Caribbean Defense Command (1941-1947) was tasked with protecting the Panama Canal, the Canal Zone, and all its access points as well as defending the Caribbean from German or Japanese aggression. To accomplish this task, it established American bases throughout the Caribbean.[60] However, the process of administering them was not without controversies. U.S. Army Major General Daniel Van Voorhis recommended placing Jamaica under the Puerto Rico Department and Antigua and St. Lucia under Trinidad. Major General James L. Collins, commanding general of the Puerto Rican Department, "objected to this grouping on the score that the Anegada Passage, between the Virgin Islands and the Leewards, could not be effectively closed unless the Puerto Rican defenses extended beyond it."[61] He also believed that Antigua and St. Lucia should be supplied from Puerto Rico. On May 29, 1941, the War Department organized the Caribbean Defense Command along those lines.[62]

"On January 2, 1942, the United States Government instructed the American representative to the Netherland Government in Exile, Anthony J. Drexel, to inform Queen Wilhelmina that this nation felt an 'imperative need that prompt action be taken with regard to the security of the islands of Curaçao and Aruba'."[63] According to Washington, "it now seemed likely that Germany would attempt to destroy the vital oil facilities in the Dutch Antilles," and President Roosevelt wanted these facilities secured.[64]

Queen Wilhelmina was annoyed with the Allies for not consulting her regarding the naming of the Commander of the Southwest Pacific, which covered the area where the Dutch East Indies was located. Given the speedy victories of the Germans in Europe and the Japanese in Asia, there was little time for formalities. On January

6, the Queen asked the United States to replace the British troops on the islands, which it did on January 12 as the first United States contingent arrived by air to Aruba. After some discussion over the exact number of American troops to be allowed, the Dutch agreed to 2,500. The troops were required to be self-sustaining while the Dutch supplied housing and other permanent facilities. The bulk of the troops arrived around January 28; the remainder followed in the coming weeks.[65] As a result of Dutch intransigence, only a small detachment of U.S. troops was accessible to counter the first U-boat attacks on January 15.

As a result, President Roosevelt expressed his frustration and irritation of the amount of time it took to negotiate with the Dutch authorities in a letter dated January 29:

> It took three months of perfectly childish negotiations before we got troops to protect the bauxite mines in Surinam. They might have been destroyed by a German aircraft carrier in the meantime. It has taken us well over a month to get troops to Curaçao and Aruba. They are not protected today, and their absolutely essential high-octane gas refineries might be destroyed by a German submarine tomorrow. Frankly, I cannot delay the troops… and I am taking sole responsibility for this move.[66]

U-boats attack the Caribbean

In early 1942, U-boats were having enormous success attacking ships off the East Coast of the United States, and on January 15, 1942, German Admiral Karl Doenitz decided to expand his operational area to include the Caribbean. He was aware of the importance of the oil and bauxite shipped from ports in Aruba and Curaçao, as the Germans had previously purchased these commodities. Operation

Neuland (New Land) would consist of a surprise, concentric, and synchronized attack on Aruba, Curaçao and Trinidad. Aruba was home to the world's largest oil refinery, and Curaçao and Trinidad were vital for the oil, aviation gas, and bauxite trade.

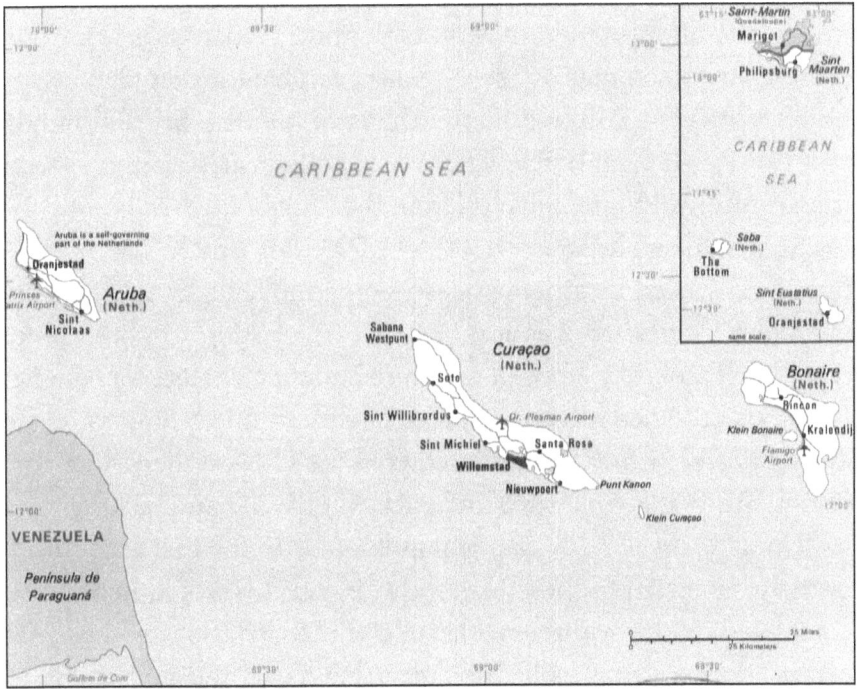

Map of Netherlands Antilles and Aruba. Contributor Names: United States. Central Intelligence Agency. Created, 1989. Published: Washington, D.C.; Central Intelligence Agency. Medium: 1 map; col.; 17 x 22 cm. Call Number. Physical Location: G5165 1989. U5. Repository: Library of Congress Geography and Map Division Washington, D.C. 20540-4650 USA dcu. Digital ID: http://hdl.loc.gov/loc.gmd/g5165.ct001540. Library of Congress Control Number: 2005631608. Language: English. Online format: image. Description: "801359 (541677) 6-89." Includes inset showing Sint Maarten, Saba, and Sint Eustatius. Available also through the Library of Congress Web site as a raster image. Original format: map. LCCN Permalink: https://lccn.loc.gov/2005631608. Additional Metadata formats: MARCXML Record, MODS Record, Manifest (JSON/LD), Dublin Core Record.

On February 16, the five selected U-boats were to attack their designated targets. The convoy was led by an elite group of captains. Günter Müller Stöckheim, commanding U-67 would operate off Curaçao; Werner Hartenstein's U-156 and Jürgen von Rosenstiel's U-502 off Aruba; Albrecht Achilles' U-161 off Trinidad, and Asmus "Nicolai" Clausen's U-129 off the coast of British Guiana and Surinam. Primary targets were the oil tankers and bauxite freighters as well as the oil refineries, most notable the Standard Oil Company of New Jersey complex at San Nicolaas, Aruba; the Trinidad Leasehold's refinery at Pointe-a-Pierre, the largest in the British Empire; and the Royal Dutch Shell Schottegat plant at Curaçao. These islands received Venezuelan oil from the Gulf of Maracaibo in shallow-draft tankers of about 1,200 to 1,500 tons which was then refined and loaded onto large ocean-going tankers. Trinidad was of particular interest to Admiral Doenitz. In addition to housing the oil refinery and tank farms, it was the transshipment site for bauxite. It was also the departure point for seaborne traffic bound for Cape Town, South Africa. The distance from the U-boats' departure port in Lorient, France to Aruba and back was 8,000 nautical miles and to Trinidad, it was 7,200 nautical miles. Due to the fuel capabilities of these submarines, these Caribbean incursions would need to be completed in two to three weeks, or else the U-boats would run out of fuel and be stranded in the Atlantic Ocean and vulnerable to Allied attack.[67]

At midnight, on the 15th of February, U-156 was inside the San Nicolaas Harbor of Aruba. At one-minute past two o'clock, U-156 torpedoed the tanker *Pedernales*. This was followed almost immediately by an explosion that lifted the ship. Next Hartenstein turned to the tanker *Oranjestad*, which was torn apart by two torpedoes. "Columns of water climbed upward alongside the ships as the tremendous concussion of the explosion startled nearly all the inhabitants of the island. Burning oil flowed out of the great holes in the sides of the two ships and soon spread over the surface of the entire harbor."[68] Hartenstein then struck the 400-ton tanker *Arkansas* which settled onto the bottom of the harbor almost immediately. He then ordered his crew to fire the 4.1-inch deck gun at the refinery. The person in charge of the deck gun forgot to remove the heavy tampion from the muzzle. This caused the shell to detonate inside the muzzle. Two sailors died in the explosion and one was wounded.

In Curaçao, the 31-ton tanker *Rafaela* was sunk by U-67. Von Rosenstiel had taken U-502 into the Gulf of Venezuela. There he sank the tankers *Tia Juana* and *San Nicolas*. The U-161 sunk the tankers *Mckihana* and *British Consul*.[69] This initial incursion into the Caribbean had been a resounding success of the Germans, as many tankers were sunk, and all the U-boats returned safely to Lorient.

Lieutenant General Frank Andrews, commander of the U.S. Caribbean Defense Command and the Panama Canal Department, was spending the night in the Aruba guest house of the Lago Oil and Transport Company, a subsidiary of the Standard Oil Company of New Jersey, when he was awakened by the first explosion of the submarine attack. A shocked General Andrews cautioned, "that it was impossible to determine whether there were one or more U-boats but added that indications led to the belief that several had joined in the attack."[70] He quickly ordered the aircraft under his command to get airborne immediately and attack the submarines. He believed that at least one of them was destroyed by depth charges.[71]

The following day he recounted the "terrible tales of shooting flames reaching mountainous proportions in Aruba harbor, and of despairing cries from men doomed to die there and of tracer shells screaming overhead."[72] The attacks of the U-boats had left 59 sailors dead or missing. Andrews added that, as ordered, the aircraft left the runway as soon as the attacks began. Upon returning, the pilots indicated that "some submarines had paid [a severe] price for the raids."[73] Did Andrews really believe that some of the submarines were in fact sunk? This is unlikely as the chain of command appeared to have been disorganized and antisubmarine warfare lacked the necessary equipment and trained personnel to combat the highly trained and motivated U-boat captains and crew.

Soon after the attack, six additional planes arrived from Puerto Rico and Trinidad. Even with these additional planes, the U.S. command was at a severe disadvantage when engaging the U-boats. They lacked radar, the crews were untrained in antisubmarine warfare, and they were armed with ineffectual 300-lb demolition bombs. However, noted General Andrews, "possibly the mere presence of the planes forced the submarines to a more cautious approach than they would have otherwise made."[74] Writing to General and Army Chief of Staff George C. Marshall,[75] General Andrews noted that "it was fortunate that we had airplanes there, otherwise the oil plants would have been in for a good shelling."[76]

After the U-boat attacks, the Allies were questioning how these submarines could travel such long distances. Where were they being resupplied from? Could there be a well-concealed base in the Caribbean, perhaps close to the Panama Canal? At the same time, Germany's Berlin Radio was flaunting the success of the attack on the tankers and the shelling of the refinery. Here is proof, they claimed, "that the United States naval and air forces are not yet strong enough to prevent German submarines from operating close to the American continent."[77] Unfortunately for the Allies, 1942 would prove this broadcast to be correct.

In California, the *Los Angeles Times* published an article that claimed that there "must" be a U-boat base in an isolated spot of the Caribbean, and "it was assumed" that U.S. planes and warships were checking this possibility. In the meantime, in order to prevent such a catastrophe from repeating, the Curaçao radio started to broadcast a warning to all ships that submarines had been sighted between Oranjestad, Aruba and San Nicolaas, Aruba. The panic created by this attack caused a disruption in the supply of oil and bauxite to Britain and the United States. It was also feared that an attack on the Panama Canal would be eminent.[78]

The Panama Canal was one of the most important strategic targets in the Western Hemisphere during the Second World War. It was vital for the U.S. war effort, as it was the most efficient means of moving men and materials from the Atlantic to the Pacific. As the fear of espionage and sabotage by Axis subversives was believed to be real, the United States expended valuable manpower and material to protect the Canal. Much of this fear was based on the large contingent of Germans and Japanese in Panamá, as well as contingents of Spanish Falange and French Vichy in the Caribbean. In order to deal with this threat — real or imagined — the U.S. military instituted anti-sabotage measures throughout the Canal Zone.[79]

By February 19, the Allied forces were alert to U-boats operating in the vicinity of Aruba and Curaçao. The element of surprise was lost as the Allies intensified air and sea patrols. "American and Dutch bombers operating from bases in Aruba and Curaçao" claimed to have sighted a submarine off Aruba that submerged as soon as it spotted aircraft flying towards it. Despite the military presence on these islands, as a precautionary measure, all tanker traffic between Venezuela and Aruba and Curaçao was temporarily discontinued. Patrolling bombers claimed (incorrectly as we now know) to have sunk two and possibly more submarines, as they claimed they saw "spreading oil slicks" and "air bubbles" after dropping depth charges. As the threat of sabotage was considered authentic, the U.S. Post Office Department instructed all postmasters in the Caribbean to forward the mail sent from Axis-controlled countries to the censorship office, unless given prior clearance from the British or American censors.[80]

Even in Brazil, there was amazement that German submarines would be operating unchallenged in the Caribbean. Military sources in Brazil were under the impression that the complete U.S. Army contingent was already stationed on Aruba and Curaçao. As previously discussed, the disagreement between the Dutch and American political leadership delayed the arrival of the troops, and when the attack occurred, the forces available were not enough, nor were they trained and equipped to mount an effective submarine counterattack. Brazilian newspapers reported being puzzled as to where the submarines were finding fuel and provisions. They could not fathom the idea that U-boats crossed the Atlantic without being resupplied. Brazilian military sources believed that the submarines' main base was in Dakar (Vichy-controlled French West Africa) and that they found shelter in either Guadeloupe or Martinique, also under Vichy control.[81]

A new U-boat attack was reported on February 20. The submarine shelled the Standard Oil refinery in Aruba with its deck gun thought they failed to set fire to the refinery or sink the two ships that had previously been damaged. "All of the shells fired from the submarine lying three or four miles offshore fell short of the oil refinery and reserves, but they whistled through the advanced post occupied by Americans; one ripped through a bachelor quarters building from end to end; another smashed through the nearby library; one Dutchman's room in the quarters was wrecked, but he escaped injury."[82] Though air and sea patrols were sweeping the Caribbean, a tanker flying the Panamá flag was reported torpedoed off Aruba. This was the ninth ship sunk in the area since the attacks started on February 15. General Frank Andrews again expressed "belief" that "Army bombers from Aruba and Curaçao may have sunk" one or more submarines.[83] However, according to an article published the following day in the *New York Amsterdam Star News*, a weekly newspaper founded in 1909 and geared to the African-American community of New York City, the "natives" of the islands in the Caribbean were "without adequate means of protection against air raids or submarine attacks."[84] The writer added that "the whole Caribbean area is said to be a 'happy' hunting ground for Nazi submarines," and "the defenseless inhabitants, who have been drawn into the orbit of total war, are without any means of protection or defense, particularly this is true in the case of the frame houses in the cities, where a shell of a bomb could set off huge and uncontrollable fires."[85] The remainder of 1942 would prove this vision to be prophetic and in sharp contrast to the unrealistic and confident depictions presented by the United States military.

The attack on Aruba had many repercussions including in Puerto Rico. Governor Rexford G. Tugwell was considering the possibility of a German attempt to "destroy the command center at San Juan which could be easily shelled from the sea."[86] The Nazis had, after all, made a special broadcast to the people of Puerto Rico. "Fellow countrymen and friends, we'll be there by February 15."[87] At the time, many Puerto Ricans thought the incident was "a joke."[88] The military and political command structure, though, were taking the submarine attacks seriously as evidenced by the island-wide mandatory blackout.

Tugwell thought that the island was under attack on February 21. General Collins had just informed him that there was an undetermined number of submarines off the San Juan harbor and that "we would have to rush our evacuation arrangements. We were," commented Tugwell, "far from ready for such an emergency. We had a bad 24 hours while planes and small boats hunted and waited. In the end, the threat was lifted as there were no more contacts."[89]

The same could not be said of the many ships and tankers that would be sunk in the Caribbean during the following months.

Operation Neuland had been an outstanding success for the Germans. In 28 days, they had sunk 41 ships, of which 18 were tankers. They also damaged 11 ships, including 7 tankers. This enormous success was coupled with the fact that not one U-boat was lost during the campaign. A motivated Doenitz decided to continue deploying his fleet in the Caribbean. This "experimental deployment" would develop into the full-fledged U-boat campaign. As far as the Allied forces were concerned, the lull they experienced by the third week of March, after the end of Operation Neuland, would not last. The U-boat attacks in February and March had "virtually brought the inter-island trade to a standstill."[90] German victories had been far too successful for them not to return.

Though the Allies had no way of knowing, the Germans would return in about a month. This gave them very little time to prepare, and certainly not enough to prepare for an elite U-boat force that had been waging war since September 1939. The naval resources were insufficient, and aircraft were not available. The U.S. naval base at Chaguaramas, Trinidad had five squadrons of flying boats, but only one was available in September 1942. The Naval Air Station at Isla Grande, Puerto Rico had a detachment of PBY Catalina flying boats. However, they had to cover virtually the whole of the Caribbean from Guantanamo in Cuba to Chaguaramas in Trinidad, an area too large for the number of planes assigned.[91]

CHAPTER II

Lopsided Affair (February–June 1942)

The U-boat war in the Caribbean was a lopsided affair. In 1942, the German submarines sunk at least 336 ships in the Caribbean (Table 1). Of these, 214 were sunk in the West Caribbean. The western Caribbean supplied the United States and British economies with oil and bauxite, essential war materials.

US troops at a training session in Trinidad. 1943. Library of Congress Prints and Photographs Division Washington, D.C. 20540 USA. United States, Office of War Information. Rights Advisory: No known restrictions on publication. Call Number: LOT 2203 (F) [P&P]. https://www.loc.gov/pictures/item/2005675142/. Retrieved November 5, 2020.

TABLE 1
SHIPPING LOSSES IN THE CARIBBEAN, 1942

Date	No.	Tonnage[1]
January	0	0
February	24	118,354
March	17	99,481
April	14	—
May	58	255,143
June	66	314,562
July	28	132,110
August	46	241,368
September	32	133,450
October	16	65,927
November	25	149,077
December	10	49,077
Total	**336**	**1,558,549**

Source: Stetson Conn, Rose C. Engelman, Byron Fairchild, *The Western Hemisphere: Guarding the United States and its Outposts* (Washington, D.C., Center of Military History, 2000), 431.

1. April tonnage not shown in source document CDC History Section, Anti-Submarine Activities in the CDC, 1941-46, Appendix B.

The Army's unpreparedness for the submarine assault during 1942 was partially due to a shortage of the long-range bombers required to seek out and destroy U-boats. Another reason was "the reluctance of air officers to employ their bombers in this fashion."[1] The Navy was also to blame as it was reluctant to employ convoys as Britain had done rather successfully since the beginning of the war. Two essential elements to counter the submarine threat were therefore missing: planes for air cover and ships for convoy escort. Even as hundreds of ships were sunk, the Army, "which had the planes, was unwilling to use them for convoy escort and patrol under the Navy command."[2]

Things began to turn against the Germans when an Enigma machine and its codebook were recovered by the British on May 9,

1941, inside the captured U-110. With the machine and codebook, the British were able to break the German code and read the secret transmissions relayed to the submarines from their headquarters. The principal source for breaking the code was the Short Signal Code book captured from inside the submarine which was used for weather reports. These were "carelessly rebroadcasted by German meteorological stations" in less secure codes that the British could read. Working backward and using the three-rotor Enigma machine, the British could soon read German messages with little delay. Unfortunately for the Allies, in January 1942, the Germans added another rotor to the Enigma and changed the Short Signal Code to such an extent that the British were unable to read German intercepts again for some time. This would have serious consequences for submarine warfare in the Caribbean.[3]

Things started to change by the summer and early fall of 1942 as the Allied antisubmarine forces received substantial reinforcements. The Navy had withdrawn some of its Catalina Flying Boats to reinforce the defenses of Alaska when the Japanese invaded the Aleutian Islands. However, enough air and surface craft were assembled in the Panamá-Caribbean area that by July 1942 a system of convoys was organized. The total sinkings dropped from 66 in June to 28 in July. In August, a Royal Air Force squadron arrived at Trinidad. By the end of September 1942, the Allies had 44 heavy bombers, 65 medium bombers, 22 light bombers, and 105 observation planes plus Navy Catalinas and RAF Hudsons in the Panamá-Caribbean area. Despite these initiatives, the number of ships torpedoed was not significantly reduced until January 1943.[4]

The views of the attackers and their victims were in stark contrast. The submariners were enjoying the fruits of their success; their victims were fighting for their lives. The aim here is to provide the reader with an understanding of the difficulties endured by some of the victims of the U-boat attacks and the lopsided battles that were taking place.

U-boats are back

After having sunk 24 ships in February 1942 in Operation New Land, the U-boats returned safely to their base in Lorient, France. U.S. military officials refused to believe that these submarines were capable of such feats. According to George Fielding Eliot — an author, commentator and military analyst who wrote for *Harper's Magazine*, *Current History*, and *The American Mercury*, and who after the war became a confidant of Secretary of State George Marshall — submarines did not have the range to attack Aruba from a port in France as they would run out of fuel before arriving at their destination. Eliot claimed (incorrectly as we know now) that submarines could not operate 4,000 miles from their base. "The officers and men of their crews," added Eliot, "must have known full well when they set out on their perilous missions that return was unlikely."[5]

What would it be like to be aboard a torpedoed tanker? Nicolas Monsarrat, author of *The Cruel Sea*, served in World War II and drew on this experience to recount this in vivid detail. Consider what would happen in World War II if a merchant ship were hit by a torpedo, wrote Monsarrat. "There would be the initial blow, followed by total confusion, then disbelief, then frenzied action. How much damage? Could the ship be saved? If so, damage control and firefighting teams would be called to action. If not, a race to lower the lifeboats would ensue."[6]

The crewmembers closer to the impacted area would probably be pulverized, burned or jellied by fire and overpressure. Others would be wounded, some severely. If the hit to the vessel was mortal, it would have to be abandoned in an orderly fashion if there was time or 'every man for himself.' The sight was horrifying and those that saw it would never forget it. "She was sinking fast," recounted Monsarrat from his experience, "and already her screws were out of the water...the cries of men in from inside [the ship], and a thick smell of oil." He would see a mass of men packed high in the towering stern [of the ship] waving and shouting as they felt the ship begin to sink.

Not all survivors made it into lifeboats. Many leaped into oil-covered water that was itself on fire, where they would be asphyxiated or burned to death. Others might be killed on impact by the falling debris from the masts or bridge wings, or they might be sucked underwater by the ship's descending bulk and drown. Those that did not die at once or who were not immediately rescued could face a slow and agonizing death. Bodies floating in the ocean would become waterlogged and sink, only to rise to the surface when they decomposed. The men in the lifeboats waiting to be rescued might have to wait for days or weeks. Many died of burns, broken bones, open wounds, and later, hunger, thirst, exposure or the heat of the tropic. Those who died were shoved overboard. Many went completely mad. They would swim from the safety of their lifeboat toward imagined rescuers. Or they might drink gallons of seawater to quench their thirst, stare at the sun, or rave and scream like madmen.[7] It was a horrible ordeal for those who survived.

In order to limit the information that could be made available to the Axis powers, the U.S. Navy prohibited news media from disclosing the names of the vessels attacked or the victims. The Cuban authorities did not partake in this censure and disclosed that the name of the American tanker torpedoed and sunk on February 28 50 miles off Puerto Plata, Dominican Republic was the *Oregon*. She was on her way from Aruba to Melville, Rhode Island, navigating unescorted and unarmed.

Ten survivors of the *Oregon* landed at Baracoa, Cuba while 16 others were rescued in Puerto Plata in the Dominican Republic. Eleven crewmen were listed as missing. After spending five and a half days at sea, four survivors on a life raft were picked up by the American tanker *Gulfpenn* and taken to Philadelphia. There they provided the authorities with details of the attack. "The submarine [U-156] sank our ship with about 200 shells and then ran down and sank two lifeboats," they asserted. "We drifted on two life rafts for nearly a week before being picked up," the survivors added.[8] The *Oregon* sunk five hours after being shelled. German Naval Records available after the war contradict this version of events. They state that the survivors were not deliberately targeted and all casualties occurred during the initial shelling of the bridge.[9]

Isla Grande Airport, San Juan, 1941. (Mapoteca: Archivo General de Puerto Rico)

After the attack on Aruba and Trinidad, Governor Tugwell and the commanding officers of the Tenth Naval District operating out of the naval base at Isla Grande expected an attack on the fortifications and bases located in San Juan, Puerto Rico. It came as a surprise that the first (and only) attack by the German U-boats in Puerto Rico did not occur there, but in Mona Island, a volcanic rock in the Mona Passage 50 miles southwest of Puerto Rico. It is a mere four and a half miles long by three and a half miles wide and of no military importance. It was said that centuries ago Mona was a pirate hideaway, but by 1942, it was a forest reserve whose only fulltime inhabitants were the family of the lighthouse keeper.

According to Remberto Casaba, assistant director of a National Youth Administration camp on the island, on March 3 about 30 shells landed on the cliffs of Mona Island where 170 youths from Puerto Rico were camping. The shells caused no damage or casualties. "The boys behaved very well," added Casaba. Forestry officials confirmed the attack, though the naval authorities made no mention of it. They dismissed this incident as merely target practice by the U-boat gunners. U.S. air and naval patrols searched the area in case the U-boat lingered, but it was long gone by then.[10]

On March 6, the Navy announced the sinking of the 5,104-ton American freighter *Cardonia* by U-126. The *Cardonia* was sailing unescorted and unarmed from Ponce, Puerto Rico to Guayabal, Cuba with general cargo. Upon seeing the submarine, it tried to escape by laying down a smokescreen, increasing speed and heading in a zigzagged maneuver toward the coast of Haiti. However, the submarine commenced firing its deck gun at the *Cardonia* and after 30 or 40 shells hit their target, the ship caught fire and stopped. Thereupon, the crew abandoned the vessel. Two torpedoes finally sunk her.[11]

Survivors of *SS Cardonia* photographed as they arrived at McCalla Field, Guantanamo Bay, Cuba, after rescue. *Cardonia* had been torpedoed, shelled, and sunk by German submarine U-126 off St. Nicholas Mole, Haiti, in March 1942. The plane is a Grumman JRF Goose. Catalog #: 80-G-63475. Copyright Owner: National Archives. Original Date: Saturday, March 7, 1942. After this Year: 1940. Before this Year: 1949. Original Medium: Black & White Photo. https://www.history.navy.mil/content/history/nhhc/our-collections/photography/numerical-list-of-images/nhhc-series/nh-series/80-G-63000/80-G-63475.html. Retrieved October 4, 2020.

Two survivors — John R. Taurin of Baltimore, Maryland and Francis Rooney of Johnston City, Tennessee — were picked up by the *USS Mulberry* two days later on March 8 and taken to the naval base at Isla Grande in San Juan. Taurin and Rooney recounted to the *Associated Press* how they survived in shark-infested waters, battling hunger, thirst and not knowing when or if they would be rescued. A 35-year-old Puerto Rican was with them on the makeshift raft but did not survive. According to Rooney, "he was all right until Monday morning. Then he lost his head. He said he wanted to get a room somewhere and insisted he had money to pay for it. All of a sudden he slid off the raft and went down."[12] This interview was permitted as the Navy had yet to enforce its censure against the publicizing of the names of the disaster victims. Twenty other members of the crew survived while 16 went missing. These 20 survivors first arrived at a Haitian village in their lifeboats and were taken to the capital city of Port-au-Prince. Later they were flown to West Palm Beach, Florida and then to New Orleans, home office of the Lykes Brothers Steamship Company, owners of the *Cardonia*.[13]

Twenty-eight-year-old Ensign Pinter of the U.S. Navy was piloting a PBY Catalina flying boat with two copilots and a crew of five from San Juan, Puerto Rico to the naval base in Guantanamo, Cuba. Pinter had limited flying experience and had been a pilot for only 16 months. His orders were to watch out for German submarines and, if found, to engage them. He didn't come across a U-boat though. Instead, he noticed what appeared to be men struggling in the ocean with a series of lifeboats and rafts[14] from the shipwreck of the American vessel *Barbara*, which had been traveling from Baltimore to San Juan, Puerto Rico with a crew of 85.

At 08:35 hours on March 7, the unescorted and unarmed *Barbara* was hit by a torpedo amidships on the port side, causing a fire that damaged the engines. The fire prevented the survivors from launching any lifeboats, so they had to jump or climb into the water and swim to the life rafts. The ship burned for two and a half hours and sank stern first about nine miles northeast of Tortuga Island, Dominican Republic."[15]

"Flying low over the raft, Pinter could see that it was a makeshift affair, only 10 feet square and crowded with the survivors. The sea was very rough and Pinter thought they might not have lasted until a rescue ship arrived."[16] Despite the sea conditions and with a fully loaded plane, he decided to make the risky rescue attempt. "The rescue was a touch and go operation from the start," Pinter acknowledged, "so I considered the alternatives, debating whether I could land and take off with the sea conditions being what they were. I estimated that the plane had already burned 300 gallons of fuel, which made it 1,800 pounds lighter, so I figured the risk was worth taking. The sea was too rough to taxi to the raft, so I had to taxi away and then sail up to it."[17] The survivors had been adrift for 60 hours without food or water and were so weakened that the plane's crew had to practically carry them into the plane and administer first aid.

The PBY Catalina had a normal capacity of seven. Now it would be carrying 17 additional passengers (16 men and 1 woman). Pinter hoped that since the plane was 1,800 pounds lighter, the weight of the survivors would not make a noticeable difference in the plane's performance. He and Aviation Machinist Mate Lewis M. Thompson, serving as copilot, tried to get the plane in the air. However, the waves only bounced it around. Pinter then shifted some weight forward and tried again.

"The plane bounced high into the air without speed," Pinter reported, "and on each bounce Thompson gave it more power as I nosed it down at the peak of each bounce and pulled back as we hit the swells and waves, easing the blow and still increasing airspeed. Finally, on one of the bounces, I gave it the maximum power available and it stayed in the air. It took us approximately 20 minutes to climb 500 feet."[18] The plane landed without further incident a few hours later at the naval base in Guantanamo, Cuba. Pinter's commander reported that this action required the highest degree of skill and was in keeping with "the finest tradition of the naval service."[19] The remaining *Barbara* survivors were picked up by a U.S. destroyer following the directions provided by Ensign Pinter. Another group of 21 survivors from the *Barbara* landed on Tortuga Island after three days at sea and were rescued by the Haitian Coast Guard. Fourteen crewmembers and eight passengers lost their lives in this incident.[20]

On March 12, U-126 struck the American freighter *Texan* which sunk off of Nuevitas, Cuba. The vessel, loaded with Cuban sugar, was streaming about 40 miles east of Nuevitas on a non-evasive course at a speed of 11.8 knots.[21] The attack came after an armed British escort ship left *Texan* to her own fate. The U-126 fired her deck gun, and as a result, an order was given to abandon ship but not before the crew sent emergency messages. Ten minutes after the attack, the crewmen abandoned the ship. When it sank, it capsized the two lifeboats and five men drowned. The next day the survivors were spotted by the Cuban fishing boat *Yoyo* and taken to Nuevitas.[22]

The U-126 then attacked the unarmed and unescorted American freighter *Colabee* 10 miles off Cape Guajaba, Cuba the same day the survivors of the torpedoed *Texan* being rescued. It was transporting 38,600 bags of Cuban sugar from Puerto Tarafa to Baltimore, Maryland. According to the *Associated Press*, all members of the crew, except for 37-year-old first assistant engineer Frank Eckman, were lost. When interviewed, Eckman said "that five members of the crew succeeded in lowering one of the lifeboats" but that it sank as soon as it hit the water. Other members, added Eckman, "jumped overboard. I heard my companions crying for help for six hours and to help them I tossed lifelines, lifesavers and other objects in the direction from where the cries were coming"[23] as he had decided not to abandon the ship, a decision which probably saved his life. "The last cries grew fainter," Eckman added, "and I heard nothing more until the tanker *Kansas* sighted the wreck and came alongside."[24] Days after the interview, other members of the crew were located. Out of 38 people, 24 had drowned. The *Colabee* was severely damaged but did not sink.

It would later be repaired and returned to service in September 1942.²⁵

April 4 found Governor Tugwell flying to St. Lucia on a DC-3 as part of the Caribbean Advisory Committee. "Just a month before," commented Tugwell, "a particularly audacious sub had run deep into this neck one evening and let go two torpedoes, sinking the *Lady Nelson* and a large freighter at the pier. [The U-boat had] turned, gone out, and lost herself without even being fired at. There had been," Tugwell continued, "gross negligence. There was then no submarine net at the harbor mouth; the pier and the ship were floodlighted for the discharge of the cargo; and the guns on the heights never seen to have been put into action."²⁶ Tugwell added that they ran alongside the ship and saw "the enormous holes full of twisted metal sheets and a litter of machinery and cargo. The stench was sickening. There were no facilities [at St. Lucia] and not even the bodies of those killed" have been removed.²⁷ Twenty-five people lost their lives in this attack. Neither Tugwell nor the Allied military would know that the U-boat that attacked that fateful day was U-161 captained by the German Ace Albrecht Achilles, who would be awarded the prestigious Iron Cross on April 5, 1942.²⁸ The *Lady Nelson* was later salvaged and converted to a hospital ship.²⁹ The U-161 would end up sinking 14 ships and damaging 6 others before being sunk in September 1943 northeast of Bahia, Brazil.³⁰

On April 17, U-66 attacked the unescorted and unarmed Panamanian tanker *Heinrich von Riedemann* traveling from Venezuela to Aruba. According to the survivors' account, after the attack they tried to board the ship to salvage her, "but the U-66 stayed around to make sure that did not happen."³¹ The ship eventually burst into flames and sank, two and a half hours after the first torpedo hit. All 44 crewmembers were rescued. Twenty-nine were brought to Trinidad aboard the Norwegian ship *Karmt*. Andrew Weiller, the ship's captain, and the remaining crew were rescued by the steam merchant *Maracaibo* and brought to Caracas, Venezuela.[32]

The U-boats were having unparalleled success in the Caribbean. Such was the speed at which ships were sunk or damaged, that the news media could not keep the public informed. The censorship enforced by the Navy made their jobs even more difficult. Under these circumstances, why would the crew and vessel owners brave the odds by trying to avoid detection by the U-boats against which they were defenseless? The Navy had not instituted the convoy system and in any case, lack of experience, leadership and equipment meant that there was little they could do to counter this menace. The ships were therefore left to their own accord. Was it a need for money, a sense of patriotism, or a lack of awareness of the dangers they faced? It was probably a combination of all three factors. In any case, the vessels continued to sail, and the U-boats continued to sink them.

Blackouts and 'milch cows'

On April 18, orders were issued to blackout the East Coast of the United States. Waterfront lights and neon signs of the seaside resorts were forced to shut down. In addition, more auxiliary vessels were produced and manned. This gave the tankers and other sailing vessels appreciable extra protection when the U-boats did find them. Taking these factors into account, in April, Admiral Donitz decided to move more of his U-boats to the easier hunting grounds of the Caribbean:

> I, therefore, decided to use all U-boats becoming available for operations from the end of April onwards in a simultaneous attack on a number of other, and widely separate, focal points for shipping off the American coast. I would thus compel the enemy to split up and scatter his defensive forces, withdrawing considerable

portions from the concentration he has just established off the east coast in order to protect other important areas which will now be equally threatened.³³

"Turn off the lights". Poster encouraging the enforcement of blackouts. World War II propaganda poster commissioned for The Office of War Information, Bureau of Graphics. National Archives and Records Administration. https://time.com/ 4591841/loose-lips-sink-ships-posters/. Retrieved October 27, 2020.

Thus, at the end of April, Admiral Donitz ordered the Type XIV U-tanker, the first of its class, to assist the U-boats posted in the Caribbean. According to Donitz, the U-459 was: "a clumsy great boat of nearly 1,700 tons. As she was not intended for offensive purposes, she carried no torpedo armament and mounted only AA guns for her own protection. She was immediately dubbed 'the milch cow' by the submariners."³⁴

The Type XIVs carried 700 tons of fuel. This meant that one of them could keep 12 Type VIIs U-boats supplied for an extra four weeks or five Type IXs for an extra eight weeks. The first submarine U-459 refueled was U-108. This occurred on April 22, 500 miles northeast of Bermuda. According to Donitz, within a fortnight she had refueled 12 Type VIIs and 2 Type IXs. There was, of course, danger in this operation as it required that a number of U-boats gather at the same point in order to carry out an operation that kept them on the surface for some time, making them vulnerable to roving aircraft. Nevertheless, the presence of these 'milch cows' meant that "in practice, we had advanced our Biscay bases anything from 1,000 to 2,000 miles further westwards."[35]

With the help of U-459 and her sister ship, U-460, as well as a large ocean-going minelayer converted to a supply ship, U-116, the number of sinkings increased from 14 in April to 58 in May.[36]

> Within a fortnight, 12 medium and 2 large boats had been refueled at the same meeting point. The 'milch cow' had been 'sold out' as we called it and turned for home. During these refueling operations, interruptions and delays on account of bad weather were, of course, inevitable. This had resulted in there sometimes being several boats at the meeting point at the same time, all awaiting their turn, and these concentrations were dangerous in themselves and always filled me with misgivings.
>
> The boats which had thus been replenished by U-459 now proceed to take up their positions for the new 'frontal' attack. Some 16 to 18 medium-sized boats were ranged between Cape Sable and Key West. A further nine were to operate in the area between the Bahamas Channel and the Windward Passage, in the Gulf of Mexico, to the south of Cuba as far as the Yucatan Straits, off Curaçao, Aruba and Trinidad, and off the Guiana coast.[37]

In April, Doenitz decided to transfer six U-boats from the U.S. East Coast to the Caribbean as the convoys system on the East Coast made for more difficult targets. The Americans, he noted, had not anticipated that U-boats could travel to such distant parts of the Caribbean. Four additional boats that were headed to the Atlantic were also diverted to the Caribbean.[38]

> It was thanks to three submarine tankers which had now come into commission, U-459, U-460 and U-116 that we were able to exploit to the full a most fruitful theater of operations, which was 3,000 to 4,000 miles away from our Biscay bases and which itself

spread over an area measuring 1,000 miles by 500 miles. Between the end of April and the middle of June, submarine tankers supplied fuel oil to 20 out of the 37 U-boats which during these months of operation had successfully been engaged in the Caribbean.

Both the success achieved and the economy of effort required were very great in this area.... In all, in May and June alone, 148 ships with a total tonnage of 752,009 tones were sunk in the Caribbean.... From the end of June, however, results in these areas began to deteriorate. Here, too, as had happened off the East Coast of the United States at the beginning of May, the convoy system was gradually introduced.[39]

The loss of 129 tankers sunk through May 1942 deeply concerned the British Admiralty as its petroleum stockpiles (oil reserves) were falling to unacceptable levels. Given the importance of the petroleum supplied by the refineries in the Caribbean, additional tankers were sent to make up for the losses incurred, though they would take a longer route from Britain along the West Coast of Africa and across in order to avoid the U-boats threatening the North Atlantic passage.

In fact, British tankers were being sunk at a faster rate than could be built. Britain needed more tankers to supply its war effort, and it did not have the shipyards to build them. Britain turned to the United States for assistance and petitioned a "loan" of 70 tankers of 10,000 deadweight tons each. Even though the United States had lost a significant number of tankers itself, and many tankers had been diverted to the Pacific theater, President Roosevelt acceded to Churchill's request. Harold Ickes, the American Oil Czar, notified the British on May 14 that their request would be met in four weeks. Instead of the 700,000 tons requested, the United States sent 854,000; 170,00 to Canada and 684,000 to the United Kingdom.

Less than three months later, on August 1 London again petitioned the United States for tankers. This time it requested 54 tankers of

10,000 deadweight tons each. President Roosevelt again promptly met this request. Within thirty days, Ickes had allocated the equivalent of 40 tankers or a total of 400,000 deadweight tons. The rest of the request was fulfilled in October and November. The total tanker assistance by the Americans to the British in 1942 was more than 124 tankers for a total of 1.24 million deadweight tons. To this end, Churchill wrote to Roosevelt on May 27 expressing his gratitude. "Without your help, our stock [of oil] would have fallen to a dangerous level by the end of the year [1942]. The action is more than generous considering recent heavy American tanker losses and the sacrifice involved in realizing so many ships."[40]

Nazist or saboteur?

On April 26 the *Alcoa Partner*, owned by Alcoa Steam Ship Company, was attacked and sunk by U-66. She was traveling towards Mobile, Alabama unescorted and unarmed carrying 8,500 tons of bauxite ore which she had loaded in Trinidad. Due to the weight of the cargo, *Alcoa Partner* sank in less than three minutes, taking 10 of her 35 crewmembers down with her. The survivors crowded into the only lifeboat they could manage to get a hold of, and 37 hours after the attack, landed in Bonaire.[41] On May 7, the unescorted Norwegian freighter *Frank Seamans*, also carrying bauxite, was torpedoed and sunk by U-162. After all her crew had abandoned the vessel and boarded the lifeboats, a second torpedo was fired which sunk the ship. As a result, there were no casualties.[42] According to the *Associated Press*, the 33-year-old steam merchant ship *Atenas*, owned by the United Fruit Company, "was attacked by two enemy submarines, [she] sank one U-boat and eluded the other."[43] This information was also published in the Costa Rican newspaper *La Tribuna*. Though unescorted, *Atenas* was armed with a four-inch stern gun that she used against the surfaced submarine, which then submerged and retired. The crew of the *Atenas* thought she had been sunk, but this did not happen. The submarine continued attacking vessels, claiming a total of 22 before being sunk herself on August 2, 1943 in the North Atlantic.[44]

Given that the U-boats were sinking merchant ships at will, what was the reaction of the crew on the ships? Why did they continue to sail? Most of the documents pertaining to discords between the crews and the owners of the vessels were subject to censorship by the military authorities. Therefore, at the time, any disagreement or discord was kept secret. Such was the case of the dispute between the crews of the Norwegian freighter M/S *Karmt* and their union delegate in New Orleans. In this case, the original document was written in Norwegian, and Navy translators translated it, as best they could, into English.

The crew of this and most Norwegian transports were members of the Norwegian Seamans Association whose main office in the United States was in New York City. On April 12, 1942, the crew of the *Karmst* summed a Mr. Eriksen, the union representative in New Orleans, demanding that their vessel be fitted with an anti-aircraft gun. The crew was short of six men, four for the deck crew and two to assist the engineer with the diesel motors. The officers of the *Karmst* refused to sail unless they had a full crew complement and the requested gun was installed. According to them, they also need three extra men to man the lookout stations throughout the 24-hour watches.

Eriksen stunned the officers, stating that if they did not sail immediately — without the gun and their crew full complement — it would be considered sabotage. He further stated that the anti-aircraft gun could not be obtained in America and therefore, if the ship did not sail, they would be considered saboteurs, and serious consequences would entail. The officers did not bulge. A few days later, the anti-aircraft gun arrived and was installed. Two gunners arrived from New York and two others from the surrounding area.

After this confrontation, the officers wrote a scalding letter to the main office of their union, stating that "we have no use for that type of representative who tries to work the members [of the union] down in the dirt and who resorts to untrustworthiness."[45] Either Ericksen is removed, they demanded, or they will leave the union. "It is always like this: if a member should be unfortunate enough to demand anything, then one is (considered) a 'nazist' or a saboteur."[46] During their heated discussions, Ericksen alleged that the crew and officers were acting inappropriately as "this was the first boat that demanded sufficient crew and that there was a boat which was to sail on the same day short of 23 men."[47] In any case, the *Karmst* left New Orleans with its stated cargo and three men short, as the officers believed that they had enough crewmembers "to have a complete watch on deck."[48] The *Karmst* made it safely to its destination, but its luck ran out before the end of the war. On April 18, 1945, just a few weeks before Germany's surrender, she was sunk by U-245 about 10 miles east-southeast of North Foreland, England. Thirty-eight out of a crew of 42 survived the attack.[49]

Why would a union delegate, whose main responsibility is to protect its members, act in such an arrogant and untrustworthy manner? At the time, Norway was under German rule, and its government in exile lived in London. It is probable that Eriksen was being pressured by either the British or the Americans to move as many ships to the Caribbean as was possible, regardless of the risks to the cargo and the crew. The original document was written in Norwegian and translated into English for the benefit of both intelligence services. In any case, Eriksen had a cozy job, he lived outside harm's way, and would probably do just about anything to keep it, as there must have been quite a few people lined up to take his place should he fail.

Dominican Republic enters the war

Once the Dominican Republic declared war on Germany and Italy on December 11, 1941, its ships became targets of the U-boats prowling the Caribbean. Such was the case of the 3,161-ton freighter *San Rafael* who encountered U-125 on May 3 and was sunk with a combination of torpedoes and gunfire. Once the ship was struck by the torpedo, the Dominican crew rushed to the four lifeboats they were able to salvage. According to the survivors, the submarine surfaced and started to fire its gun at the *San Rafael*. In the meantime, the crew started rowing their lifeboats away from the scene as quickly as possible while members of the submarine pointed their machine guns at them. The attack occurred so quickly that they were not able to send an S.O.S. Once the submarine left, they were completely alone, at the mercy of the sea. Seven days later, in what seemed to the crew as an eternity, they were picked up by a small fishing boat and taken to Isla de Pinos, Cuba.[50] The entire crew of the U-125 would be lost on May 6, 1943, almost a year to the day of the sinking on the *San Rafael*, in the North Atlantic northeast of Newfoundland.[51]

The Dominican Republic would lose its second freighter later that month. On May 15, *Presidente Trujillo* was headed for Pointe-à-Pitre, Guadeloupe and then to Fort-de-France, Martinique with 300 head of cattle. It also transported 600 bags of rice and a distillery earmarked for San Juan, Puerto Rico. The vessel arrived at Pointe-à-Pitre, Guadeloupe where 150 cattle disembarked. Once the cattle had safely gone ashore, *Presidente Trujillo* left for its next port of call, Fort-de-France, where the remainder of the cattle disembarked.

The provisions carried by the *Presidente Trujillo* were of utmost importance to Vichy-controlled Martinique and Guadeloupe, as food was scarce. U-boats routinely circumvented these islands, and a large contingent of French naval forces was stationed there. There were

SS Pennsylvania Sun (U.S. Merchant Marine Tanker, 1938) burning after she was torpedoed by the German submarine U-571 about 125 miles west of Key West, Florida on July 15, 1942. Photographed from a Naval Air Station, Key West, aircraft. *Pennsylvania Sun* was saved and returned to service. Official U.S. Navy Photograph, now in the collections of the National Archives. Catalog #: 80-G-61599. https://www.history.navy.mil/content/history/nhhc/our-collections/photography/numerical-list-of-images/nara-series/80-g/80-G-60000/80-G-61599.html. Retrieved October 4, 2020.

rumors among the people working at the docks that the food transported on the *Presidente Trujillo* was intended for the submariners, and for that reason, the vessel was not attacked until it had offloaded its provision.

On Thursday, May 21 at 11:20 A.M. *Presidente Trujillo* left Fort-de-France bound for San Juan. It was attacked by U-156 seven miles outside of the port, traveling parallel to the coastline. The ship broke in two and sank in about four minutes. Fifteen survivors were picked up by local fishermen who could not help but hear the loud explosion. The remaining 24 crewmembers perished. The survivors were taken to a nearby hospital where they believed the French had interned others. One Colombian patient warned them that Axis submariners in Martinique were intent on poisoning them. The next day he "suddenly" died. Seventy-two hours later, the survivors were flown to the Dominican Republic.[52]

Attacks continue

On June 8, the *Chicago Daily Tribune* reported the sinking on May 12 of the Norwegian tanker *Lise*. As was required by the Navy, the vessel was identified only by its nationality. One of the survivors, chief engineer Nils Oversen, was interviewed by the Navy after his rescue. "I was awakened by the shelling and found the engine room deserted. I found the bodies of several shipmates on deck. I and seven others fled in a lifeboat and later saw the ship burst into flames and settle stern first after an explosion. We drifted three days in shark-infested waters until we were rescued."[53] Although Oversen and his seven companions believed they were the only survivors, there were indeed others.

An updated account sheds more information on this attack. On May 12, the unescorted *Lise* was torpedoed by U-69 and then shelled. The crew of the *Lise* tried to engage the submarine with their gun. However, either as a result of not having the proper training or mechanical malfunction, the gun proved useless. The crew was ordered to abandon the ship. The tanker sank one hour after its encounter with U-69.

Twenty-one crewmembers — not the seven reported by Oversen — survived the attack. He would not have known this at the time since the remaining crewmembers headed toward Curaçao and were picked up by the Dutch armed whaler *Femern* and the Dutch steam merchant *Socrates*. On June 7, the survivors that arrived at Curaçao boarded the passenger steamship *Crijnssen* for New York. It was torpedoed on June 10 by U-504. All the *Lise* crewmembers onboard survived a second sinking, along with 93 of the 94 people onboard. Some were later flown to the United States. Others boarded the *Lebore* which was sunk on June 14 by U-172 despite being armed.[54] All the *Lise* crewmembers onboard survived their third sinking in 33 days. They were picked up two days later by the destroyer USS *Erie* and taken to Cristobal, the Atlantic terminal port adjoining the city of Colon, Panamá. The USS *Erie* would be lost on December 5, 1942, after being struck by a torpedo from U-163 while she was escorting a convoy from Port-of-Spain, Trinidad to Guantanamo, Cuba.[55]

USS Erie (PG-50) taken December 2, 1942, at Willemstad, near Curacao, West Indies, where she had been towed after having been torpedoed on November 12, 1942 and later abandoned. She eventually sank on December 5, 1942. Note extensive damage by fire and hole astern. Catalog #: 80-G-30867. Copyright owner: National Archives. Original Date: Wednesday, December 2, 1942. https://www.history.navy.mil/content/history/nhhc/ our-collections/photography/numerical-list-of-images/nhhc-series/nh-series/80-G-30000/80-G-30867.html. Retrieved October 4, 2020.

Prisoner on a U-boat

An American seaman of the *Lebore*, Archie Gibbs, 36, of Roscoe, Texas told of being held prisoner aboard U-172 for four days. No lifeboats or life rafts were nearby when the *Lebore* sunk, so Gibbs was asked by the crew of U-172 if he wanted to stay in the water or go aboard the submarine. "What else could I do?" he stated. "I started swimming towards the submarine," he continued recounting, "when a big German grabbed me and hustled me up the conning tower. He stuck a pistol that looked like a Big Bertha under my nose and asked me if I knew what I would get if I didn't answer questions. I told him 'I know my Germans' and then I told the name [of the ship], but they didn't get out of me our destination."[56]

Gibbs was taken below and made to lie on the floor on the torpedo tube compartment. "I could detect a groundswell at about 1:00 P.M. June 17," recounted Gibbs, "when the Germans opened fire with the anti-aircraft gun on the deck. Two bombs exploded near [the submarine]. I surmised that a Navy plane had surprised [us on the surface]. Later, the crew offered to share their rations with Gibbs, but he could not eat them "because the food was lousy." He added that there were hints that the Germans did not like the food either, as one man smashed a plate of cheese on the table and splattered it all over the compartment.

Gibbs experienced the U-172 attacking other vessels and herself coming under attack. The submarine had to zig-zag frantically until the hatch was closed in order to crash-dive. It lay for hours in extremely deep waters in order to evade her pursuers. "It was hot and miserable," noted Gibbs, "before surfacing again and again. Two more torpedoes were placed in the compartment that night, yet no ships were attacked even after the torpedoes were placed in the tubes, ready for firing."[57] With no advance notice, at 9:00 A.M. on

June 19 Gibbs was told to put on his lifebelt and get his bag which contained his possessions and to go on deck. A warning shot from the anti-aircraft gun halted a small trading boat near the submarine, and Gibbs was ordered to swim to the little craft. Upon reaching landfall Gibbs told the press that "the sub crewmen acted like men who knew they had a dirty job to do and wanted to get it over with and go home. One sailor who entered the crew's quarters with a 'Heil Hitler' got a calling down from another crewman who growled 'Nix on the heil'."[58]

U-172 was an extremely successful submarine. It sunk 26 ships for a total tonnage of 152,080. She was finally caught and sunk on December 13, 1943 in the Atlantic, west of the Canary Islands. Out of a crew of 59, 46 survived the attack.[59]

Supermen?

Allied and Axis propaganda would convey the image that the crews of the U-boats were resolute and confident with "unshakeable faith in victory."[60] Gibbs did not observe this during his four days as a prisoner aboard the U-172. In fact, the British interrogators had observed similar attitudes as the U-172 crew as early as 1941 among the survivors of U-131, U-134, and U-574, which had been forced to surface as a result of depth charge attacks in December 1941. According to the interrogators, these U-boat men expressed doubt about the ultimate success of the U-boat campaign. Many spoke "with loathing of their service in the U-boat," which they found vastly different from the propaganda they had been led to believe. Some said that they never would have joined the U-boat service if they knew then about the boredom, misery, and sheer terror they would experience.[61]

A letter from Josef Dick, a member of the crew of U-181, to Jordan Vause, author of *U-Boat Ace: The Story of Wolfgang Luth* gives a glimpse of what the crews of U-boats might have endured. This narrative was particularly relevant given the extreme heat they endured while sailing in the Caribbean. "At the beginning of a long patrol," commented Dick, "the submarine would be so crammed with provisions that the space under the eating table was used as storage. We would not have space to put our legs while eating. Traffic continually clogged the single passageway and torpedoes were stored in every conceivable place, including the steel canisters on the weather deck."[62] Continued Dick:

> The boat had a definite smell to it — a pungent mix of diesel fumes, battery acid, food, unwashed clothes, and sweat. There was the inevitable green mold that grew on the bread and shoes....The heat was intense...not just in the engine room. It caused rashes and blisters and contributed to ringworm and lice. It made the food spoil faster. The best efforts of the cook could not prevent food from tasting like diesel fuel or insects from proliferating. ? Little black bugs crawled through the rice and cockroaches scurried all over the galley, oblivious to diesel oil, acid, seawater, overpressure, vacuum and the unending persecution of disgusted crewmen.
>
> But neither the smell nor the heat nor the wet were real problems; submariners in every navy had been dealing with them for 40 years, the real problem was boredom. It bred discomfort and arguments; it made men careless and slow to respond. It could be fatal.[63]

Neutral Brazilian ships attacked

The American steamship *Hampton Roads* was sailing from Tampa, Florida to San Juan when, on June 1, it was attacked by U-106. The unescorted and unarmed vessel, which was carrying 3,320 tons of phosphate rock, was stopped by two warning shots northwest of

Cape San Antonio, Cuba. The crew was given six minutes to abandon the ship before she was sunk.

As the crew of the *Hampton Roads* was struggling to survive, they saw a Brazilian ship "hove into view and stream toward the lifeboats about the time the second torpedo was fired."[64] At the time Brazil was a neutral nation, so the crew of this ship figured that if they displayed their flag prominently, they would not be attacked. "Go away!" the Americans shouted, "there's a submarine here. Get away as fast as you can." "We'll pick you up," the Brazilian crew replied. "No," insisted the Americans, "don't do it. You'll be sunk." William J. McCarthy of New York, Second Mate of the *Hampton Roads*, said it required half an hour to persuade the rescuers to leave the scene. The next morning an airplane dropped a message to the lifeboats and another Brazilian ship sailed by a few hours later. Again, the crew of the *Hampton Roads* warned them away.[65] Twenty-three survivors were picked up by the *Alcoa Pathfinder* seven hours after the sinking and taken to Curaçao.[66]

Regardless of their neutrality, Brazilian ships were being targeted in mid-1942. Such was the case of the *Alegrete*, which despite having the Brazilian flag visibly displayed, was attacked and sunk on June 1 by U-156.[67] This blatant disregard for their neutrality coupled with pressure from the U.S. moved Brazil to declare war on Germany on November 22, 1942.

Congress approves of the Navy's performance

Between February and April 1942, 55 ships were sunk in the Caribbean without the loss of any German submarine. In May, 58 more ships were sunk. June would see an alarming increase to 66 ships sunk in a single month. It is therefore hard to believe that some members of the U.S. Congress lacked the information or understanding of these submarine attacks and the *de facto* blockade of many of the islands in the Caribbean. Though this may be the case for Carl Vinson, a Democratic congressman from Georgia who chaired the influential House Naval Affairs Committee since 1931.[68]

On June 3, at the request of Chairman Vinson, Vice Admiral Russell Wilson, the navy chief of staff to Admiral Ernest J. King, the commander of the U.S. fleet, appeared before the House Naval Affairs Committee to discuss the general aspects of the naval war, and in particular the anti-submarine warfare. As a result of these talks, Vinton stated that he had confidence in the Navy and its conduct of anti-submarine warfare. "The country does not realize that the Navy has other demands [in addition to anti-submarine warfare] in nearly every part of the world. There are those who, nevertheless, believe that our military effort is too widespread and should be concentrated on fewer areas."[69] Vinton added that it "is obvious that Admiral King has more information and more experience on which to base decisions in such matters than any other person. As an example of such decisions, concerning submarine warfare, there is the question of having a number of escort vessels inadequate to fully protect both troop transports and coastal cargo vessels."[70]

According to Vinson,

> the defeat of the submarine menace involves four essentials: organization, materials, personnel, and training. An organization cannot be suddenly built up and expanded 50-fold with smoothness and full efficiency. However, the anti-submarine warfare organization has now passed thru its period of growing pains, is well established, and is functioning effectively. Vice Admiral Adolphus R. J. Andrews at New York oversees the eastern sea frontier, Rear Admiral James L. J. Kauffman at Miami oversees the gulf sea frontier, and Vice Admiral John H. Hoover at San Juan, the Caribbean Sea frontier. In each of these frontiers, there is unity of command vested in the Navy over all Army aircraft engaged in

anti-submarine warfare, and the Army and Navy are established together in joint operational centers. The Army is cooperating wholeheartedly."[71]

In a statement previously approved by the Navy, Vinson declared on June 8 that "the enemy [Germany] is building more submarines but cannot build them in the proportion [required as] we are increasing our means of combating them. The Naval Committee has full confidence that we shall defeat the submarine."[72] In his statement, Vinson mentioned that the U-boats had "largely withdrawn from the Eastern Seaboard and [were] operating farther out to sea,"[73] in other words, in the Caribbean. Vinson added that the construction of vessels needed to combat the submarines was behind schedule, but it was "approaching a more satisfactory solution."[74] Unfortunately for the residents of the multiple islands in the Caribbean, many of whom were American citizens, it would take over one year, or until August 1943, for the U-boats to retreat from the area. Once this was accomplished, the islands would be able to start obtaining the foodstuff and essential supplies need after the blockade.

Manufacturing war material

The United States had geared toward a war economy since 1940, though after the attack on Pearl Harbor, it increased production of war matériel in an unprecedented manner. General Motors (GM), for example, started war production only 29 days after ending the civilian line. This would be one of the great success stories of the Second World War. In the spring of 1939, the Army had barely 15,000 vehicles, yet by the end of 1942, the Army would be requisitioning 800,000 vehicles of some 330 different types, not counting tanks. By the war's end, American automakers would produce 50 percent of all aircraft engines, 38 percent of aircraft propellers,

47 percent of all machine guns, 87 percent of all aerial bombs, 80 percent of tanks and tank parts, one half of the diesel engines for ships, submarines and other naval craft as well a 100 percent of the Army's trucks, half-tracks, and other vehicles. They would also supply trucks and other armaments to the Soviet Union and the British.[75] It was GM that discovered 8 Liberty ships could carry the same number of dissembled 2.5-ton trucks as 100 Liberty ships if the trucks were assembled. With 40,000 employees in their Overseas Operation Division, GM was perfectly suited to assemble these trucks wherever they were most needed.[76]

General Electric (GE), the fourth largest corporation in 1940, was also instrumental in the production of war material. GE would expand its facilities for military production and produce propulsion plants for warships, turbo-superchargers for airplanes, searchlights, military radios, radar sets, naval gun directors, and motors for operating the ramps of LSTs and similar boats. The company designed and built 300 new types of electrical lamps, manufactured heated flying suits as well as designing a new torpedo for the Navy. It also provided the turbines for 10 of the Navy's carriers, 37 of its 43 cruisers, and 200 of its 364 destroyers.[77]

Between July 1940 and August 1945, the United States produced $183 billion in war matériel, of which aircraft and ship accounted for half that figure. American shipyards launched 27 aircraft carriers, 8 battleships, 807 cruisers, destroyers and destroyer escorts, 203 submarines, and 52 million tons of merchant shipping. Factory output included 88,410 tanks and self-propelled guns, 257,000 artillery pieces, 2.4 million trucks, 2.6 million machine guns, and 411 billion rounds of ammunition, plus 324,750 aircraft, averaging 170 per day. The U.S. not only armed its military forces, it also was instrumental in assisting the Soviet Union and Great Britain. In fact, when they first met Tehran in 1943, Joseph Stalin proposed a toast "to American production, without which this war would have been lost" — a tribute from the leader of a Communist state to the forces of American capitalism.[78]

Attacks on U-boats

The *New York Times* reported that the first actual sinking of a U-boat in the Caribbean occurred on June 12, 1942. At the time, the name of the American vessel involved was withheld in compliance with the Navy's policy. According to the article submitted by *United Press*, "the gun crew of an American merchant ship, most of them youths of 20 or less, [had] sunk an Axis submarine after a brief running gun battle."[79] The newspaper article added — incorrectly as we now know — that this raised the total number of submarines sunk to "three and possibly five."[80]

"Braving withering burst of machine-gun fire that swept the decks of their vessel, the gunners fired at the submarine until it was pierced by two shells and made a crash dive."[81] Coast Guard officials stated that "the most gratifying aspect of the battle was the courage of the gun crew, despite its youthfulness, while firing at almost point-blank range."[82] The submarine in question was reported to have risen to the surface at dawn, only a few yards from the American vessel. This exposed the submarine to a broadside from the Americans. The gunners acted instinctively and quickly firing their weapons at the U-boat until two shells eventually bored into the submarine, one of them reportedly below the waterline. The submarine responded with machine-gun fire, but this did little damage and did not deter the Americans from continuing to fire their weapons at the U-boat. The submarine then crash-dived so precipitately that one member of the crew manning the machine guns was left on the deck. He was apparently not rescued. Afterward, the Americans reported an oil slick on the spot where the battle occurred, confirming what they believe to be the remnants of the submarine. Authorities refused to say precisely where this sinking occurred, only pointing out that it had taken place in the Greater Antilles, an area that encompasses Cuba, Haiti, the Dominican Republic, Jamaica and Puerto Rico — a 1,300 miles sweep from the Gulf of Mexico through the Caribbean and the Atlantic Ocean.[83]

Current documentation states that it was the *U.S. Coast Guard Thetis* that sunk the U-157 with depth charges rather than guns in the Gulf of Mexico north of Havana, Cuba. All 52 sailors aboard the submarine were killed in the attack.[84] The day before she was sunk, U-157 had attacked the unescorted American tanker *Hagan* about five miles off the north coast of Cuba. Thirty-eight crewmembers out of a total of 45 survived. Their lifeboats drifted for 13 hours before reaching Cayo Verde and Cape Roman in Cuba.[85]

On June 21, U.S. Admiral King wrote to General Marshall regarding the state of the submarine warfare:

> I have long been aware, of course, of the implications of the submarine situation as pointed out in your memorandum of 19 June.... As you are aware, we had very little in the way of anti-submarine forces...at the outbreak of the war.... We had to improvise rapidly and on a large scale.... We armed our merchant ships as rapidly as possible.... The measures were worth something, but the heavy losses that occurred up the middle of May on our East Coast give abundant proof, if proof were needed, that they were not an answer to our problem.... The situation is not hopeless.... If all shipping can be brought under escort and air cover, our losses will be reduced to an acceptable figure. I might say in this connection that escort is not just *one* way of handling the submarine menace, it is the *only* way of handling the submarine menace; it is the *only* way that gives any promise of success.

Thus, after some 2.25 million tons of lost shipping, and ignoring the recommendations of his British counterparts, Admiral King realized that convoys and escort air cover were, after all, the only method of beating the U-boats. Admiral Donitz, promoted in March 1942 as a sign of Hitler's favor for the successful exploits of his U-boats in the Caribbean and elsewhere, remarked that as the convoy system has been introduced in the Caribbean since the beginning of May "it became obvious that in the near future the main effort in the U-boat war would have to be switched back to wolf-pack attacks on convoys."[86]

The *Los Angeles Times* reported on June 23 that merchant ships sailing off the East Coast of the United States had been traveling in protected convoys "for the past 30 days."[87] Although not officially reported, the newspaper suspected that the convoy system would be expanded as quickly as new anti-submarine crafts became available. Once the Navy was in possession of these vessels, it was expected that convoys would not only operate out of the coastal waters from Maine to Florida, but they would also travel in the Gulf of Mexico and the Caribbean.

According to the information supplied by the Navy at the time, by June 1942 shipping losses in the Atlantic both to the United States and its Allies were 293 ships. Of these, 130 — 44 percent — were attacked off the coast of the United States. Eighty-seven of these were sunk in the Caribbean and 21 in the Gulf of Mexico. The remaining 55 ships were sunk off Canada and South America.[88] Once the war was over, these numbers were revised upwards. By the end of June 1942, the actual number of ships sunk in the Caribbean (including the Gulf) was 179.

On April 18, U-201 torpedoed the Argentine tanker *Victoria*.[89] Kapitänleutnant Adalbert Schnee, upon realizing that he had attacked a neutral ship reported his mistake, was ordered to cease the attack and leave the area. All 39 crewmembers survived. Following this incident, the government of Argentina lodged a strong protest to both Germany and Italy as a thorough investigation revealed that the *Victoria's* damage had indeed been caused by a torpedo and not a mine. On June 17, the German government confirmed its involvement and sent a formal apology.

A few days later, on June 23, the Navy Ministry of the Argentine government announced that the freighter *Rio Tercero* was sunk 175 miles from New York despite prominently displaying the Argentine flag, a total disregard for the neutral stance of that country.[90] Buenos Aires officially characterized this incident as "very serious."[91] Thirty-six survivors, including one passenger, reached New York aboard a naval patrol vessel. This act escalated the tension between Argentina and Germany. Days later, there were demonstrations outside of the German Embassy in Buenos Aires, and public sentiment against Germany went to an all-time high. Germany also acknowledged responsibility for this attack, offered to pay reparations, and gave assurances that no further raids would be forthcoming.[92]

June 28 would be a terrible day for American vessels. The freighter *Raphael Semmens*, traveling from Bombay, India to Trinidad and carrying 7,500 tons of manganese ore, licorice, wool, and rugs was traveling unescorted and unarmed when she was attacked and sunk by U-332. Eighteen crewmembers out of 37 lost their lives. The unescorted *Sam Houston* with 10,000 tons of Army supplies was sunk by U-203 with a loss of eight crewmembers. The tanker *William Rockefeller*, owned by Standard Oil Company of New Jersey and escorted by the *USS CG-460*, was hit and sunk by U-701 off the East Coast. There were seven survivors out of a total of 46 sailors. U-701 was later sunk by depth charges from an aircraft. The armed freighter *Tillie Lykes* en route from Galveston, Texas to San Juan was torpedoed and sunk 100 miles south of Santo Domingo, Dominican

Republic by U-154. All 33 crewmembers perished.⁹³ In total, four U.S. ships were sunk on this day.

The following day, June 29, the *Empire Mica*, a British tanker sailing in the Gulf of Mexico was attacked and sunk by U-67. Captain Hugh Bradford Bentley, of Bristol, England, recounted his harrowing ordeal. "I sighted a periscope off the port beam two or three seconds before the first torpedo struck amidships. It set the ship on fire and knocked out the communication system so that no general alarm could be sounded. Everything became red, yellow and orange — a technicolor scene."⁹⁴ Captain Bentley continued his recollection of these tragic events.

> We made for the other side, but before we had crossed over another fish clipped us. The second torpedo hit further aft and made it impossible for the gun crew to use [the gun]. Violent explosions were set off by both torpedoes. The ship was making eleven knots, too fast for the lifeboats to be lowered. Third Engineer J. Steel displayed 'particular heroism' in staying at his post at the cost of his own life to stop the engines so that the boats might be lowered. Two lifeboats caught fire before they could be lowered and the men in them were burned to death. Others were caught in their bunks by the fire.

Thirty-three crewmembers lost their lives in this attack. The 14 that survived were picked up by a Coast Guard vessel and taken to Panama City, Florida. Nine of the survivors were in serious conditions due to the burns and bruises they experienced from the attack. The following day, British radio reported that the British Director of Anti-Submarine Warfare had arrived in the United States to advise his counterparts regarding the best methods for combating the German U-boats.⁹⁵

Berlin Radio, in German-language broadcast for Europeans, stated that the enemy had "strongly increased" their defenses against the

U-boats in the Caribbean, the Gulf of Mexico, and the East Coast of the United States. They added that:

> The fight against the enemy supply shipping and patrol and escort vessels…assumed particular fierceness…. The enemy has strongly increased his submarine defense and convoy protection and is using for the battle against the ever-greater submarine danger all available craft.
>
> It could be observed that along the East Coast of the United States small vessels were used for coastal patrol and also for convoy service. Blimps of the American Navy and all types of land and seaplanes [were] patrolling the 3,000-kilometer-long south and southeast coast of the United States in order to discover the positions of [our submarines].[96]

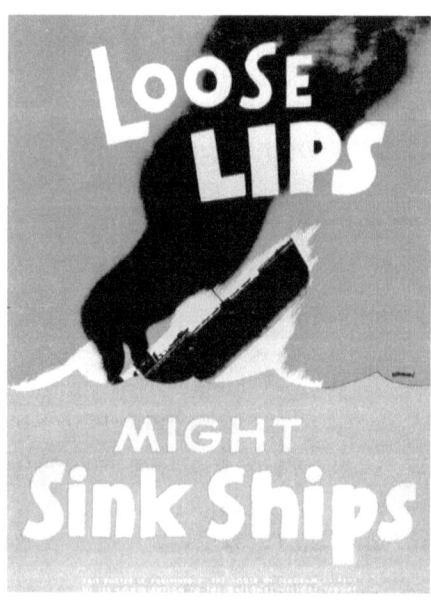

World War II propaganda poster commissioned for The Office of War Information, Bureau of Graphics. National Archives and Records Administration. https://time.com/4591841/loose-lips-sink-ships-posters/. Retrieved October 27, 2020.

While sinking in the Caribbean did not immediately cease, they dropped after June.[97] In August 1942, many U-boats shifted toward their old hunting grounds: the main convoy routes across the Atlantic. From then on, ship losses in this region would never reach similar levels. The Atlantic coastal and Caribbean campaigns had, nevertheless, been an undoubted success for Donitz and his U-boats. In Churchill's words: "For six or seven months, the U-boats ravaged American waters almost uncontrolled, and in fact almost brought us to the disaster of an indefinite prolongation of the war. Had we been forced to suspended or even seriously restrict for a time the movement of shipping in the Atlantic, all our joint plans would have been arrested."[98]

Espionage: real or imagined?

Due to the appalling number of ships sunk in May and June 1942, (58 in May and 66 in June), the U.S. military forces became convinced that the Germans were receiving information on the whereabouts of the ships in the Caribbean, such as sailing routes, dates, tonnage and cargo. On July 2, the *New York Times* reported that 20 people were "suspected of subversive activities, including supplying fuel and information to Nazi submarines" and rounded-up. The arrests were made in the Canal Zone and in British Honduras. Among those arrested were "Colon cabaret girls, Panama Canal laborers, and a prominent businessman of British Honduras."[99] According to Army, Navy and British Intelligence services and Army observers in Central America and the Canal Zone, George Gough, merchant and coastwise shipper known as "the King of Belize" was suspected of heading the ring.[100] The Army believed that he operated a fleet of 10 coastal schooners from the port of Belize in British Honduras. The Army was also aware of his other many enterprises.

British Honduras, according to Army sources, was an ideal location for this sort of activity. "It had beautiful night club hostesses who could 'wangle' information from dockworkers and pass it to the spies who would then transmit it to the submarines."[101] Army sources stated that "it would have been impossible without land-based refueling" for the U-boats to operate so far from their base in France.[102] It seems somewhat inconceivable that at this stage of the war (July 1942), the U.S. military continued to believe the U-boats were refueled by collaborators in the Caribbean and did not know that Germany had developed the 'milch cow' submarines specifically for this purpose.

In any case, Gough had fled to British Honduras when he learned of the arrest in Panamá. The Army rushed to round-up the suspected collaborators living in Belize, yet Gough, learning about this clandestinely, escaped. He was eventually captured by Navy patrol planes as he was fleeing aboard his vessel *La Laguna*. This was believed to be the first instance "where a crew of aviators was placed aboard a ship captured by planes."[103] While many believed this ring was broken, they also felt others would fill the void. "We must understand," said Lieutenant General Frank M. Andrew, commander of the Caribbean defense and the person in charge of the investigation, "that the enemy expected us to smash this ring sooner or later, and most likely has preconceived plans to place another echelon into operation. Our intelligence agencies will leave no stone unturned on ferreting out evidence of any such act. We will destroy the enemy before their activities can be used to their further advantage."[104]

Military authorities believed at the time that Gough and his cohorts had a hand in the astonishing number of ships sunk in June. These ships were attacked in the vicinity of where Gough's boats were operating. Investigating officials declined further comment except to stipulate their belief that there was a connection between these attacks and the delivery of supplies, fuel and information to the German submarines by these vessels.[105]

At the same time this operation was disclosed, President Roosevelt ordered a military trial for eight Nazis accused of entering the United States inconspicuously aboard a German U-boat with the intent of sabotaging critical military installations. The eight were taken into custody by the Federal Bureau of Investigation (FBI) in various parts of the country not long after they arrived. A military commission was convened to try the saboteurs. It was composed of seven generals, including Major General Frank R. McCoy, a former commander of the Fourth Corps Area, who presided, Major General Blanton Winship, former Governor of Puerto Rico from 1934 to 1939, and Brigadier General Guy V. Henry, also former Governor of Puerto Rico from 1898 to 1899.

Given the significance of this event, President Roosevelt issued a proclamation denying the accused the right to be tried by a civil court. They would be tried instead in a military tribunal where the decision rendered could not be appealed. It would also be conducted in secrecy and the judges would be empowered to condemn those found guilty to death. President Roosevelt requested that he be personally informed of the verdict, something that normally would be under the Secretary of War's purview.[106]

The trial was held in secret at the Justice Department starting in May 1942. The would-be-saboteurs pleaded innocence and insisted they had no intention of engaging in sabotage. The prosecution asked for the death penalty. On July 27, the defense rested and thereupon the seven generals prepared a report and sent it to President Roosevelt along with the 3,000-page trial transcript. On August 8, six of the eight German agents were executed at the District Jail in Washington, D.C. The other two were sentenced to hard labor: one for life and the other for 30 years. Their sentences were commuted in 1948.[107]

The FBI was also actively involved in the arrests of other saboteurs in Havana, Cuba. In September 1940, the Cuban Nazi Party headed by anti-Semitic Juan Prohias was abolished, and 700 Germans and 1,370 Italians were jailed.[108] Heinz Lunning, a German nationalist, was arrested on August 6, 1942. In his residence, Cuban authorities found transmitters and receivers for shortwave radio. They believed he communicated by radio with German submarines sailing close to the coast of Cuba. The two Cuban merchants' ships sunk — the *Santiago de Cuba* and the *Manzanillo*, both by U-508 — were attacked on August 12, six days after Lunning's arrest. According to Thomas D. Schoonover, author of *Hitler's Man in Havana*, Lunning was poorly trained and awkward at his work and gathered little information worth reporting,[109] so it was probable he had nothing to do with the attacks. In any case, the Cuban authorities were pressured by the FBI to try Lunning. He was put on trial and after two months, found guilty and sentenced to death. He was executed by a firing squad on November 10, 1942 in the moats of the Castle of the Prince in Havana.[110]

Lunning was not the only spy operating in Cuba. Fernando Penne Schmidt, a German-born naturalized Cuban citizen, was detained on charges of espionage in late 1942. Schmidt worked as a pilot in the harbor of Havana, overseeing the safe navigation of the ships inside the treacherous waterways of the bay. This would provide him with ample knowledge of the comings and goings of all maritime transportation. During a search of his living quarters, compromising information was found, including Axis propaganda materials and maps marking strategic points in Cuba.[111]

This assistance of the Cuban intelligence was in line with the promise President Fulgencio Batista of Cuba made to President Roosevelt during their meeting in December 1942. While in Washington, they discussed cooperation on issues of internal security and subversive activities. Batista referred to the fact that Cuban authorities, on his orders, had rounded up Axis spies. He promised, as had happened with Lunning, "that all would be punished as soon as they were discovered."[112]

In October 1942, Radio Berlin broadcasted a report detailing that a U-boat captain (the report omitted the names of the captain and the U-boat) had landed in Curaçao, been served at an American hotel (also not named), and even attended the Cinderella theater, without being recognized. According to some sources, "this report was highly likely true, and it is only one of many such reports. With the extraordinary freedom that the U-boats enjoyed, they could easily have landed teams of trained saboteur and commandos and taken off again," though the source of this report is not identified,[113] and given the failures previously detailed of the saboteurs infiltrating the continental United States, this scenario seems unlikely. Also, it does not seem plausible that a U-boat captain would risk his crew and his boat for a night out in town. As a result of these and other similar reports, American intelligence "found themselves embroiled in literally hundreds of investigations, none of which produced results…. They lived in an atmosphere of constant rumor and suspicion…that made the Caribbean Command an intelligence nightmare."[114]

German espionage was not limited to the Caribbean, as demonstrated by the case of Max Stephan, a German-born restaurant owner in Detroit, charged with 12 counts of covert acts. He was accused of assisting Hans Peter Krug, a fleeing Prisoner of War (POW), by offering him food, shelter, money and entertainment on April 18 and 19. This act constituted "aid and comfort" to an enemy of the United States in time of war.[115] Oberleutnant Krug was a German POW held by the British at Camp 30 in Bowmanville, Canada. He had been taken there after being shot down during a bombing raid over England. Krug escaped on April 17 dressed as a Canadian worker and made it to Detroit, where he met Stephan. After leaving Detroit, he traveled to San Antonio, Texas where he was arrested by the FBI. While Krug was returned to the camp, Stephan was found guilty of treason and sentenced to death. President Roosevelt commuted his sentence to life in prison. He died there in 1952.[116]

In Brazil, President Getúlio Vargas ordered "thousands of enemy aliens…sent to hundreds of internment camps."[117] Nine Gestapo agents were arrested in the State of Santa Catalina, where an espionage ring under the direction of Theodore Fredrich Schlegal operated several secret radio stations that transmitted valuable information to Berlin. They were concealing their espionage by operating an importing firm named "Herman Stolzco." At the conclusion of their trial, all were sentenced to prison terms.

Count Edmondo di Robilant, a former official of the Italian Latin airline in Brazil, was said to have operated a secret transmitter which informed Rome of the movements of Allied transports. He was said to be operating under the orders of Italian Naval Commander Enzo de Vicino. The transmitter was set up at Jacarepaguá in the State of Rio de Janeiro. After each transmission, the radio was stored in an iron box and buried. The Brazilian authorities discovered it during one of the times it was transmitting. All the Italians in the spy ring were given jail sentences. Throughout the country, police were rounding up those they considered to be carrying out "subversive activities," such as those posing as farmhands, domestic servants, and small retailers. Many innocent victims were rounded up in these anti-Axis sweeps.

CHAPTER III

Beginning of the End (July 1942–July 1944)

As soon as the United States started employing convoys to protect the routes between the mainland and the Caribbean, the number of ships sunk decreased dramatically. Doenitz noticed this change and in June 1942 transferred many of his U-boats.

> At the end of June, a group of new boats left Germany and was ordered first to a meeting point southeast of Bermuda, where a 'milch cow' would replenish fuel. The boats were then to make for the Caribbean Sea. In the meanwhile, however, the introduction of the convoy system had led to changes — to our disadvantage — in the conditions under which boats could work independently. As wolf-pack tactics could not be applied in these narrow, coastal waters, which were now under strong and constant air patrol, I decided to compromise and to use this new group for independent [enterprises].[1]

Despite all the improvements in antisubmarine warfare, the Caribbean was still a dangerous place to sail in mid-1942. On July 3, 1942, the Panamanian freighter *San Pablo* was attacked at 8:00 P.M. by U-161 in Puerto Limón, Costa Rica. The 3,305-ton vessel of the Balboa Shipping Company was discharging a cargo of the United Fruit Company when the attack started. According to offi-

Pre-sailing convoy conference at Naval Operating Base Norfolk, Virginia, July 26, 1943. Ship masters and involved Naval officers listen as the convoy escort commander explains that his warships have ordered to shoot out unauthorized lights if necessary. Note expressions. Master at extreme left, with captain's shoulder boards, is master of *SS Booker T. Washington*. Catalog #: NH 95337. Copyright Owner: Naval History and Heritage Command. Original Date: Monday, July 26, 1943. After this Year: 1939. Before this Year: 1945. Original Medium: BW Photo. https://www.history.navy.mil/content/history/nhhc/our-collections/photography/numerical-list-of-images/nhhc-series/nh-series/NH-95000/NH-95336.html. Retrieved October 4, 2020.

cial sources, the port had been blacked out for several nights.² However, German sources claim otherwise. They state that the port was fully illuminated.³

Officials at Puerto Limon were horrified when they realized that 23 stevedores, all locals, were trapped in the burning hull. It sank within an hour, killing all of them. Due to the shallowness of the harbor, the upper deck was still visible. Some officials speculated that the submarine must have been informed of the presence of the

Puerto Ricans waiting to buy bread. 1942. (Colección Fotográfica del Departamento de Instrucción Pública del Archivo General de Puerto Rico)

San Pablo from someone near the coast, possibly by a ring of collaborators.[4] On January 9, 1943, the *San Pablo* was raised and after temporary repairs, taken to Tampa, Florida to repair the damage from the U-boat attack. After careful examination, she was declared a total loss and, on September 25, sank as target practice nine miles south-southeast of Pensacola, Florida.[5]

Food is scarce

The marked reduction in food and basic necessities imported to the islands of the Caribbean took an enormous toll on their economies throughout 1942. On July 13, for instance, the government of Cuba ordered further reductions in the use of electrical power as the fuel shortage became more acute. U-boats had prevented the arrival of shipments of petroleum, and the reserves were being depleted at a rapid pace. As a result, the Government announced that radio stations must reduce their broadcasting time to less than 14 hours per day. The police were instructed to enforce the requirement that all lights be turned off by 11:00 P.M. and that all exterior lighting be removed. Government offices, private office buildings, and movie theaters were ordered to reduce their electrical consumption for lighting and ventilation systems by half.[6]

Previously, on June 10, Rexford G. Tugwell, Governor of Puerto Rico, had addressed listeners to his nightly radio address to Puerto Rico and other Caribbean islands regarding similar challenges:

> War has reached our shores and the enemy lurks in the Caribbean. Despite the blockade from the German submarines, there will be enough food for the island. Ships are already being loaded [with foodstuff and other provisions and headed to Puerto Rico]. Trains are rolling southward in the United States to ports of embarkation. Food will come safely, partly overland under the protection of the Army and Navy, and they will insure us against the worst hazards of the present submarine menace.

Tugwell had just returned from Washington where he had attended conferences with President Roosevelt and members of the Anglo-American Caribbean Commission.[7] The Commission, created on March 9, 1942, was tasked with "encouraging and strengthening social and economic cooperation between the United States of America and its possessions and bases in the area known geographically and politically as the Caribbean and the United Kingdom and the British Colonies in the same area."[8] In its first communiqué, it announced that it would concentrate efforts primarily on matters pertaining to labor, agriculture, housing, health, education, social welfare, finance and economics. One of its first meetings was held in Jamaica. There, officials experienced in supply management devised a plan to supply the eastern part of the British Caribbean islands up to and including British Guiana. Called the "Land- Water- Highway," its route was customized to evade German submarines as it reduced the exposure to them by 800 miles.

> The first section of the Highway was a shuttle service between Florida and the Gulf [of Mexico] ports and [La] Havana, Cuba. The other links in the system were a railroad from [La] Havana to Santiago de Cuba, on the eastern end of the island; a small boat service across the narrow straits separating Santiago de Cuba and Port-au-Prince, Haiti; a truck service from Port-au-Prince across the island [to] Santo Domingo [and] San Pedro de Macoris, Dominican Republic; and another small boat service from San Pedro de Macoris to Mayagüez, Puerto Rico.[9]

One of the challenges faced by shipping companies supplying the islands — besides the obvious threat from the U-boats — was the lack of available freighters, as many had been requisitioned by the armed forces to transport bauxite, copper and other essential metals need by the American smelters. Consequently, the island's private-sector income suffered because their economies depended on the exports of such homegrown stapes as sugar, coffee, and tropical fruits. This limited their available capital to purchase local goods and services. Added to this was the 'first call' by the armed forces and the construction companies working on military projects for the foodstuff that arrived.

The supplies shipped to Puerto Rico proved insufficient to feed a population of close to two million. Other islands in the Caribbean suffered similar fates. In Cuba, Haiti, the Dominican Republic, and the British West Indies the reserves of flour, beans, rice and lard and imported staples critical for the survival of the population were near exhaustion. The Central American nations of Guatemala, Honduras, Nicaragua, Costa Rica and Panamá expected a food crisis during the fall or winter of 1942.[10] All were looking to the United States for assistance. Unfortunately, the U-boats interfered with the Americans' ability to supply these critical items.

U-boats attack

The 7,551-ton American freighter *Warrior* was traveling from Philadelphia to Trinidad with 10,080 tons of general war supplies and food when it was attacked by U-126 on July 1, 125 miles east of Trinidad. Four Navy gunners and three crew members died in flames that shot high into the air.[11] Despite this, four armed guards fired four rounds from the forward 3-inch gun at the submarine's periscope but were killed in the process.[12] U-126 suffered no damage. The ship settled rapidly by the stern and sank within five minutes.

William R. McDonough, of Mobile, Alabama and captain of the *Warrior*, believed that the submarine's commander must have had information in advance about his ship's itinerary. "In my opinion, there was a lot of monkey business about this torpedoing. The crew of the submarine knew we carried a valuable cargo and [our] destination and route were known to them."[13] Four hours after the attack, the 49 survivors were picked up by the destroyer *USS Herbert* and taken to Trinidad.

Survivors of the armed Norwegian freighter *Beth*, sunk May 18 by U-162, voiced a similar opinion. They had departed Trinidad and were on their way to Freetown with 10,109 tons of fuel oil. The *Beth* was traveling on a non-evasive course at 9.5 knots in a dark night and was about 135 miles east-southeast of Barbados when it was attacked. As the survivors were rowing away from their sinking ship, the submarine surfaced, and its commander demanded to know the name of the ship, the tonnage, and its nationality. "I am the captain of the ship," replied Hans Gulliksen, when asked by Jürgen Wattenberg, captain of the U-boat. Wattenberg had trouble understanding him, so Gulliksen had to spell out his name for him. Thereupon, Wattenberg "told him the name of the port from which they had sailed and their intended destination and asked if that information was correct." Gulliksen confirmed that it was. This pretty much corroborated the crew's suspicions that the U-162 had prior information about their voyage.

The only casualty of this attack was Sigurd Swendsen, the 60-year-old boatswain. He was last seen during the launch of a lifeboat and probably fell into the water and drowned or was crushed between the boat and the side of the ship. Thirty-one others survived. The U-boat approached the lifeboats and asked if anyone was injured and whether they needed any assistance. The survivors refused help and U-162 subsequently left the scene. Some lifeboats sailed towards Barbados and made landfall 36 hours later. The others landed on Tobago on May 20.[14] There the locals thought that the island was being invaded by Germans, until "the survivors succeeded in persuading them this was not the case."[15]

Up to this point in the war, the U-boat campaign had sunk approximately one-third of the American Merchant Marine. At the outbreak of the war, in September 1939, the U.S. Merchant Marine had 1,400 vessels with an aggregate of 8.25 million tons. At the time, most of the sailings were along the East Coast of the United States. During the first half of 1942, the U-boats were sinking ships faster than they could be replaced. The American shipyards could build only one ship for every three that the U-boats were sinking. This, of course, had a detrimental effect on the economies of the Caribbean islands.[16] Up until July 1942, only two U-boats has been sunk in the Caribbean. As mentioned before, U-157 was sunk on June 13, 1942 by the U.S. Coast Guard cutter *Thetis*. No member of that crew survived the attack. The other submarine was U-153.

The history of the demise of the U-153 is complicated, with many parties having claimed the kill. Due to the censorship applied by the Navy, the press and historians were only allowed access to this information after the end of the war. The U-153 was either sunk by Army Air Force Squadron No. 59 based in Curaçao on July 6 or by the 2,000-ton Buchanan class destroyer *USS Lansdowne* on July 13. From the few radio reports logged at the U-boat headquarters, it appeared that U-153 was near the Colombian coast. This, however, is difficult to ascertain as there are few references in the U-boat command diary. Neither No. 59 squadron nor the *USS Lansdowne* sighted wreckage or had definite proof they had sunk the submarine. U-boat headquarters noted on July 15 that the U-153 had failed to reply to numerous messages. As a result, on August 1, U-boat headquarters assumed it was lost. It is ironic that it was not possible to pinpoint the location of this submarine, as the positions of the two purported attacks were 500 miles and eight days of sailing apart.[17] All aboard the U-153 were lost.[18] On March 26, 1943, almost a year after the U-153 was lost, the Army awarded air metals to the crew of the plane who purportedly sunk the submarine. "The pilot, Captain Marshall E. Groover, of Ball Ground, Georgia was cited for having maneuvered the light bomber so skillfully that it was in position for a direct attack on the U-boat" before it had a chance to submerge. Sergeant John E. Badzik, of Donora, Pennsylvania, and Corporal Ralph D. Tobias, of Nappanee, Indiana were also awarded medals.[19]

After torpedoing the unescorted American freighter *Tachirá* which was carrying 2,100 tons of cacao and coffee from Colombia to New Orleans, Hans-Ludwig Witt, the captain of U-129, questioned the 34 survivors. Captain Sverre Gram of the *Tachirá* told Navy officers upon his rescue the following recount of his ordeal: "As we were rowing away from the sinking *Tachirá* the submarine came to the surface and approached with their machine guns trained on our lifeboats. The submarine commander was dressed in blue shorts. He was deeply tanned and had a heavy beard. He spoke English with a strong accent. He asked whether we had passed through the Panama Canal, to which I replied in the negative, and the subject was dropped."[20] According to Gram (who at the time did not know the number identifying the U-boat), the U-129 was large and painted light gray, with a blue and gold coat of arms painted on the conning tower and a flag bearing the swastika flying from the stern. Five men were killed when the torpedo struck the aft portion of the ship, tearing the stern away. "Two minutes later, at about 9:50 P.M.," added Gram, "the ship went down."[21]

July 1942 would be a turning point for the U-boats in the Second World War. The tonnage sunk for July in all theaters of the war was 365,398 while that of August was 110,801.[22] The U-boats would continue to have some successes in the Caribbean, as the tonnage sunk in July was 132,110 and in August it increased to 241,368.[23] For a while anyway, the Caribbean would represent a significant portion of the ships sunk by the U-boats: 36 percent in July and 54 percent in August. These came at an exceptionally low cost to the Germans. In July, only the U-153 was lost and in August, U-94. On the other hand, 37 U-boats were lost in July and 25 in August in all other theaters of the war. On average, each of these U-boats sunk around 10,000 tons in July and 4,800 in August; a far cry from the performance of the U-boats in the Caribbean.

On July 17, Lieutenant General Frank Andrews, commander of the Caribbean defenses, held a press conference in which he stated

Convoy in the Gulf of Mexico photographed May 29, 1944, with a PBY flying patrol overhead. Catalog #: 80-G-238408.Copyright Owner: National Archives. Original Date: Monday, May 29, 1944. After this Year: 1939. Before this Year: 1945. Original Medium: BW Photo. https://www.history.navy.mil/content/history/nhhc/our-collections/photography/numerical-list-of-images/nhhc-series/nh-series/80-G-238000/80-G-238408.html. Retrieved October 4, 2020.

that the "new anti-submarine defense measures" had proven very effective, although he would not discuss the nature of these measures.[24] Doenitz, however, had quickly realized that it was the use of the convoy system that had been effective in reducing the overall number of ships sunk after June. Secretary of the Navy, Colonel William F. Knox, also stated that the "convoy is the one really effective antidote to direct attack" by a U-boat. "The experience in each theater had been the same," added Knox. "Where merchants ships have not been convoyed, or where the convoy escorts have been inadequate, U-boats have inflicted heavy losses.... As soon as the convoy system has been put into full operation, it has been the

U-boat themselves that have suffered the heavy losses, and they have been driven to seek areas further afield, where merchant shipping is less adequately protected."[25]

A *New York Times* reporter and an *Associated Press* photographer were invited by the Navy on July 29 to go onboard a naval vessel commanded by Lieutenant Commander John. F. Walsh which was leading his first convoy of merchant ships across the Caribbean. Commander Walsh, a native of Washington, a former instructor of ordnance at the Naval Academy in Annapolis and a veteran of the foreign service stated that: "[the U-boats] may sink ships, but from now on they [will have to] fight for every one they hit."[26] He made these comments after engaging in the first of several skirmishes he would encounter on his voyage. "So successful was Walsh and his officers in outguessing and outmaneuvering the U-boats," commented the *New York Times* reporter, "that not one torpedo was fired at the convoy or a subsequent one escorted northbound for the United States. Nor," he added, "on other convoys plowing at frequent intervals."[27]

Walsh explained his strategy in the following terms. "I ignore submarines which posed no threat and only engage those that do." Such was the case when he ignored a submarine positioned 30 miles from the convoy yet sent his destroyers at flank speed to a point 50 miles out as he believed that it was possible that the U-boat was trailing the convoy. The destroyers attacked with depth charges, but whether the submarine was destructed or escaped was difficult to ascertain. However, Walsh and his officers believed that with this strategy, they could drive the U-boats away and avoid attacks on his convoy. "All of our action was crowded into a few scattered hours," assured the reporter. "There were many days of peaceful sailing, the routine of which was interrupted only once when the ship's doctor, Lieutenant D. J. McCarthy, of Savannah, Georgia, performed an emergency appendectomy, a difficult surgery feat aboard a tossing warship."[28]

As for the effectiveness of the measures being taken, in a press conference held on August 3, Rear Admiral Clifford Evans Van Hook, commander of the 15th Naval District, quoted Admiral Doenitz's recent radio broadcast. Doenitz was cited as saying that the battle in American waters was no longer a simple matter, as the Americans had learned, rather quickly, to defend themselves. Van Hook reacted to this broadcast by stating unequivocally that the United States was providing sufficient and adequate escort of the convoys traveling to and from the Caribbean.[29] Escort groups were comprised of cutters, sloops and sometimes corvettes. "We believe that the U-boats have been forced to seek other water," commented another Navy official.[30] They, of course, were referring to the dramatic reduction in the number of ships sunk between June and July. Unfortunately for the Allies, this number increased to 46 in August despite the measures being taken, though from then on it would continue to decrease.

The Navy's official policy was not to disclose the statistics regarding the ships lost until quite some time after the actual attack occurred. For this reason, articles published during the second half of August point to spectacular success in battling the U-boats when the opposite was true. The number of ships attacked and sunk during those two weeks had increased. Navy officials were quoted as saying that "there has been a very definite decline in the rate of sinkings during the last two weeks" as more planes are available to search out the U-boats. Yet, not having timely data available, they might not have realized the inaccuracy of these statements, and the harm they could possibly inflict to both themselves and the civilian population. Even in July, when Van Hook claimed that the Caribbean "had been particularly free from effective attacks on shipping," the U-boats claimed 28 victims.[31]

According to Governor Tugwell, "information even in the Navy was not too good. We had a few patrol planes, but they were old Army B-18s, short-range but dependable; and we had some YP boats which were converted yachts and not very dangerous really, although it was amazing how they frightened the submarines."[32] Tugwell would walk along the San Juan harbor which was fitted with a submarine net and a small tender anchored at the center, wondering when the next shipment of food and critical supplies would reach the island. "In the week since I [returned], no merchant ship had come in."[33] The comforting words of Rear Admiral Van Hook and other Navy officials did little to assuage Tugwell's concerns. As Governor of Puerto Rico, an American colony, he was responsible for the wellbeing of its citizens.

His concerns were not unfounded. In August, German submarines were again having success in the Caribbean. Doenitz explained why:

> In August...our captains found from experience, however, that they were never attacked by the patrolling aircraft when they were inside the protective screen of the convoy or in close vicinity of the escort vessels. Accordingly, our boats proceeded with circumspection, steering the general course as the convoy and avoiding any major change of direction. This, presumably, was because in these circumstances the aircraft were unable with their locating gear to tell the difference between their own ships and our U-boats.
>
> In September the success achieved in the Caribbean by these surprise tactics came to an end, and the U-boats were withdrawn towards Trinidad and the coast of Guiana. Further marked success was achieved in this month against the heavy but sporadic traffic in those areas [32 ships were sunk that month].[34]

At the time, there were 12 U-boats operating in the Caribbean, including the Italian submarine *Tazzoli*. These U-boats would be responsible for sinking 46 ships with a total tonnage of 241,368 while losing only two submarines in the process. The first U-boat sunk in August was a new Type IXC built in 1941. The U-166 was under the command of the inexperienced captain Hans-Günther Kuhlmann with an equally inexperienced crew. They had been ordered to lay mines close to the Delta of the Mississippi River which flows into the Gulf of Mexico. The waters along the Delta were very shallow, and there was a lot of commercial and military ships traversing the area. The U-166 spent three days in the area reporting on the traffic, enough time for the authorities to realize that there was a German U-boat close by laying mines. When it sunk the 5,000-ton freighter *Robert E. Lee*, the Navy was able to triangulate the U-boat's position. As these submarines were forced to surface in order to charge their batteries and refresh the air inside, U-166 was forced into a compromising position. When the U-boat surfaced, aircraft from Coast Guard Squadron 212 were waiting for him. The U-boat was sunk in very shallow waters, which might have given the crew ample opportunity to survive; however, it is possible that the escape compartment might have been damaged in the attack, as none did.[35]

On July 24, the Commanding Officer of the Marine Corps Air Station in Saint Thomas, U.S. Virgin Islands, Lieutenant Stephen J. Donovan, sent a report to Admiral Hoover with information obtained from the survivors of the *S.S. Sam Houston* which was attacked and sunk by U-203, a fearful submarine which sunk 21 ships and damaged three before being itself sunk on April 25, 1943.[36] The dreadful account of the *Sam Houston's* demise was relayed to Donovan by the ship's [unnamed] captain.

> At 0945, on Sunday, June 28, we were traveling north of Sombrero Island, Anguilla, when we were struck by a torpedo. It hit the starboard side, about midship, between the engine room and the

number four deep tank. Every piece of machinery and instruments were immediately disabled, engine, radio, lights, etc. Fire immediately swept up through the quarters and fire and smoke filled the passageways.

It was immediately obvious that the ship was doomed, and preparations were made to abandon it. The motor launch was blown up and inboard with the explosion. This first boat launched on the port side was lost but not upset. The other boat was loaded with the injured first and then with the uninjured, to the number of 29. This boat was launched. The starboard launch was tangled and fouled with spare and gear of the broken motor launch. When the water got to the main deck, we managed to get [the lifeboat] away carrying 14 men.[37]

The captain added that two men had died of burns the night of the accident and were buried at sea. Another died the next morning and another that afternoon. The bodies of these last two were returned to the submarine base in Saint Thomas.

The information gathered by Lieutenant Donovan from the survivors specified that the lifeboats were difficult to launch due to their design configuration. The survivors added that sun exposure did not seem to be a serious factor. Though Donovan noticed that the survivors did exhibit a tan, they were not seriously hurt. They also did not seem to be emotionally affected. The red sail of the lifeboats aided in their rescue. "No one suffered from lack of food or water. There were not enough blankets in the lifeboats. Those severely burned were burned on nude areas. The rated capacity of the lifeboats of 31 was far overrated. Even with 14 men on the boat, they were overcrowded and uncomfortable. The chocolate bars stored in two of the boats had been stolen."[38]

Given the difficulties the *Sam Houston* survivors had with their lifeboats, Lieutenant Donovan proposed the following enhancements to the Senior Medical Officer in San Juan and the Chief of the Bureau of Medicine and Surgery in Washington. All lifeboats should be equipped with a medical kit and supplied with an antiseptic ointment for the treatment of eye burns. They should have concentrated vitamin capsules, concentrated canned fruit, morphine, a catch basin for rainwater, a light-colored cover to protect against sunburn, and an increase in the allotment of blankets. The inside of the lifeboat should be painted with a color that contrasts with that of the water, like yellow and a red or pink sail with an S.O.S. painted on or its radio equivalent should be included. A severe penalty should be imposed for the theft of any item stored in the lifeboats.[39] Though these were excellent suggestions, they do not seem to have been followed through, as attested by the suffering of the many survivors of later sinkings.

On August 1, the unescorted and neutral Uruguayan freighter *Maldonado*, traveling from Montevideo to New York, was attacked and sunk west of Bermuda by U-510. The freighter was carrying tinned meat, hides, wool and fats. The survivors were interviewed by *Associated Press* after their ordeal, some of whom had to wait 15 days before being rescued by the U.S. Coast Guard. They recounted how Karl Neitzel, the submarine commander, took Mario Gianbeuo, the *Maldonado*'s captain, prisoner and left the remainder of the crew on their lifeboats to fend for themselves. This was the second Uruguayan vessel sunk by the U-boats, despite the country's neutral stance. According to Andres Cikoto, *Maldonado*'s First Officer:

> We first sighted the submarine about 6:30 P.M. and for four hours she paralleled our course during which time we floodlighted our Uruguayan flag painted on our side. Then about midnight she fired a shot across our bow, then fired three shells at us and blinked the signal "boats."
>
> Our whole crew of 49 piled into four lifeboats and rowed away. The submarine fired one torpedo into her and then started to cruise about among our lifeboats.

The commander in the conning tower [Karl Neitzel] called for the captain and the chief engineer, the captain's boat rowed over to the submarine and the captain was taken aboard. As the chief engineer was about to step aboard, the submarine got underway and submerged.

The submarine then fired a second torpedo into the freighter breaking it in half and sinking it immediately. For a few days, we were able to keep together but after several nights we lost contact with each other. We did not experience much hardship, except for the small water ration of six ounces per day.[40]

The sinking of the *Maldonado* and the detention of captain Mario Gianbeuo lead to massive demonstrations in the capital of Montevideo. Doenitz's U-boat headquarters was severely criticized in Uruguay for permitting the sinking of its neutral bound and unarmed freighter. Karl Neitzel — though his name was not known to the Uruguayan authorities — was criticized for being inexperienced and for not following the Prize Rules and for capturing a Uruguayan national. Gianbeuo was returned unharmed in September 1942. He made his way through Switzerland and arrived in Uruguay the following month.[41]

On August 13, the *Los Angeles Times* reported the sinking of two Cuban merchant ships, the 1,865-ton *Santiago de Cuba* and the 1,025-ton *Manzanillo* in the Gulf of Mexico. Five crewmen were reported dead while 26 were missing.[42] Meanwhile, *The Atlanta Constitution* recounted that indignant Cubans reacted harshly to this news. President Fulgencio Batista expressed his anger over these attacks in a formal statement "and called on all Cuba to honor the victims. The Cuban newspaper *Prensa Libre* urged the government in no uncertain terms to apply the law of a tooth for a tooth and an eye for an eye."[43] After searching the area for survivors, only the bodies of Cuban crew members were found. They were taken to Havana and interned in the Capitol's *Cementerio de Colon*.[44]

Cuban ships, however, were not the only ships targeted by the U-boats. The next day, August 14, three British ships were sunk off the coast of Cuba by U-598. Even though they had the protection of a convoy, U-598 fired a spread of torpedoes that sank the *Michael Jebsen* and the *Empire Corporal* and damaged the *Standella* northwest of Barlovento Point, Cuba. Forty crewmembers out of a total of 47 onboard the *Michael Jebsen* survived. The freighter was carrying 2,750 tons of sugar from Barbados to Trinidad. The *Empire Corporal* was carrying 4,532 tons of motor spirit and 4,745 tons of white spirit from Curaçao to Key West, Florida. Forty-nine out of a total complement of 55 survived and were transferred to the naval base at Guantanamo.[45] Meanwhile, reacting to this sudden surge in sinkings during his visit to San Juan, Lieutenant General Frank M. Andrews, commander of the American defenses in the Canal Zone, stated that there was no "strong evidence" indicating that the U-boats were getting supplies from the Caribbean. He did not believe, moreover, that there were clandestine bases in the Caribbean used to repair the submarines and to furnish them with ammunition.[46]

Three Allied ships were sunk on August 17, the British *Fort la Reine*, the Egyptian *Samir*, and the American tanker *Louisiana*. The *Fort la Reine* was transporting 5,200 tons of general cargo and 4,100 tons of grain and lumber from Vancouver, Canada to the Naval Base at Guantanamo when it was sunk by U-638 west of Haiti. Minutes later, U-638 caught up with the *Samir* which sank five minutes after being attacked.[47] The *Louisiana* was traveling unescorted from Trinidad to Rio de Janeiro, Brazil, with 92,514 barrels of gasoline and oil when it was attacked by U-108.

According to Navy sources, August marked the resumption of large-scale submarine activity in the Caribbean after the lull in July. Prior to that time, the U-boats had found the Caribbean "a happy hunting ground," but with the introduction of the convoy system in

July, and the dramatic reduction in the number of ships sunk that month, it was hoped that the battle with the U-boats was finally being won. August proved this hope premature.

The U-boats were being more cautious in their tactics by torpedoing their victims at night, as demonstrated by the August 17 strikes. Several hours before the *Louisiana* was attacked, its Radio Operator Theodore Hergenrader, 38, of New Orleans was awakened by the automatic radio alarm warning him that the *Samir* had been sunk by a submarine about 20 miles away. "I watched through my glasses as smoke billowed up and the ship went down in about a minute. There was a big loss of life," he added, "I don't know how many, but it was about 25."[48] Shortly thereafter, the *Louisiana* was struck by a torpedo and, according to Hergenrader, sank in four minutes. When interviewed after his rescue, he claimed that the attack was the work of two submarines working in conjunction. "Submarines have changed their tactics," he recounted to the *United Press*. "They just lie [and] wait for passing ships. When the ships come, they spring up, make a quick attack, and then go back to waiting again."[49] In a broadcast recorded by the *Associated Press*, Berlin Radio reported that the increase in the number of ships sunk in the Caribbean showed the "intensified continuation of the U-boat blockade" in the Gulf of Mexico and the Caribbean.[50]

The unescorted Dutch freighter *Moena* was traveling from Bombay, India to Trinidad when on August 24, it burst into flames upon being torpedoed by U-162 100 miles east of Barbados. "The whole aft end of the ship became enveloped in flames, and the survivors [were] just plain lucky," recounted Chief Officer J. Wols, 40, a Dutch military veteran. "It's a wonder we didn't all die," he added. The *Moena* sank four minutes after the crew had launched their lifeboats. Out of a crew of 87, 83 survived and were picked up the following day by the British motor merchant *Cromarty*. They were then taken to Trinidad.[51]

The 46 ships sunk in August came at a loss of only two U-boats. U-654 had sunk three ships and one warship before she was sunk by depth charges from a U.S. B-18 Bolo aircraft north of Colon, Panamá on August 22. All 44 crewmembers were killed in the attack. A few days later, on August 28, U-94 was sunk after being rammed on the surface by the Canadian corvette HMCS *Oakville* and by depth charges from a U.S. Catalina aircraft as it tried to submerge. Twenty-six sailors out of a total complement of 45 survived and were taken prisoner. U-94 had sunk 26 ships on her 10 patrols starting in August 1940. Her captain, Otto Ites, 24, was awarded the Knights Cross for this achievement.[52]

U-162's demise

During the beginning of September, there were only six U-boats in the Caribbean, so U-171 was ordered to the Gulf of Mexico. U-558, U-164, and U-217 patrolled the area in the vicinity of Trinidad while U-66 was in the area east of Trinidad. At this point, the United States and its Allies had become sophisticated submarine hunters, so much so that no single U-boat could successfully challenge a strong escorted convoy with unlimited air support. U-162 paid the ultimate price by not adapting to the changing environment.[53]

On September 1, Captain Wattenberg of the U-162 sent his last message to U-boat headquarters. That evening, he made the fatal mistake of attacking, inadvertently, three British destroyers. The HMS *Pathfinder, Quentin,* and *Vimy* were proceeding to Trinidad to pick up a convoy of tankers. All three ships were fitted with ASDIC and depth charges, both for firing off the launchers and from the rails at the stern.[54] ASDIC, known as Sonar to the Americans, was the primary underwater detection device used by the Allies throughout the war. It was basically a transmitter-receiver that sent out a highly directional sound wave through the water. The length of time from the transmission to the return of the sound provided a rough estimate of the distance to the target.[55]

On September 3, all three ships were roughly 50 miles northeast of Trinidad. Wattenberg's inexperienced hydrophone operator probably did not inform him that he was about to attack not one but three destroyers. U-162 dived to prepare for the attack but was quickly detected by the *Pathfinder*'s ASDIC operator. U-162 fired torpedoes but missed the *Pathfinder*. Then *Pathfinder* regained the ASDIC contact and started to depth charge the submarine. It is probable that leaks started appearing all over the submarine, including the engine room. Wattenberg decided it was time to leave the area as fast as possible and for some time was able to evade his pursuers. He headed towards the Caribbean islands, exactly opposite the direction the destroyers guessed he would travel. Needing air to recharge the batteries and give his crew some rest, Wattenberg ordered the U-boat to surface. The destroyers were then able to locate the submarine. After the *Vimy* rammed the U-boat and it lost navigational control, Wattenberg ordered his crew to abandon the sub. *Pathfinder* and *Quentin* picked up 49 survivors, including Wattenberg. They were taken to Port-of-Spain and then to the St. James POW camp. After a couple of weeks, they were flown to the United States where they ended up picking cotton in Arizona for the next four years. During this period, 25 Germans escaped from the camp including Wattenberg, who was only recaptured after an extensive search lasting 36 days.[56]

In September 1942, Doenitz decided that the easy successes the U-boats had been having in the Caribbean since the beginning of the year had come to an end. The U-boats were withdrawn toward Trinidad and the coast of Guiana. In any case, U-boats still managed to sink 32 ships in September, though it was a far cry from the 66 sunk in May, their highest total. Doenitz credits this success to the "efficiency and fighting spirit" of the U-boat captains. He was, however, concerned about the increasing air cover the Allies had managed to achieve in such a short span of time. "These ever-increasing difficulties which confront us in the conduct of the war can only lead, in the normal course of events to high and, indeed, intolerable losses, to a decrease in the volume of our success and to a diminishment, therefore, of our chances of victory in the U-boat war as a whole."[57]

Laconia incident

On September 12, 1942, the tragedy of the sinking of the *Laconia* by U-156 under captain Werner Hartenstein would change the nature of the relationship between the attacking U-boats and the victims of these attacks. It would also be one of the reasons Doenitz was accused of war crimes in the Nuremberg Trial in 1946. The 19,695-ton British armed liner carried a British crew of 436 men, 268 British service personnel, including 80 women and children, 1,800 Italian POWs, and 160 Polish ex-prisoners of war serving as guards for the Italians. Appalled at consigning so many soldiers to death by drowning, Hartenstein began a rescue operation and asked Doenitz for authorization to continue. On receiving the news, Doenitz, with Admiral Erich Raeder's approval, allowed the rescue operation, as the Italians were German allies.

The torpedoed *Laconia* had sent an SOS signal indicating that she had been attacked. The broadcast gave her position. Since he was sure the Allied forces had heard this broadcast, Captain Hartenstein broadcasted the following message in English: "If any ship will assist the shipwrecked Laconia Crew, I will not attack her

German submariners rescuing the survivors of the torpedoed British liner *Laconia*. Shown is the shuttle service for shipwrecked persons from the *Laconia* between U-156 (foreground) and U-507 (background). Deutsches U Boot Museum, Cuxhaven.

provided I am not being attacked by ship or air force. I picked up 193 men.... German submarine."[58] On September 15, U-506 and U-507 joined U-156 in the rescue mission. The next day, as reported by U-156 in the captain's War Diary, they were attacked by an aircraft despite displaying a large Red Cross flag four yards square on the bridge facing the line of the aircraft flight. The aircraft flew away and returned half an hour later and attacked again. The War Diary of U-156 read as follows:

> Aircraft of similar type approached. Flew over at a height of 250 feet slightly ahead of boat and dropped two bombs at an interval of about three seconds. While the tow for lifeboats was being cast

off, the aircraft dropped a bomb in the middle of these boats. One boat capsized. Aircraft cruised round in the vicinity for some little while and then dropped forth bomb some two or three thousand yards away. Realized that his bomb-racks were now empty. Another aircraft. Two bombs one of which with a few seconds delayed action exploded directly beneath control room. Conning tower disappeared in a mushroom of black water. Control room and bow compartment reported making water. Ordered all hands to don lifejackets. Ordered all British to leave the boat. Next, all Italians away, as the battery begins to give off gas.

Sent out war emergency message on four wavelengths, each repeated three times. Returned to the lifeboats, to which I transferred all remaining survivors. (Some of them required a little gentle persuasion). Reports regarding leaks canceled. No leak.[59]

When confronted with this unexpected and surprising situation, the pilot, Lieutenant James Harden, had called his control at a new U.S. Army Air Force base in Ascension Island for instructions on how to proceed. The officer in charge passed the request up the chain of command who in turn called Washington. As he could not get through, he made the decision that would have a profound impact on the survivors of submarine attacks for the remainder of the war. He passed along the order to sink the U-boats.[60] Upon hearing that his prized U-boats were attacked on the surface despite visibly displaying a Red Cross flag, Doenitz issued an order that under no circumstances should a U-boat commander should risk the safety of his ship, which meant that all rescue operations were to be abandoned. "Do not rely on enemy showing slightest consideration," he added.[61] On September 17, Doenitz issued his most controversial order:

> All attempts to rescue the crews of sunken ships will cease forthwith. This prohibition applies equally to the picking up of men in the water and putting them aboard a lifeboat, to the

righting of capsized lifeboat and to the supply of food and water. Such activities are a contradiction of the primary objective of war, namely, the destruction of enemy ships and their crews.[62]

From this point on, survivors of ships sunk by U-boats would receive no mercy. Afterward, there were instances of U-boat captains machine-gunning survivors, as happened with U-852 when it sunk a steamer in Greece full of passengers and shot the survivors in what became known as the Peleus Affair. We found no such instance of this occurring in the Caribbean.

By the end of 1942, the U-boats had sunk a total of 1,662 ships with a loss of 88 of their own. Yet the average number of ships sunk per U-boat was dropping. In 1941, the average U-boat sunk 37 ships, while in 1942, that number was reduced to 19. The U-boats were therefore starting to pay a heavier price for their incursions as the Allied antisubmarine tactics became more successful.[63] How does this performance compare with the results achieved in the Caribbean?

U-boats sunk 336 ships in the Caribbean during 1942, and the Caribbean accounted for a whopping 20 percent of the total number of ships sunk by U-boats in 1942.[64] The average U-boat in the Caribbean sunk 46 ships. The first eight months of 1942 were even more impressive, as 253 ships were sunk with an average of 51 ships sank per U-boat. Doenitz knew this would not last.

The tide turns

The first U-boat sunk in the Caribbean, as previously noted, was U-157 on June 13. U-153 was sunk on July 3 northwest of Aruba by aircraft while U-166 was sunk on July 30 southeast of New Orleans. There were no survivors from either submarine. U-94 and U-654 were sunk in August, the first on August 22 and the latter on the

28th. Both were sunk north of Colon, Panamá by aircraft. Nineteen sailors survived the sinking of U-94 while none survived on U-654. U-162 was sunk on September 3 while U-512 was sunk on October 2. The last U-boat sunk in 1942 was the U-512 which met her fate north of Cayenne, French Guiana by depth charges from an aircraft. There was only one survivor. All told, seven U-boat were lost in the Caribbean and the Gulf of Mexico in 1942.[65]

The cost in human lives of the 336 ships lost in the Caribbean is staggering, especially when compared to the few lives lost by the Axis in this pursuit. According to Gaylor Kelshall's book *The U-Boat War in the Caribbean*, the merchant marine sustained a 17 percent loss rate compared to 9 percent for the Navy and Air Force and 6 percent for the Army. Shipwrecked survivors faced sharks, heatstroke and thirst. The Allied Command post at Trinidad estimated that 1,167 crewmembers survived the sinking of their ship. Most of these were rescued during the second half of 1942. During the first half, the United States was unprepared for this effort. If we assume that each ship carried a crew of 50, then the 336 ships that were sunk would have impacted a total of 16,800 sailors. If, as the record demonstrates, the loss rate for the merchant marine was 17 percent, then we can estimate that 2,856 crewmembers were killed in the U-boat attacks, and 13,944 were saved. This is in comparison to the 272 U-boat sailors who lost their lives on the seven U-boats sunk during the same time period. The irony that U-boat sailors were saved by the Allies while their victims were left to die was not lost on those who rescued them.

Captain Jürgen Wattenberg had an interesting history before taking command of U-162. He was a former navigation officer aboard the *Admiral Graf Spee*, the German pocket battleship scuttled in Uruguay in 1939. He escaped from Argentina and returned to Germany where he was given command of the submarine until it was sunk on September 4, 1942. The 49 survivors of the U-162 were taken into custody by the British and confined to Port of Spain, Trinidad before being transferred to American custody and taken from Trinidad to Miami and later to Washington, D.C.

> After a brief stay in Fort Meade, Washington, Wattenberg, his officers, and his crew were interrogated at Fort Hunt in Alexandria, Virginia. Most of the crew were then sent to Crossville, Tennessee, and later Papago Park, located outside of Phoenix, Arizona. There Wattenberg and several of his officers would make national headlines when, two days before Christmas 1944, they were among the 25 participants in the largest POW escape that occurred in the United States.[66]

Life as a POW in America

The United States would, throughout the war, become a place where German POWs of all branches of the military were interned. All would be accorded the rights bestowed on them by the 1929 Geneva Convention, though none of the Axis powers recognized or abided by the Geneva Convention. In May 1942, the United States had only 32 POWs, 31 Germans, and 1 Japanese. In August 1942, Lord Halifax, the British emissary to the State Department, persuaded Washington to accept an emergency batch of 50,000 German POWs from Britain. However, large numbers began to arrive in May 1943 after the defeat of Rommel's Afrika Korps. By spring of 1944, the Army was handling more German and Italian prisoners than there had been American soldiers in the entire pre-war Army. Ultimately, there would be 378,898 Germans and 51,455 Italian POWs in the U.S. Surviving U-boat men comprised a small portion of them.

Including all auxiliary camps, 10,000 German POWs were interned in Florida, and Camp Blanding was the largest POW camp in the state. The first contingent of U-boat men arrived at Camp Blanding on September 24, 1942. Early in the war, naval intelligence was particularly interested in interrogating these U-boat captives, and naval intelligence was surprised to find them willing to provide valuable information regarding submarine tactics and capabilities. As hard-core Nazis interned with them might suspect them of collaborating with the Americans and turn on them, U-boat POWs were frequently placed in an anti-Nazi compound, both for their protection and so they would not be "contaminated" by other German POWs.[67]

Life in the POW camp was regimented, but the prisoners were not subjected to the rigors of war or the excruciating treatment given American POWs in German camps. Daily routines began with reveille at 5:30 A.M. Prisoners headed toward breakfast prepared by German cooks. They were housed, feed, and clothed in a similar fashion to the Americans guarding them. The United States adhered strictly to the Geneva Convention in the hope (unsuccessful as we now know) that the American POWs would be extended the same treatment.

After breakfast, the Germans could use the soap, toothpaste, shaving cream, and razors they purchased with the money the United States government provided them in the form of canteen coupons. Between 7:00 A.M. and 4:30 P.M., Monday through Saturday, they would perform manual labor and get paid for their work. Some of these tasks included agricultural work and assisting the undermanned military base. They would get lunch at noon and finish working at 5:00 P.M. After dinner, they could play sports, see an American movie, attend an English, math, or American history class, or relax in the POW-run canteen.[68]

Lend-Lease programs in the Caribbean

Since the beginning of the Lend-Lease Program on March 11, 1941, the U.S. Government and private shipyards, under the direction of the Navy's Bureau of Ships, repaired, converted and overhauled vessels for the Allied nations. Cuba and the Dominican Republic were significant beneficiaries of this program. However, in addition to the technical difficulties involved, there were language and cultural barriers to overcome. In the case of these islands and other Latin American nations, their primary and official language was Spanish.[69]

A colorful ceremony was celebrated in Miami, Florida on March 22, 1942 whereby 10 speedy Coast Guard anti-submarine patrol boats were transferred from the United States to Cuba. Captain H.H. J. Benson, commander of the Seventh Naval District read the orders of transfer while the national flag of Cuba was simultaneously raised over each vessel. Commodore Julio D. Arguelles, chief of Cuba's Navy, remarked that Cuba was proud to be an ally of the United States of America in these difficult times. Benson added that this transfer "is a further emphatic demonstration of the joint action of the countries of the Americas against the common foe, the Axis."[70] "We of the United States Navy," observed Benson, "are happy to work with you in avenging the death and destruction which the foe has wrought in these waters of our frontier."[71] He noted that all of the Cuban crews had been trained at the sub-chaser school in Miami.[72]

In comparison to the vast scale of the Lend-Lease Program, the assistance given to the Dominican Republic in the form of weapons, supplies, and expertise was minuscule. However, the Dominican Republic obtained 12 coastal patrol boats, 19 airplanes, 3,000 old Enfield rifles without ammunition, and some equipment for general use. As in the case of Cuba and other Allied countries, this assistance came at a cost. These nations would have to declare war on Germany. In the case of the Dominican Republic, its two merchant ships, the *San Rafael* and the *Presidente Trujillo*, were sunk by U-boats in May 1942.[73] Cuba also lost two ships to U-boat attacks, the *Manzanillo* and the *Santiago de Cuba* both sunk on August 12, 1942.[74]

Rafael Trujillo, the previously mentioned dictator of the Dominican Republic, was initially enamored by Hitler's spectacular rise to power. He changed his military's attire to resemble Nazi and Italian fascists uniforms. However, he needed to remain on friendly terms with the United States not only for military reasons but also for economic ones. The Dominican Republic's economy was largely dependent on sugar exports to the United States. At the July 1938 international conference sponsored by President Roosevelt on the rescue and relocate of millions of displaced people, mainly German and Austrian Jews fleeing the Nazis, only one of all the countries in attendance offered to open its doors to the fleeing refugees, and that was the Dominican Republic, which offered to take in at least 100,000 Jewish refugees. Trujillo hoped that this generous offer would ingratiate him to Roosevelt, and he would no longer have to worry about a possible military intervention by the United States.[75]

This was not an unreasonable concern. The United States had already intervened militarily in almost all the countries in the Caribbean. Between 1898 and 1914, this interventionist policy was principally aimed at setting the conditions for the opening of the Panama Canal. The inauguration of the Canal in 1914 coincided with the start of the First World War in Europe. This created a vacuum of power in the Caribbean which the United States gladly filled. Though the United States had intervened militarily in that region before the war, after 1914, these increased. It intervened in the Dominican Republic (1906, 1914, 1934), Haiti (1914), Colombia (Panamá) (1901), Panamá (1902, 1904, 1920, 1921, 1925),

Cuba (1898, 1909, 1912, 1922, 1933) and other countries of the region including Nicaragua, Mexico, Guatemala, Costa Rica, and Honduras.[76]

Victim and perpetrator meet

In mid-August 1942, the 6,466-ton motor freighter *Laguna* was torpedoed by U-94 captained by 24-year-old Otto Ites, one of only a few U-boat captains to receive the prestigious Knights Cross. The torpedo tore a 40-foot hole on the side of the ship, yet she remained afloat. Only 250 tons of the 8,000 tons of valuable cargo were lost as a result. Surprisingly, Ites did not pursue his victim. If he was out of torpedoes, why did he not sink the freighter with his gun? Maybe he was concerned for the safety of his submarine given the increased risks of attacking a ship that traveled as part of an escorted convoy system that the U.S. Navy had recently begun to implement. In any case, the *Laguna* was able to make a 1,600-mile trek to Galveston, Texas where she would undergo repairs. Sidney Grant, captain of the *Laguna*, praised the 24-hours-a-day repair work undertaken by the American crew in order to patch his ship quickly so that it can continue to service the needy population of the Caribbean islands. "As we arrived in Galveston," remarked captain Grant, "there was a gang on the quay waiting to get busy. Those guys worked day and night until the damage was repaired."[77]

A few weeks after torpedoing the *Laguna*, U-94 was sunk east of Jamaica by depth charges and finally by being rammed by the Canadian corvette *HMCS Oakville*. Twenty-six crew members out of 45 survived. One of these was Captain Ites. By sheer coincidence, Captain Grant and Captain Ites saw each other in the United States. It is difficult to pinpoint where, as Ites was taken to Miami and later to Camp Blanding in Florida while Grant must have stayed in

Depiction of the Jewish refugee settlement in Sosua, Dominican Republic. 1940-1945. Museum of Jewish Heritage, New York, N.Y.

Galveston where the *Laguna* was being repaired. What we do know is that they met and that Grant asked Ites for his age and that of the crew. "I am 24 years old," answered Ites, "and the average age of the crew is 18 and a half."[78] The censors only allowed this report to be circulated on January 9, 1943, almost five months after this event took place. The whereabouts of Sidney Grant are lost to history. Otto Ites returned to Germany after being liberated from the POW camp in the United States and studied to become a dentist.

U-boat attacks continue

The *New York Times* reported that 29 American seamen, survivors of the United Fruit Company freighter *Olancho* (whose name was not disclosed due to the Navy's censorship requirements) arrived in Key West, Florida on March 23, 1943. According to the sources, seven men were missing and presumed lost. "Three of them were on duty in the engine room when a single torpedo [from U-183] plowed into the ship 75 feet from the stern," recalled W. W. Falkes, the third mate, from Houston, Texas. "The first I knew of the presence of a submarine was a terrific impact like a dull thud, and then the stern dropped about three feet," added Falkes. "The entire stern was beneath the water in three minutes and four of the missing men were believe to had been trapped in their bunks. The ship took water so fast [that] two lifeboats and two rafts launched within four minutes floated away from the ship without having to be lowered."[79]

Survivors of the torpedoed Dutch freighter *Ceres*, traveling with a convoy of 16 other ships, was en route to Curaçao with 3,386 tons of general cargo, including foodstuff, machinery, helium and a motorboat, described to the *Associated Press* how a sudden hit destroyed their vessel, after which they spent 11 days aboard the *USS Biddle*, chasing the submarine that had sunk them. The Tenth Naval District confirmed the survivors' account, stating that "during the first three days after the rescue, the escort vessel [the Navy did not disclose the name of the *USS Biddle* in its statement] engaged in running fight with a pack of submarines, dodging torpedoes from all quarters and dumping 'ashcans' [depth charges] on all sides."[80]

The torpedo explosions killed three crewmembers of the *Ceres*. According to Navy sources, an hour after the sinking, the *USS Biddle* picked up the survivors and during the next three hours, three torpedoes grazed the ship while she zigzagged through the darkness. The following night, the officers aboard the *USS Biddle* estimated that they were attacked by 10 U-boats. Lewis Williams, of Northford, Connecticut, was a gunner's mate on the *Biddle*. He recalled that "there was firing all night long. No one saw the sub, but we had plenty of contacts. After the third day, the U-boats gave up the chase."[81] Those aboard the destroyer thought they had sunken her.

The *Cities Service of Missouri* was the last ship in the second column of the same convoy. It was struck by one torpedo at the stern

USS Biddle (DD-151) off New York City in the early 1920s. Collection Photo : L45-27.08.01. Accession # : L45-27. Catalog #: L45-27.08.01. Tags: NHHC_Tags:epublishing_tags/new_york_city. https://www.history.navy.mil/content/history/nhhc/our-collections/photography/numerical-list-of-images/nhhc-series/naval-subjects-collection/l45—us-navy-ships/21-40/l45-27-08-01-uss-biddle—dd-151-.html. Retrieved October 4, 2020.

which ripped a ten-foot hole, damaging the bridge and the wheelhouse. The vessel stopped to assess the damage, and Captain John B. Martin ordered a portion of the ships flooded in order to balance her weight. U-68 launched a second torpedo which demolished the engine and then surfaced to finish her off.[82] Captain Marin recounted his ordeal in Miami a few days later. "I surveyed the damage [done to the ship after the first torpedo hit] and decided that I could get the ship to a port barring another attack. I asked for volunteers to stay aboard and not one man left. I then ordered the engines cut off in a move to fool the enemy into thinking the ship was sunk. Just as I ordered the crew to go down and prepare to get underway, another torpedo demolished the engine room."[83] "Lieutenant J.

Feeney, of Scranton, Pennsylvania, the gun crew commander, was blown against the mast and fell injured [in] the bridge. But he dragged himself to the rail and directed the fire against the submarine, which has been sighted aft. We continued to fire," added Martin, "until our communications were disorganized, and our ammunition was wet. Then I gave the order to abandon ship."[84] Lieutenant Feeney was lowered into one of the lifeboats and recovered from his injury. He was cited for bravery by Lieutenant General George Brett, Commanding General of the Caribbean Sea Frontier and the Panama Canal Department. Two members of the crew were killed in the attack while 52 were rescued by the destroyer escort USS *Biddle*.[85]

The *Ceres* and the *Cities Service Missouri* were part of a 16-ship convoy that left the naval base at Guantanamo for Curaçao. It was escorted by destroyers USS *Leary*, USS *Biddle*, Patrol Craft USS *PC-567* and USS *PC-627*. Despite these escort vessels, the U-68 surfaced and chased the convoy. It fired three torpedoes; one hit the tanker *Cities Service Missouri* and the other two, fired about thirty minutes later, hit the *Ceres*. The USS *Biddle* picked up the survivors of both ships and eventually took them to Willemstad, Curaçao. The U-68 left the scene unscratched, though her luck did not last. On April 10, 1944, she was sunk northwest of Madeira, Portugal by depth charges from U.S. aircraft from the escort carrier USS *Guadalcanal*. Only one crewmember survived. Throughout her career, which started in February 1941, the U-68 sunk 32 Allied ships: a remarkable feat.[86] The *Ceres* and the *Cities Service Missouri* were two of the eight ships sunk in the Caribbean during March 1943. For the first three months of 1943, a total of 17 ships were sunk: six in January, five in February, and eight in March. Though it is not an insignificant number, it is a far cry from the staggering numbers of 1942.[87] Donitz commented that those days were long gone as the antisubmarine defenses had been considerably strengthened by the advent of radar,[88] though he forgot to mention in his *Memoirs* that airplanes also were instrumental in this "change of fortunes."

Cuban Navy and the U-176

Obtaining reliable information on historical events, especially when it pertains to ongoing armed conflicts, is challenging not only for intelligence agencies at the time but also for historians attempting to provide a thorough narrative after such events have transpired. Such is the case of deciding where the credit lays for the sinking of U-176 off the coast of Cuba. Was it the U.S. Navy or the Cuban Navy?

On May 23, 1943, the Navy reported that Lieutenant Gordon R. Fiss, of Virginia Beach, Virginia was piloting a patrol bomber protecting a convoy "several months ago" when he sighted a German U-boat.[89] "The submarine was approaching the convoy from the rear," noted Fiss.[90] The lookouts on the submarine spotted his aircraft and it attempted a crash dive. Fiss quickly put his plane in a dive and released depth charges before the U-boat was fully submerged. These damaged the submarine, making her incapable of submerging, so she surfaced. Thereafter, she was destroyed by gunfire from a surface vessel. The Navy awarded Lieutenant Fiss the Distinguished Flying Cross for this accomplishment.[91]

Many in the Cuban Navy had been trained at the sub-chaser school in Miami. One of these was Mario Ramirez Delgado, captain of the *CS-13*. On May 13, 1943, a squadron of antisubmarine patrol boats sailed from Isabela de Sagua towards La Habana in order to protect the freighter Honduran *Wank* and the Cuban freighter *Camagüey*, both loaded with sugar. All were on high alert as a German U-boat had just two days earlier sunk the Cuban freighter *Mambi* with a loss of 19 crewmembers and the American freighter *Nickeliner,* with no loss of life, near Nuevitas, Cuba. The loss of the *Nickeliner* was a huge blow to the Allied effort as it transported 3,400 tons of ammonia water. No other American vessel had this capability. Ramirez Delgado recounted what happened on that fateful day:

> It was 5:15 in the afternoon and the convoy traveled at a speed of eight knots. Suddenly we saw an American hydroplane of the 'Kingfisher' type that quickly dove and then circled various times, flapping his wing, and shutting his engine and then turning it back on. This was an established code which signaled the presence of a submarine. In order to further assist the Cuban boats in locating it, the aircraft dropped smoke bombs where the submarine had been spotted.
>
> I ordered this patrol boat to approach the spot marked by the aircraft at full speed. A few minutes later, the sonar operator detected the submarine's propeller at an approximate distance of 900 yards. We could hear the submarine trying desperately to escape.
>
> At the appropriate distance, the CS-13 launched three depth charges programmed to explode at 100, 150 and 250 feet. These were set by calculating the submergence rate of the submarine. Four explosions were detected. The last one was so strong that the bow of our vessel sunk beneath the waves and seawater flooded the engine room.
>
> At that moment, the sonar operator reported hearing a sound that reminded him of one made when opening a waterlogged and airtight recipient at once. After that, the sound slowly faded. In order to make sure the submarine had been sunk; I ordered that two additional depth charges dropped in the location of the supposed sunken submarine. These were set to explode at 250 feet.
>
> Minutes later, we detected a pool of a dark substance whose viscosity and smell was like petroleum. We obtained a sample so that we could have proof that we had sunk the submarine.[92]

Ramirez Delgado added that "we stayed in the area a while longer, but the sonar did not detect additional propeller sound. We, therefore, sped away to join the convoy. Once in La Havana, I notified the Secretary of the Navy of what had transpired and he, in turn, called the President of Cuba, Fulgencio Batista. I later talked with Batista as he was interested in knowing the details of the operation. For reasons which I still do not understand, Batista asked that this operation not be made public. And so, until the end of the war, Cuba's involvement in the sinking of U-176 was not known."[93]

"During the depth charge attack on the submarine," Ramirez Delgado added, "the American pilot stayed in the area in case the submarine suddenly surfaced, and his assistance would be need. From his vantage point he could follow all the details of the operation. Once it was clear that the submarine had been sunk, the pilot flapped his wings, and flying at an exceptionally low altitude, congratulated us."[94] He later left for his base in the United States. In 1946, Mario Ramirez Delgado's effort was finally recognized by the Cuban authorities and he was awarded the *Mérito Naval con distintivo rojo* for the sinking of the U-boat.[95] German naval records available after the war confirm the loss of U-176 on May 15, 1943 with all hands being lost. U-176 had sunk 11 ships during its time at sea. The only two ships sunk in May, the *Mambi* and the *Nickeliner* were both sunk by U-176.[96]

U-boats shift to Trinidad and Puerto Rico

In March 1943, three U-boats patrolling the Caribbean were responsible for the eight ships sunk. By May, only the U-176 was stationed in the Caribbean. In June, it was replaced by U-157 which was lost before sinking any Allied ships. In July, as a result of the success of the Allied aircraft in the North Atlantic, Admiral Doenitz decided to shift operations to safer waters and ordered 13 U-boats to make a concerted attack on shipping in the vicinity of Trinidad and Puerto Rico. These 13 submarines were only able to sink six Allied ships at a cost of four U-boats. Two of these, U-159 and U-359 were sunk in the Caribbean. By the middle of August, all but a few had been withdrawn from the Caribbean, as losses continued to mount. In August, U-615 was also sunk by Allied forces. After July 1943, only seven additional ships were sunk: four in November and three in December, for a total of 35 in 1943.[97]

Declassified naval records of both the United States and Germany shed light on the demise of these submarines. On July 15, 1943, U-759 was sunk south of Haiti by depth charges from a U.S. aircraft with all hands being lost. On July 26, U-359 was sunk east of Jamaica by a U.S. PBM Mariner aircraft. There were no survivors. This submarine had not been successful in sinking any Allied ships in its three patrols. Two days later, on July 28, U-159 was also sunk by a U.S. PBM Mariner aircraft with all hands lost. This U-boat was responsible for sinking 23 ships during its five patrols starting on October 4, 1941.[98] The sinking of U-615 on August 17 received extensive press coverage, though due to the censorship policy in place, the Navy reported this attack on November 21, three months after it had occurred.

The *Washington Post*, the *New York Times*, and the *Chicago Daily Tribune* all reported on November 21, 1943 that "a fierce battle was fought in the Caribbean which finally ended, after 10 hours of combat, with the enemy sub [U-615] and an American plane and blimp destroyed."[99] Six Navy planes — five Martin PBM Mariners and a Lockheed Ventura — made repeated attacks on the surfaced German submarine from early afternoon to nightfall. One of the Mariner aircraft and its crew of 10 was lost, two others were severely damaged, and a Navy K-2 blimp was lost when it ran out of fuel returning to the base in San Juan, Puerto Rico, though its crew was rescued.

When the submarine was first sighted on the surface, 25-year-old Lieutenant Anthony R. Matuski of Long Island, New York, flying a PBM Mariner aircraft, attacked and severely damaged the U-boat so that "its speed was reduced to a crawl and its stern was down."[100]

Martin PBM-3R Mariner transport aircraft's cockpit during a flight to Jamaica, August 1943. Photographed by Lieutenant Junior Grade Wayne Miller, USNR. Catalog #: 80-G-377237. Copyright Owner: National Archives. Original Creator: Photographed by Lieutenant Junior Grade Wayne Miller, USNR. After this Year: 1939. Before this Year: 1945. Original Medium: BW Photo. https://www.history.navy.mil/content/history/nhhc/our-collections/photography/numerical-list-of-images/nhhc-series/nh-series/80-G-377000/80-G-377237.html.

However, the German crew manned the antiaircraft batteries and started shooting the Navy planes attacking them. Matuski initially reported that he observed "no damage to plane or personnel." However, minutes later, he radioed: "Damaged! Damaged! Fire!" That was the last message received from his aircraft before it crashed in the sea killing all 10 crewmembers [*Chicago Daily Tribune* reported nine]. Twenty-two-year-old Lieutenant John W. Dresbach of Kingston, Ohio, also flying a PBM Mariner aircraft was hit by U-615 and though mortally wounded, managed to release his bombs before turning over his command to the copilot. The radioman of another Mariner, Third Class Paul Raymond Lanigan, was slightly wounded.

A plane piloted by Lieutenant David Crockett, 27, of Nashville, Tennessee was ordered to the battle scene when Matuski's plane was lost. He arrived two hours after Lieutenant Matuski's last report and spotted the U-boat moving slowly and with blue smoke trailing from the stern. He attacked and, though his plane ran into heavy antiaircraft fire, was able to discharge his bombs alongside the U-boat, causing severe damage to the craft. In a second attack, a shell from the submarine's antiaircraft guns tore through a gasoline line in the plane, and a fire started in the right wing. Despite the obvious risk to his plane and crew, Crockett continued to dive while machinist Anthony S. Creider of San Diego, California crawled inside the wing to extinguish the fire. The bombs were released, which further damaged the U-boat.

A Navy blimp, returning to the naval base in San Juan, located the battle and, though almost out of fuel, offered to assist. Lieutenant Crockett, who was directing the battle, ordered the vulnerable airship to leave the vicinity as he directed other planes to pick up any survivors of Matuski's drowned plane. The blimp, skippered by Ensign Wallace A. Wydeen of Minneapolis, Minnesota, served as an observer for several hours and used up so much fuel that it was compelled to make a forced landing. At nightfall, an ancient Army B-18 bomber located the submarine at 11:00 P.M. with the aid of flares dropped by Crockett's plane. The plane, piloted by First Lieutenant Milton L. Wiederhold, 23, of Brenham, Texas, attacked the U-boat. Following a large explosion, the submarine sunk within the hour. The next day a destroyer [not identified in the report] picked up the 43 [reports at the time only mention 40] German survivors.[101]

U-615 was the last U-boat sunk in the Caribbean (Table 2).

By the end of 1943, the war had shifted to other theaters. The Caribbean was no longer newsworthy. The few articles that were published were short and lacked the details furnished in the ones published previously. In 1944, only three ships were sunk in the Caribbean: one in March, another in June, and the last one in July. After that, the U-boats vanished from the Caribbean.[102s]

TABLE 2
U-BOATS SUNK IN THE CARIBBEAN

Date Sunk	U-boat	Survivors	Killed	Location	Ships Sunk
1942					
June 13	U-157	0	52	North of Havana	1
July 6	U-153	0	52	Northwest of Aruba	3
July 30	U-166	0	52	Gulf of Mexico	4
Aug 22	U-654	0	44	North of Panama	4
Aug 28	U-94	26	19	East of Jamaica	26
Sept 3	U-162	2	49	Northeast of Trinidad	14
Oct. 2	U-512	1	51	North of French Guiana	3
		29	319		55
1943					
May 15	U-176	0	52	South of Haiti	2
July 15	U-759	0	47	South of Haiti	2
July 26	U-359	0	47	East of Jamaica	0
July 28	U-159	0	53	Southeast of Haiti	23
Aug 7	U-615	43	4	Northwest of Grenada	4
		43	203		31
Grand Total		72	522		86

Source: ww.uboat.net. Retrieved May 2, 2020 at Guaynabo, Puerto Rico

CHAPTER IV

Gibraltar of the Caribbean

Puerto Rico was war booty acquired from Spain during the last stages of the Spanish-American War of 1898. Since its "discovery" by Christopher Columbus in 1492, Puerto Rico had been a military bastion of the Spanish Empire, relegated to a second- or third-class colonial property after Spain lost its Latin American Empire during the first decades of the 19th century and concentrated its wealth on Cuba and its other possessions. The Treaty of Paris in 1899 officially ended the war and gave the United States possession of Puerto Rico and its nearby islands in addition to the Philippines and several islands in the Pacific. Puerto Rico includes three other smaller islands: Vieques at 50.7 square miles; Mona at 21 square miles; and Culebra at 10.4 square miles. They are relatively near some of the ports of the main island of Puerto Rico: Culebra is 20 miles east of Fajardo; Vieques, 10 miles southeast of Ensenada Honda; and Mona, the farthest away, 50 miles southwest of Mayagüez. In 1940, Mona was practically uninhabited while Culebra had a population of 738 and Vieques a population of 10,981.[1]

Puerto Rico's strategic location was of utmost importance to the United States, which expected that military bases on the island would help to secure the naval and air routes to the United States, the Gulf of Mexico, and the Panama Canal. The protection and defense of the Canal had been of great concern to the United States

Aerial view of El Morro and San Juan Bay, 1948. (Colección Fotográfica del Departamento de Instrucción Pública del Archivo General de Puerto Rico)

since the start of the Second World War in 1939.[2] Yet, no new major military base construction had been undertaken in Puerto Rico since 1898. Many of the existing military and naval facilities that were inherited from Spain through the Treaty of Paris were old and antiquated. "The only new major naval presence was the naval base in Culebra that was acquired in 1899 by presidential decree, but it had not been developed or fortified. Culebra, however, had been used in the late thirties to test the new amphibious landing craft that would later be used in the island-hopping campaign in the Pacific."[3]

By early 1939, war loomed both in Europe and the Pacific. The United States, concerned about the defense of the Panama Canal

Landing area for amphibious planes. Isla Grande Naval Base, 1939. (Colección Fotográfica del Departamento de Instrucción Pública del Archivo General de Puerto Rico)

and the entire Caribbean region, started a program of acquisition and construction of bases in the Panama Canal Zone and throughout the Caribbean. Bases in Cuba, Haiti, and Puerto Rico were either expanded or built from scratch.[4]

Construction of the Naval Base at Isla Grande

Puerto Rico lacked an airport capable of projecting airpower in the region. "The main operating airport was the Pan American aerodrome in Isla Grande, which had been in operation since 1928 and was used for international flights."[5] In addition to this shortcoming,

Puerto Rico exhibited others, including endemic infections, malaria, and smallpox as well as poor road infrastructure, water and sewer facilities, and an energy supply inadequate for the population of close to two million. A huge investment by the military would have to be undertaken to solve these problems, and quickly, given the tensions in Europe and Asia.[6]

On October 30, 1939, a month after the start of hostilities in Europe, the Navy awarded the contract for the construction of the San Juan Naval Base to the Arundel Corporation and Consolidated Engineering Co. Inc. based in Baltimore, Maryland after they successfully competed with "the most outstanding construction firms in the United States."[7] The contract was negotiated and awarded on a cost-plus-fixed-fee basis.[8] Valued at $8.5 million, it was one of Washington's most expensive construction projects outside the continental United States.[9]

Two million cubic yards of mangroves along the coastline of San Juan Bay had to be filled thereby eliminating the islands of Isla Grande and Miraflores. On this newly created expanse of land, the construction firms planned to build a naval base which included two seaplane hangars, a hangar for ground aircraft, warehouses, officer accommodations and maintenance buildings. Part of the filling came from the dredging of San Juan Bay, and the rest was obtained from the nearby Buena Vista quarry, owned by the island government. This quarry was in the Hato Rey neighborhood of Río Piedras, north and east of the road from Río Piedras to Barrio Obrero, near the Martín Peña Bridge and, therefore, near the base under construction. The insular government did not charge the Navy for the fill; it only requested that all excavation be backfilled to avoid standing water and a mosquito infestation.[10]

In January 1940, the contract for dredging the San Juan Bay was awarded to the local construction firm of Rexach Construction.

After only three months, Arundel and Consolidated Engineering had a serious disagreement with Rexach Construction which resulted in the termination of the contract. The stateside firm of Standard Dredging Co. was hired to replace it. Subsequently, engineer Félix Benítez Rexach, president of Rexach Construction, sued the Arundel Corporation and asked that federal prosecutor A. Cecil Snyder investigate if Arundel had been pressured by Washington or its cronies to hire Standard Dredging. At the time Benítez Rexach was building the prestigious Hotel Normandie, which was estimated to cost $2,000,000. It was inaugurated on October 10, 1942.

Other construction projects s

The military buildup in Puerto Rico began in early 1939 with the construction of essential infrastructure projects, accomplished by the Works Projects Administration (WPA), a brainchild of Roosevelt's New Deal programs. On January 14th, *El Mundo*, the newspaper with the largest circulation in Puerto Rico, announced the construction of a bridge connecting both sides of the Río Grande de Loíza in Trujillo Alto, a municipality in close proximity to San Juan.[11] The following week another article noted that eight regional airports would be constructed around the island.[12] Also, a 2,000-foot underground tunnel connecting the old Spanish fortification of San Felipe del Morro with forts San Cristóbal and San Jerónimo was to be built. Ironically, the last time these forts were used in battle was against the United States in the Spanish-American War of 1898.[13] Prior to that, they were instrumental in heading off the British invasion of 1797 under General Ralph Abercrombie and Admiral Henry Harvey, whose objective was to capture both Puerto Rico and Trinidad. After their successful takeover of Trinidad, the British thought that Puerto Rico would also fall, but this was not to be.[14]

As the United States did not want to appear threatening to its colonial neighbors — the French in Martinique, for example — keeping the appearance of neutrality was an important aspect of the Roosevelt Administration's foreign as well as domestic policy. As part of this policy, officials of the Department of the Interior flatly denied that the construction of seven regional airports in Dorado, Vega Baja, Arecibo, Mayagüez, Santa Isabel, Salinas and Ponce had anything to do with President Roosevelt's defense programs, even though they acknowledged that in case of war, these airports could play a significant role in the defense of Puerto Rico. The WPA, instituted to provide jobs and economic stability, made similar comments regarding the construction of the tunnels below Old San Juan. According to the WPA, these tunnels were of no military value; the fact that they could accommodate a contingent of soldiers and that they were illuminated was just a coincidence.[15]

The WPA was also deeply involved in the eradication of malaria. Officially, this was presented as a civilian project designed to improve the health of the local population. While the local population certainly benefited from this effort, the need to eradicate malaria from the point of view of the military establishment was critical in reducing the number of sick days and possible deaths of military personnel who would be stationed in Puerto Rico in the event of war.[16] Another aspect of these military preparations were the many safeguards taken by the United States in order to prevent acts of sabotage. One of these was to use FBI agents in the field to fingerprint all laborers working on federally funded construction projects. Those who refused were fired on the spot.[17] The FBI also kept a close watch over communists and nationalist groups, as well as foreign individuals and organizations such as the Spanish Falange. The Falange, sponsored by the pro-fascist Francisco Franco government in Madrid, had a large following in Puerto Rico.

The FBI was not the only organization keeping tabs on the Falangistas. According to a survey prepared by the FBI's Puerto Rican Department, Lieutenant Colonel C. S. Ferris relayed that "approximately 5,300 individuals, including women and children," had retained their Spanish citizenship under the terms of the Treaty of Paris which ended the Spanish-American War of 1898. Ferris "conservatively" estimated that 75 percent of these were pro-Franco. It was believed that they were not militant as they had not served in Franco's armed forces during the Civil War. The report added that a greater percentage of the Spaniards in Puerto Rico were "of the better class, influential land-owners in several types of industry, including sugar, tobacco, rum, and fruit growing. This element constitutes a potential threat."[18] Ferris included a statement by the Spanish consul at a dinner celebrating the German invasion of the Netherlands, Denmark and Luxemburg, in which he stated that things were going to change in Puerto Rico once he was in charge. "Everything is ready and well planned," he added.[19]

On April 14, 1940, Puerto Rico Governor William D. Leahy transferred the islands of Monito and Desecheo to the Navy; the latter would be used for bombing practices. On April 25, the Legislative Assembly of Puerto Rico authorized another transfer of 110,077 square meters in Puerta de Tierra, south of Fernández Juncos Avenue, land that had been recently dredged from the San Juan Bay. The Government also authorized the transfer of "mangroves and bodies of water around the bay of San Juan" and "nine plots of mangroves and submerged land located in the Hato Rey and Monacillos neighborhood of Río Piedras, Pueblo Viejo, Guaynabo and Palmas de Cataño," equivalent to 1,679 acres and valued at almost $500,000. Four days later, another transfer was authorized "of a plot of land based in La Puntilla, a neighborhood in Old San Juan." At this point, the Government of Puerto Rico had transferred land valued at $14,292,857 to the U.S. Government.

On May 24, Governor Leahy assured President Roosevelt that, thanks to all of the military installations being built in Puerto Rico, it would be "extremely dangerous for any government to invade the United States, Central, South, or North America." According to Leahy, the bases would be completed within two years, although they could be completed quicker, just as the naval base at Isla Grande was completed in 14 months, 16 months earlier than anticipated, though with a cost overrun of one million dollars and a final tally of $9.5 million. Upon completion, Arundel and Consolidated Engineering received $9.2 million in contracts to build naval bases in St. Thomas, St. Lucia, and Antigua.[20]

Other projects included the construction of 450 housing units for army and navy personnel, slated to begin May 27, while in June another announcement foretold the construction of bases in Ceiba and Vieques at an estimated cost of $42.5 million.[21] On September 19, the Army and the National Guard of Puerto Rico announced the construction of a permanent campground in Tortuguero, Vega Baja at a cost of $2.0 million. On October 26, the construction of an Army-Air Force base in Juana Díaz, on the southern portion of the island near Ponce, was begun. It would be named Losey Field.[22]

Air raid shelters in San Juan

Following the Imperial Japanese Navy's airstrike on the American naval base at Pearl Harbor on December 7, 1941, the possibility of a similar attack on Puerto Rico was considered. Puerto Rico was, on one hand, a military bastion of the United States. On the other hand, despite the large number of military installations that were completed or being built, Puerto Rico had no means of protection against airstrikes, and the population lacked underground shelters as well as a civil evacuation plan. Consequently, on December 16,

1941, Puerto Rico Civil Defense President Jaime Annexy convened an emergency meeting to form a technical committee whose role would be to build shelters against a possible air attack. Sergio Cuevas, the Commissioner of the Department of the Interior, chaired the committee. One of its first acts was the recruitment of Dr. Honorato de Castro, given his extensive experience in civil defense matters. Having served in the Spanish Armed Forces during the Spanish-American War of 1898, he had detailed knowledge of all Spanish fortifications and military installations. Civil and military engineers provided the Committee with an estimate of $332,000 for building the required air raid shelters. Eight-five percent of this amount would be subsidized by WPA funds, the remainder would be paid for by the Federal Department of the Interior. This project would therefore be funded in its totality by the U.S. Government.[23]

On February 4, WPA took over the supervision of the construction of the shelters from the Civil Defense. Part of the construction work had already begun. A system of trenches covered with wood had been completed in the strip of land between Paseo de Covadonga and Ponce de León Avenue, behind the Insular Capitol. On the southern portion of what remained of the old Spanish wall that circumvented the island of San Juan, close to the 19th-century La Princesa prison, construction of four tunnels had begun on the wall of the Puerta de San Juan, one of the entrances to Old San Juan. Behind the Casino of Puerto Rico, ditches were dug to explore the possibility of a tunnel, built under the Spanish regime, between the Castle of San Cristóbal and the Marina. In addition, with the consent and cooperation of the military authorities, the existing tunnels in the fortifications of San Juan were inspected. This revealed that there were seven tunnels in San Cristobal Castle that were inside the U.S. military zone. One of them stretched from the courtyard of the first house of the Castle to the Marina, below Avenida Muñoz Rivera, and passed through the Casino of Puerto Rico, until it collided with one of the columns of this building.

The Civil Defense also approved the construction of steel-clad tunnels through the northern section of the Spanish wall in the La Perla neighborhood with the approval of the Compañía del Ferrocarril (Railroad Company) that owned the area where the air raid shelters were to be located. Underground shelters that could be used in case of a hurricane were also built.[24] In El Fanguito in metropolitan San Juan, the shelters were built above ground as the high water table in this area did not allow for any other type of shelter to be built.[25]

At a meeting held in La Fortaleza on May 14, 1942, it was agreed "unanimously to minimize activities related to the design and construction of air-raid shelters."[26] As discussed previously, the main threat to Puerto Rico, and the Caribbean in general, came from the U-boats and not from hostile aircraft. In fact, during May 1942 when this decision was made, 55 ships were sunk. The staff was furloughed and Dr. Honorato de Castro was allocated $300 for his services.[27] On July 16, 1943, Sergio Cuevas recommended the closure or elimination of all the air-raid shelters.[28]

Borinquen Army Airfield

The idea of building an airbase in Puerto Rico originated during discussions of the newly constituted Air Board. This Board was headed by General Henry H. Arnold, a pioneer airman who was taught to fly by the Wright Brothers and during the Second World War was the commanding general of Army Air Forces overseeing war strategies against Germany and Japan. He visited Puerto Rico in March 1939 and returned on June 2 to inspect prospective sites for an airbase. Word leaked out to the local press that the site being considered was adjacent to the coastal town of Aguadilla, in the western part of the island. Once his site visit was concluded, General Arnold recommended the construction of four new major air bases, one of which would be in Aguadilla. This new base would triangulate with MacDill Army Base in Florida and one in Panamá. It would also provide a link with the region of Natal in the 'Brazilian bulge' and serve as an alternate route to the Far East via Africa. Given the speed at which the events in Europe were happening, the investment for the base was approved even before the final report was submitted.[29]

The base required the expropriation of 3,818 *cuerdas* (a *cuerda* is slightly less than an acre).[30] These started on September 6, a few days prior to Leahy assuming the governorship of the island. Construction started on September 8. By October, 2,000 laborers of the WPA were employed in the construction.[31] Puerto Ricans whose land was expropriated felt mistreated by the military.

In August 1940, the Government of the United States allocated $1.2 million for the construction of the airbase later named Borinquen Field. This amount included the airstrip and the required infrastructure to maintain the airplanes, auxiliary vehicles, and military personnel. There would be underground storage tanks to stockpile diesel and gasoline and aboveground warehouses to store explosive materials. Separate housing for the officers and the enlisted personnel was also included. During the war, Borinquen Field would serve as a stopover for flights departing to Europe and Africa. It also provided air cover for the shipping lanes between the Dominican Republic and St. Lucia, and as previously mentioned, this proved essential during the U-boat attacks in 1942 and 1943.[32]

This base was the main facility in a network of interconnecting airfields located in Puerto Rico. The Army and Navy went on to

Dry dock at the Roosevelt Road Naval Base in Ceiba, Puerto Rico, 1943. (US Navy)

build seven other airstrips on the island. In the south, the Ponce Air Base (later incorporated in Fort Losey) worked in conjunction with the existing Mercedita airfield used by the Marine Corps. Auxiliary regional airfields were built in Salinas, Dorado, Vega Baja, Arecibo and Mayagüez. The Navy would also build an airfield in Ceiba and Vieques as part of the Roosevelt Roads facility. However, in 1940, the only operational airbases were Borinquen Field and the Army base in Ponce. During this time, the Army was also building a National Guard training center in Vega Baja named Camp Tortuguero. In addition, there were a significant number of other military installations being built,[33] including the already mentioned naval base at Isla Grande, a major expansion of Fort Buchanan in

San Juan, the Salinas Training Center, Fort Bundy in Fajardo, Camp O'Reilly in Caguas, Amelia Farm in Cataño, and others.[34] These military investments were crucial to maintaining the lifeline of goods for the inhabitants of Puerto Rico during the shipping blockage of 1942 and 1943 due to the threat of U-boats.[35]

Roosevelt Roads

The military base at Ceiba was officially named Roosevelt Roads on May 8, 1941. The original plans called for the construction of a dry dock capable of doing maintenance work on large battleships and aircraft carriers. A large airstrip would be capable of handling the bombers from both the United States and Great Britain, should either fall to the German juggernaut. The base would include a large portion on the island of Vieques in order to be able to realize amphibious training exercises and for bombing practice. Due to its strategic location, Roosevelt Roads would become known as the Pearl Harbor of the Caribbean. Sixty percent of the Atlantic Fleet exercises would involve Roosevelt Roads. As ship repairs could be performed in Puerto Rico, vessels stationed in the Caribbean could forgo the 2,000-miles trip to Norfolk, Virginia where they would normally travel for maintenance. At the time when Roosevelt Roads was being designed and built, the likelihood that the British and French naval forces would fall into German hands was a real possibility.

The United States budgeted $35.0 million for the construction of the facilities in both Ceiba and Vieques. $23.3 million was to be allocated to the construction of a seawall between Ceiba and Vieques.[36] "I [had] been told years before," commented Tugwell regarding this base, "that Coral Bay at the eastern end of St. John [U.S. Virgin Islands] was to be the fleet anchorage…. That was supposed to have been one reason for our acquisition of [these islands] from Denmark [in 1917]. But later maneuvers had centered on the larger protected area with Culebra and other islets on the north, Vieques to the southeast and Puerto Rico to the west."[37] Tugwell continued:

> A sea wall was to be built across miles of sea from Vieques to the Puerto Rican coast at Ensenada Honda. Vast magazines were to be cut into the Vieques hills, a marine base was to be established on Culebra and a great home port with dry docks, machine shops, and so on was to be centered at Ensenada Honda, just under El

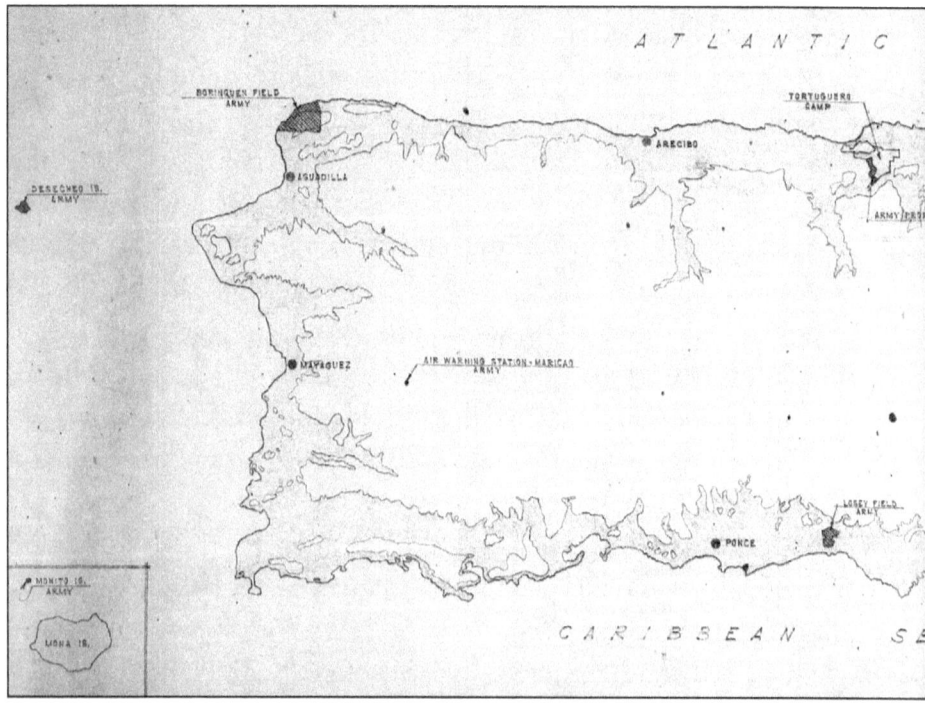

Map prepared by the Planning, Urbanizing and Zoning Board of the Government of Puerto Rico showing the Federal Properties on the island, December 1947. (Mapoteca del Archivo General de Puerto Rico)

Yunque [rain forest]. The Navy eye obviously conceived of a fleet concentration in this stretch of water — a conception which was to be made obsolete by the experience at Pearl Harbor. It would take some time for the lessons to sink into the naval consciousness, but gradually the plan [for Vieques] would be changed to a more modest repair base and magazine.... The rejuvenated Navy would not want fleet concentrations — though there would always be a need for dry docks, landing fields, magazines, and machine shops.[38]

In order to protect the base from air or naval attacks and possibly sabotage, coastal artillery was installed, and troop barracks were constructed simultaneously. The emplacements were intended to defend

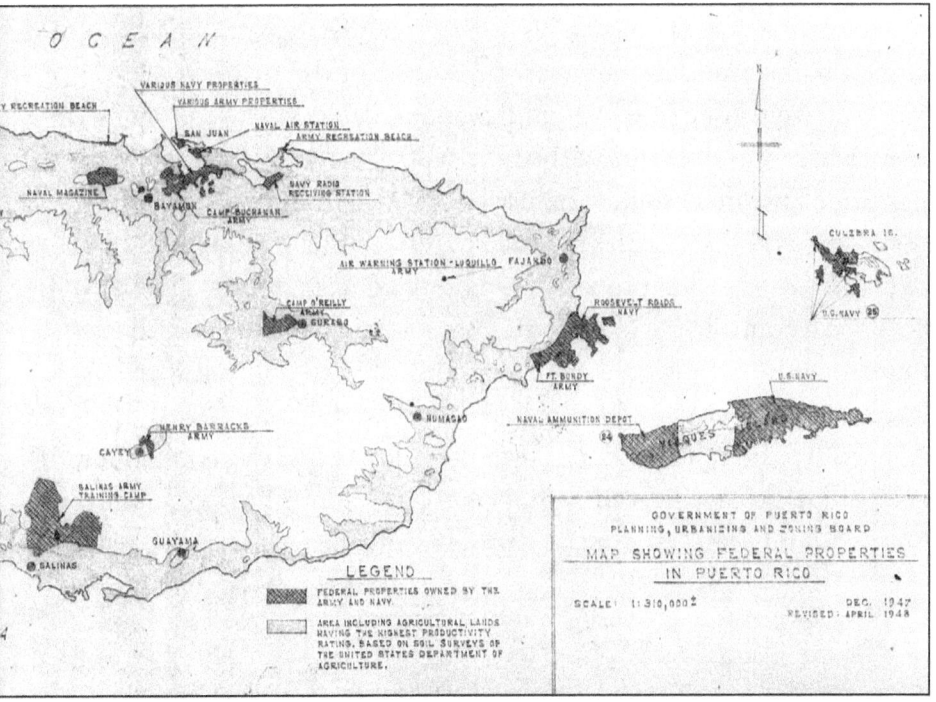

ships entering or leaving the base and had a range of 35,000 yards. Antiaircraft guns were also installed as well as radar equipment.

The base was built on 8,600 acres obtained from the local government and from forced expropriations. Construction started in May 1941 and would slow down dramatically by mid-1943, as by then the submarine menace had subsided, the Axis were losing the war and, therefore, there was no need to continue building the base or for having a large contingent of troops on the island. In any case, during those 18 months of frantic construction, 120 housing units were completed, as well as a network of roads, distribution centers, storage tanks for diesel, warehouses for explosive devices, an aqueduct, a dry dock — 1,100 feet long, 155 feet wide, and 45 feet deep — making it one of the largest dike-style dry docks in the world. The construction of the sea wall between Vieques and Ensenada Honda had started, though only 7,000 feet of the planned 40,700 foot wall were completed before it was abandoned.

The base was outfitted with three 6,000-feet landing strips with lighting. The area around them was paved to ensure the safety of the planes and the vehicles required to service them. Also built were structures to store maintenance supplies and make repairs. The airport had a control tower with antennas for communication with the numerous aircraft it would need to guide and was equipped with the latest electronic gear of the day. A fire control station was built adjacent to the tower and a cistern provided the water required for the pumps. A landing strip, a fully equipped control tower, marine barracks, and munitions depot were built on Vieques as well.[39]

Expropriations

The U.S. Army and Navy expropriated 53,484 acres in Puerto Rico between 1939 and 1943. The largest and most controversial ones were the expropriations on the island of Vieques. There the Navy expropriated two-thirds of the island. The existing population was relocated to the remaining third of the island, sandwiched on both sides by the Navy and forbidden to trespass on Navy land. In Ceiba, the Navy expropriated 8,000 acres for the Roosevelt Roads Naval Base. The number of expropriations by the military was substantial (Table 3).

TABLE 3
U.S. MILITARY EXPROPRIATIONS IN PUERTO RICO, 1939–43

Army	City	Acres
Salinas Training Center[1]	Salinas	7,114
Borinquen Army Airfield[1]*	Aguadilla	3,818
Fort Bundy[1]	Fajardo	2,547
Losey Field[1]	Ponce	1,038
Fort Buchanan[1]	San Juan	983
Camp O'Reilly[1]	Caguas	906
Henry Barracks[1]	Cayey	530
Camp Tortuguero[1]	Vega Baja	525
Amelia Farm[2]	Cataño	353
Cataño Intermediate Airfield[2]	Cataño	309
Navy Radio Station[2]	Hato Rey	140
Fort Brooke[1]	Isleta de San Juan	132
Army Gasoline Storage[2]	San Juan	70
Army Terminal[2]	San Juan	33
Punta Brava	—	27
Army drum and Tank loading[2]	San Juan	16
Army Recreational Beach[2]	Boca de Cangrejos	15
Army Barracks[2]	Parada 81/2. San Juan	6
Punta Escambrón[2]	San Juan	6
Bayamón Rifle Range[3]**	Bayamón	n/a
Total		**18,568**

TABLE 3 (continued)
U.S. MILITARY EXPROPRIATIONS IN PUERTO RICO, 1939–43

Navy	City	Acres
Roosevelt Roads[5]	Vieques	22,000
Roosevelt Roads[6]	Ceiba	8,600
U.S. Naval Magazine[2]	Sabana Seca	2,100
Navy Fill Area[2]	Isleta de San Juan	700
Radio Receiving Station[2]	Carolina	672
Naval Air Station[2]	Isla Grande	400
Culebra Naval Bombing Area[2]	Culebra	276
Navy Beach Club[2]	Isleta de San Juan	58
El Morro[2]	Isleta de San Juan	50
Tenth Naval District[2]	San Juan	27
San Cristóbal[2]	Isleta de San Juan	25
Coast Guard[2]	Isleta de San Juan	5
Navy Officers Quarters[2]	Isleta de San Juan	3
San Patricio Housing[3]	San Patricio. San Juan	n/a
Naval Hospital[3]	San Patricio. San Juan	n/a
Navy Recreation Beach[3]	Punta Salinas	n/a
San Geronimo Reservation[4]	Isleta de San Juan	n/a
Radio Range Station[3]	Toa Baja	n/a
Total		34,916
Total acres expropriated		53,484

Sources: Private archive of Dr. Jorge Rodríguez Beruff, 1 through 4 from the "Private papers of Admiral William D. Leahy."

1. "Memorandum for fleet Admiral William D. Leahy from Lt. General A. C. Wedemeyer," April 13, 1948;
2. Puerto Rico Planning Board. "Need for a study of land holdings of armed forces in Puerto Rico," April 13, 1948. 6–9;
3. Robert B. Carney. Deputy Chief of Naval Operations. "Resume of Naval Properties." April 15, 1948;
4. Tenth Naval District, "Special Puerto Rican Insular Government and Federal Property Conference." April 19, 1948;
5. Ayala y Bolívar, "Entre dos aguas…", 54–57;
6. Piñero Cádiz, Puerto Rico: El Gibraltar del Caribe, 28; Rodríguez Beruff states that the land acquired was 15,000 acres (Política militar, 169); we think he was referring to the land expropriated in Vieques.

* In 1947 name changed to Ramey Air Force Base.
** Converted to a military cemetery

The expropriations left most of the people of Vieques, Puerto Rico without their livelihood, as many were employed in the sugar industry. (Colección del periódico *El Mundo*, Universidad de Puerto Rico, Recinto de Río Piedras)

All these expropriations had three things in common. The first is that nobody wanted to part with their lands. In almost all cases, the acreages were used to grow sugarcane or to cultivate crops for food consumption and were the livelihoods of the landowners. Second, local people were not satisfied with the compensation offered by the military as this was usually below the appraised value of the land. Third, many of the people living on the expropriated properties were *agregados* (sharecroppers) who lived on a parcel of land, built their houses, raised their families, and developed a tight community. The only reason they were allowed this 'privilege' was due to their employment as laborers in the sugar plantation. The owners of the land received the compensation offered by either the Army or Navy, but the *agregados* received none. Therefore, with the stroke of a pen, they lost their land, their home, their community, and their livelihood.[40]

During Spanish colonial times (1492–1898), Vieques was on the frontier between Spanish power and British powers. The island was too close to Puerto Rico for the Spanish to allow the British to settle there and too close to British-ruled islands to be settled by the Spanish. Thus, during most of the Spanish colonial period, Vieques remained uninhabited. It was only settled under the Spanish regime in the 1830s when Puerto Rico was experiencing a sugar-plantation boom, and the slave trade was flourishing.[41]

From the start, Vieques was a plantation society, not a society of free peasants such as existed in other parts of Puerto Rico in the 18th century. Land concentration and social polarization, together with extremes of wealth and poverty, were thus structural features of Vieques from its inception. This colonial legacy lasted in Vieques into the 20th century, and it conditioned the economic evolution of Vieques in the period of U.S. colonialism after 1898. Many of the landless workers of Vieques in the 20th century were descendants of the slaves of the 19th century. Still others were descendants of a population of black workers from the eastern Caribbean who had migrated to Vieques in the 19th century and had formed a sugar proletariat in the plantations.[42]

At the beginning of the twentieth century, Vieques had four sugar *centrales* (sugar mills): Santa María, Arcadia, Esperanza (also known as Puerto Real), and Playa Grande.[43] By the time of the Navy expropriations in 1941, only Playa Grande was functioning. Land ownership was concentrated in the Eastern Sugar Associates, which owned 11,00 acres, and Juan Ángel Tio, who owned 10,000 acres along with the Playa Grande sugar mill. Tio purchased Playa Grande from the Bank of Nova Scotia in 1939 after it had gone into bankruptcy and receivership in 1936. The previous owners of Playa Grande, the Benitez and Rieckehoff families, retained 5,735 acres.[44]

Tio purchased the mill and the tract of land, including improvements, crops, livestock, vehicles and farm implements for $500,000. Once the "negotiations" with the Navy commenced, he sold the livestock for $50,000. He also sold the cultivated sugar cane while the Navy allowed him to remove all the equipment and to sell it since it had no use for sugar processing equipment. On this basis, the Navy valued the land at $400,000. Since, according to the Chief of the Bureau of Yards and Docks, Tio had "indicated [he wanted] a figure far in excess of that amount," he recommended that the Judge Advocate General approve "that the property be acquired by condemnation."[45] The final offer would be even lower, around at $370,000.

This pre-colonial land concentration made the negotiations for the expropriations much easier for the Navy, as they only had to deal with three owners. According to the Navy:

> Of the 21,000 acres, 10,000 acres or nearly half were acquired from Juan Tio, owner of Playa Grande mill and sugarcane lands in the western, central, and eastern sectors. Another substantial portion, nearly 8,000 acres, was acquired from Eastern Sugar Associates who had owned and operated the Esperanza sugar mill and lands in the east-central sector. Lands of two other major families, Benitez and Rieckehoff, brought the total to over 19,000 acres or 90% of this first series of acquisitions.[46]

The expropriation process began several months before Pearl Harbor, but the attack was the event that made landowners accept the expropriation without further litigation. As traditional usufruct rights were not considered during the expropriations, the Navy compensated the owners of the properties without being concerned about the fate of the *agregados* (sharecroppers) or other rural workers who were settled on the land.[47] The Navy paid Tio an average price of $37 per acre while the going price was $60. In fact, after World War II, when the Navy expropriated additional lands in Vieques, it paid $122 per acre.[48]

Workers who lived on the land of the landowners typically had subsistence plots, as part of the usufruct rights.[49] On this scale, it was not possible to make a living without recourse to wage labor in the sugar fields at harvest time. These plots were therefore critical for the livelihood of the *agregados* during the idle season of the sugar industry, which lasted from June through November. The expropriations affected the expelled populations as it could no longer count on this food supply.[50] "As we were *agregados*, they just told us to leave," noted one interviewed *agregado*.[51] By the Navy's own conservative estimate, the expropriations dislocated an estimated 4,250 to 5,000 people or 40 percent to 50 percent of the island's population.[52] They would be relocated along with the rest of the inhabitants of Vieques onto the remaining third of the island. Another round of expropriations would materialize in 1947-1948, during the Cold War, and make matters worse for the inhabitants of Vieques.

The experiences of landowners and *agregados* in the other parts of Puerto Rico were similar in nature, though not as dramatic as those suffered by the inhabitants of Vieques. In Ceiba, the landowners were opposed to the expropriations but fighting the military — particularly in times of war — proved fruitless. Most of those affected, as in Vieques, were *agregados*, illiterate laborers, or sustenance farmers. In the case of Ceiba, the Government of Puerto Rico stepped in and provided each family with one acre adjacent to the base. This would provide them with the needed shelter and 'hopefully' employment on the base or in the nearby restaurants, bars or hostels that the military personnel might patronize.[53]

Barrio San Antonio in Aguadilla, expropriated in 1939 for the constructions of the Borinquen Air Field, was described in 1922 as "a very active and promising little district, with several industrial establishments, and…during the active season, there are over 1,000 women employed in the little factories."[54] Three years later, it had a church, a post office, a movie theater, and a bakery. The lands expropriated from Barrio San Antonio were among the most productive on the island. Therefore, when the Army offered to pay the owners $200 per acre, they refused. (This was, of course, much more than what the Navy offered to pay in Vieques in 1941). The owners claimed that the value of the land was about $600 to $700 per acre, including the inventory of the sugarcane growing on the land and the improvements they had made. They demanded a 'just' compensation. As in the case of the other expropriations, the military had the final word, and the owners had to settle for the amount originally offered to them. The *agregados* would get nothing. They would have to try to find employment in the base or the ancillary businesses that developed around it.[55]

Puerto Rican pilot Carlos Esteva doing practice simulations at Fort McClellan, Alabama. 1943. (Private archive of Teresa Rozas de Esteva)

CHAPTER V

War Economy

The Second World War brought about major changes in the Puerto Rican economy. After the beginning of the war in Europe, the prices for basic necessities in Puerto Rico skyrocketed. The entry of the United States in the war caused an immediate and dramatic reduction of imports to the island. Between 1941 and 1942, the annual value of imports was reduced by 37 percent, from $143,700,000 to $90,400,000. A closer look at the imported monthly tonnage divulges the trauma inflicted on the inhabitants of Puerto Rico. On average, 112,933 tons were imported every month of 1940. During the first months of 1942, this amount was reduced to 91,153 tons, in April to 50,863, and in September it dropped to 7,263. This represents a reduction of 94 percent when compared to the average monthly tonnage imported in 1940 and a 22 percent reduction in imported food in an island dependent on these imports. Though a substantial portion of domestic food consumption was satisfied by local producers, after 1898, food imports were critical to adequately feed Puerto Rico's population.[1]

In order to avoid a possible famine, large quantities of imported industrial and commercial materials were replaced by food items.[2] In 1940, for example, 33 percent of the imported tonnage was food. In 1942, this increased to 57 percent. However, these efforts proved insufficient, as food shortages continued, and what was available was sold at exorbitant prices.³

Both federal and local authorities tried to solve this situation through price controls and eventually rationing and the impositions of quotas. This created countless controversies between the Puerto Rican government and merchants, especially for rice, a staple food in the Puerto Rican diet. On April 16, 1942, Dr. Antonio Fernós Isern, who ran the Food and General Supply Commission (*Comisión de Alimentos y Abastecimiento General*), informed members of the Puerto Rico Chamber of Commerce that the government would impose a profit ceiling of 7 percent on the sale of rice. The merchants replied that their accounting system did not allow them to "accurately determine the profit margin" of each item, as they sold a diverse product line.⁴ The following day, in the face of the uncertainty of rice shipments, Governor Tugwell ordered its

Local food vendors show off their produce at the market in historic Ponce, Puerto Rico. Circa 1945. (Archivo Histórico Fundación Luis Muñoz Marín)

rationing. From that day on, merchants could only sell the quantities stipulated by the government.[5] As a result of the tension this controversy was generating, the government considered importing additional quantities of rice on airplanes at considerable cost.[6] Tugwell and his staff only considered this option when, as a result of the U.S. Government's decision to freeze the price of rice, almost 800 local importers decided it was no longer viable to sell it at a profit and stopped importing it.[7]

A perturbed Filipo L. de Hostos, spokesperson for the many importers affected by the government's imposition, claimed that the Tugwell administration was singling them out for placing profits above the welfare of the island's inhabitants.[8] In any case, the struggle between the local government and rice traders was intense. The Government purchased 9,000 sacks of rice thinking that by competing with the rice traders, the price of this commodity would stabilize.[9] Paul Edwards, local director of the Office of Price Management (OPA), applauded Tugwell's brash initiative. He believed that it would "motivate" the importers to reduce their expected profit margin on the sale of rice. Edwards added that the U.S. Government was prepared to subsidize any loss suffered by the rice importers.[10] The day following Edwards' statement, the Director of the OPA in Washington stated that the price freeze for rice in Puerto Rico and the U.S. Virgin Islands would be lifted. Washington had come to the realization that given the strategic importance of Puerto Rico, food riots and similar disturbances could seriously detract from the war effort.[11]

Hence, the importers saw an opportunity to raise the price of rice, and that is precisely what they did. This increase had such an impact on the island that the Federal Government, recognizing that many of Puerto Rico's problems were not truly known in Washington, decided to buy a number of food products, including rice, at market prices and sell them to local traders at discounted prices, thus absorbing the loss. Commercial establishments were not obliged to buy from the Federal Government, but if they did, they were required to sell at the prices set by OPA.[12] Despite all the controls that were implemented, many distributors continued to violate them.[13]

On November 13, OPA warned that it would "severely punish" wholesalers, distributors or importers that violated the prices specified by law. The price of rice was not to exceed eight cents per pound.[14] In addition, the consumer should not pay more than eight cents per pound for dried beans, six cents per pound for onions, six cents per pound for butter, and ten cents for each can of evaporated milk.

It is important to note that high prices had serious repercussions on the majority of the population. Even before the war began, the typical wage in the industry that employed most of the island's labor force, sugarcane, was insufficient to obtain adequate nutrition. Most of Puerto Rico's inhabitants, therefore, walked barefoot, had no income to pay for medical care, and lacked a permanent home. The average salary provided only 12 cents to cover each family member's daily nutritional requirements. In comparison, at the same time, U.S. farmers budgeted 16 cents a day on average to cover the cost associated with feeding a hog.[15]

Between December 1941 and October 1942, the prices of items that made up the basic diet of the Puerto Ricans rose dramatically. The price of ham increased by 32 percent, butter by 29 percent, rice by 26 percent, pork by 22 percent, and flour by 20 percent. On average, between the start of 1941 and the end of 1942, the retail cost of food in Puerto Rico increased by 53 percent, while in the United States, the increase was only 16 percent. Between June 1939 and December 1941, the price of cod, one of the most economical

Puerto Rican WACS travel on a military plane for basic training in Fort Oglethorpe, Georgia. October 6, 1944. (Colección de Fotografías del Periódico El Mundo, Universidad de Puerto Rico, Recinto de Río Piedras)

proteins the island's population consumed, increased by 130 percent. In the face of this situation, Senator Luis Muñoz Marín, president of the Puerto Rican Senate and founder of the recently constituted Popular Democratic Party (PPD), vehemently complained in 1942 to Paul Gordon in the Federal Department of Interior when 300 to 400 boxes of cod were left stranded in the port of New York for "lack of space" at the same time that beer and other alcoholic beverages were being shipped at regular intervals to the numerous military bases in Puerto Rico.[16]

The increase in tonnage dedicated to transporting food led to a reduction in imports of wood, cement, steel, building materials, and fertilizers. This reduction had an immediate and adverse effect on construction, manufacturing, and farming. As a result, unemployment rose sharply. In July 1941, official statistics recorded 99,100 unemployed workers, 16 percent of the workforce. A year later, in July 1942, there were 165,600 unemployed; the following month it increased to 210,800, and in September it increased again to 237,400. This represented 37 percent of the island's labor force.[17] As noted above, these unemployed laborers not only had to contend with the loss of their wages, they also had to face the large increase in the price of food.

Training civilian personnel for the war effort

The role of the Federal Government in the creation of jobs on the island would become more critical during the war years as the sugar industry waned. During those years, 38 percent of the total labor force worked in the sugar industry. It paid 15 cents an hour during the 1939–1940 fiscal years increasing to 20 cents during 1944–1945.[18] Due to the seasonality associated with this industry, employment averaged seven months out of the year. The sugar cane workers and their families would have to survive the remaining months on whatever savings they might have and by bartering crops or animals they might own. During the Second World War, the labor situation changed dramatically, as more Puerto Ricans were employed in civil or military endeavors by the Federal Government, and employment in the sugar industry was affected by the shortage of fertilizers, the low pay rate, and the appalling work conditions.[19]

The skill level required to work in the sugar industry (cutting sugarcane being the most prevalent form of employment) was low, as most of the farm work was performed with simple hand tools. This contrasted with the skill level required in the construction industry.

The military, at the time, was involved in the construction of bases, hospitals, housing developments, airports, aircraft hangars, and the infrastructure (electricity, water, sanitary facilities) for human habitation. These efforts required a significant number of carpenters, electricians, mechanics, and other technically skilled workers who were simply not available on the island. Therefore, a significant amount of technical retraining would be required.[20] In some cases, continental employees were brought to Puerto Rico to train local workers and to supervise the construction process.

Photograph shows American troops in a segregated soft drink stand. Trinidad, British West Indies. 1942. Call Number: LOT 2203 (F) [P&G]. Repository: Library of Congress Prints and Photographs Division. Washington, D.C. 20540. Photographs received from the U.S. Army Signal Corps. U.S. Office of War Information negative nos. 57107ZC; control card no. 2115. Transfer: Office of War Information. Overseas Picture Division. Washington Division; 1944. Forms part of the Farm Security Administration-Office of War Information photograph collection (Library of Congress). Bookmark for this Record: https://www.loc.gov/pictures/item/2005675142/. View the MARC Record for this item.

In addition to the lack of technical skills, the language barrier was another obstacle faced by military contractors. Private contractors hired to build the base, such as the Arundel Corporation, a Baltimore-based company that was awarded the contract to build bases at Isla Grande, Roosevelt Roads in Ceiba, and Mosquito Bay in Vieques, and federal agencies such as the WPA, employed stateside personnel, most of whom had no working knowledge of Spanish while most locals had none of English. This situation resulted in clashes, misunderstandings, and strikes.[21] Much of the work required to retrain the Puerto Rican laborers fell on the insular government, although the funding was provided by the Federal Government. The island's Department of Education set up vocational training programs and industrial schools adjacent to the construction sites in order to provide hands-on training. By May 1941, approximately 9,000 Puerto Ricans were enrolled in these programs. Unfortunately, this training was not available when the construction of the military programs began in 1939, forcing many stateside contractors to hire mainland companies and personnel.[22]

Tensions reach a boiling point: racism and discrimination

The war brought numerous additional tensions within the Puerto Rican community. The lack of food and the exorbitant prices of what was available added to the stress of knowing your loved ones were in harm's way. Added to that was interacting with the racism of the military and its contractors. Jim Crow laws were not known or applied in Puerto Rico where many of its inhabitants were of mixed race. When both the military and its contractors started to discriminate against Puerto Ricans in favor of white Anglo-Saxons, things usually did not go well.

Puerto Ricans complained that the Arundel Corporation practiced various forms of discrimination, and when they protested, they were summarily fired. At the time, the U.S. Armed Forces were segregated, and "despite Roosevelt's insistence that it recruit African Americans, the Navy understood that this would be for kitchen jobs and the like, as it was unthinkable to impose on U.S. white soldiers the burden of cohabitation with blacks in ships or submarines."[23] Race and racism affected all of the branches of the U.S. Armed Forces. The companies hired by the military would share in this culture. This would have severe consequences on the working relationships between the continentals and the mixed-race Puerto Ricans working on the construction projects.[24] According to the census data from 1930, 1935 and 1940, the nonwhite population of Puerto Rico was 25.7 percent, 23.8 percent and 23.5 percent respectively.[25] Even though these were the 'official numbers', in reality the non-white percentage was much higher.

Puerto Ricans began registering for the draft on November 20, 1940, five weeks later than in the United States.[26] Upon recruitment, the Army segregated Puerto Ricans into "white" and "black" units, something that was completely unheard of in Puerto Rico. The Army established racial quotas of four whites to one black. A distinction was made between "whites" and "white Puerto Ricans" even though "white Puerto Ricans" were American citizens with the same rights and privileges as the other "whites." The Army described a white Puerto Rican "as light-colored people of Latin origin," while blacks "were said to be dark-skinned and of a different racial origin."[27]

By the end of 1941, Army personnel stationed in Puerto Rico convinced themselves that Puerto Ricans were drastically inferior physically and in other ways to the continental troops.[28] Despite the massive unemployment on the island, and the desire for many to join the military, 163,141 applicants were rejected. The most common cause stated by the Army was "mental deficiency," meaning the applicant "failed to meet the minimum intelligence standard."[29]

It was therefore easy for Arundel and other private contractors to adhere to the same racist code of conduct set forth — unofficially — by the Army and Navy.

During the construction of the naval base in Vieques, for example, Arundel and its subcontractors would not permit Puerto Ricans to drink cold water, as it was reserved exclusively for the continentals. The summer months in Puerto Rico are hot, with temperatures reaching 95 degrees Fahrenheit. Lack of water can lead to dehydration and other severe health problems. The fact that Puerto Ricans could not drink cold water under these circumstances led to several altercations between the locals and the continentals. Another point of discord was the salary differential between locals and continentals. According to a report issued by the insular government's House of Representatives, Puerto Rican workers claimed that continentals were paid $1.57 per hour to drive a truck while they were paid only $0.50 and obliged to work 10 hours a day as opposed to the regular eight. The discord regarding this wage differential was critical. As food prices had skyrocketed, the additional pay could make the difference between feeding their family or having them go going hungry. On another matter, the report documented the complex nature of seating arrangements on buses in the Jim Crow world, a concept foreign in Puerto Rico. The unwritten rule regarding the seating procedures on military buses was that if a Puerto Rican (white or black) sat in a seat designated for continentals, he was made to get off at the next stop and promptly fired.[30]

The construction records for the Caribbean projects of the Navy listed the number of workers hired and specified different nationalities, distinguishing, for example, U.S. citizens and people from the British West Indies. Additionally, the typology used by the authorities drew distinctions between different kinds of U.S. citizens, distinguishing "continentals" from Puerto Ricans and U.S. Virgin

Islanders. Thus, for example, 220 continentals and 7,580 Puerto Ricans worked in construction in the San Juan area. In St. Thomas, the report lists four kinds of workers: 950 Virgin Islanders; 200 Puerto Ricans; 1,000 "Aliens (Tortolans, Anguillans, etc.);" and 50 "continentals."[31] By itself, the fact that the authorities drew distinctions between different kinds of U.S. citizens was not necessarily problematic. These distinctions were useful in calculating the impact of a project on local employment, for example. But this was not their primary purpose. The typology differentiating U.S. citizens also reflected unequal treatment by race or ethnicity, especially in housing and pay.

Scholars debate whether "race prejudice" existed in Puerto Rico. Some deny its existence and point to the extensive "race mixing" among the island's population as evidence of its absence. Others insisted that Puerto Ricans exhibited their own version of racial prejudice. "Whether race prejudice among Puerto Ricans was refuted or affirmed, early studies all point to the pervasiveness of race-mixing, coupled with a lax definition of whiteness (relative to the United States)."[32] However, during this time period, the racial segregation implemented in Puerto Rico was an American institution. Not surprisingly, this would therefore be a source of significant tensions between Puerto Ricans and continentals, particularly the military and its contractors, who constituted the most significant 'immigration' seen on the island for decades. These problems became so serious that as late as 1948, Governor Jesús T. Piñero (the first Puerto Rican Governor and the last to be named by presidential decree in 1946), noted the irony of the situation caused by the racist policies of the Navy by pointing out that though it was interested in remaining in Puerto Rico, no Navy recruiting station was set up on the island during the war, despite the huge unemployment that prevailed. Piñero added that, unfortunately, racism had become one of the most intractable issues in the relations between the Navy and the Puerto Ricans.[33]

The armed forces of the United States only began to end segregation after Truman's Committee on Civil Rights recommended in 1947 legislation and administrative action "to end immediately all discrimination and segregation based on race, color, creed or national origin in…all branches of the Armed Services." And yet, it took decades for de-segregation to advance in the armed forces. During World War II, despite Roosevelt's insistence on recruiting African Americans, it was understood that this would be for kitchen jobs and the like. By mid-1944, over 38,000 blacks were serving as mess stewards, cooks and bakers. These jobs remained in the eyes of every African American "a symbol of his second-class citizenship in the naval establishment."[34] Not surprisingly, this culture, foreign to Puerto Ricans, permeated the practices of the contractors that the United States military brought to the island and conflicts ensued.

One of the major points of contention between the continentals and the Puerto Ricans was the wage differential. This provoked a noteworthy conflict with the Puerto Rican trade unions, some affiliated with their stateside counterparts. By 1940, Puerto Rico's labor movement had undergone a significant transformation ushered in by two labor battles in 1937: the strike of 600 operatives at the Red Star Manufacturing Company (a button factory) and a strike of the drivers of the White Star Bus Line in San Juan. Four workers were killed during the drivers' strike. Members of the Communist Party of Puerto Rico played a key role in these mobilizations.

On May 31, 1940, 112 delegates from 42 unions organized a new labor federation: the *Confederación General del Trabajador*. By October, it claimed 80,000 members in 59 unions. As food prices continued to increase, unionized workers demanded higher wages. This led to increased tensions in the unionized labor market.[35]

On January 19, 1942, a month after the Japanese attack on the American naval base at Pearl Harbor, and while American patriotism was running high, Puerto Rican workers went on strike, and all construction work was stopped at naval bases in Isla Grande, Vieques, and Roosevelt Roads in Ceiba.[36] A total of 4,000 workers went on strike; 2,000 of these assembling at the Sixto Escobar Park in San Juan in order to strategize.[37] Due to the intervention of the Department of Labor of the Insular Government, a meeting was held between the officials of the base and the striking laborers. The next day, an agreement was reached, and the workers returned to work.[38] However, the strikes continued. On February 23, strikes began in Vieques and Roosevelt Roads. On February 25, a mediation commission was convened to put an end to these labor protests. The following day, the strikers met with naval and local authorities. The strike concluded on March 2, and two days later, Arundel and Consolidated Engineering formally accepted the demands of workers, thereby increasing their wages an average of 12% to 18% and agreeing to overtime pay.

As a result of these strikes, naval construction jobs began to pay approximately $2.25 per day or 40 percent more than the sugar cane industry. The need for additional workers to satisfy the rush in naval construction was evident as demonstrated by the fact that in Vieques, besides the 1,700 local laborers employed, 1,000 Puerto Ricans were 'imported' from the main island as well as 250 continentals from the United States.[39] However, labor disputes continued. On May 23, 1943, the Brotherhood of Electricians sent a letter to Arundel Corporation notifying them that a strike was forthcoming if wages were not increased. The grievances over wage discrepancies continued, particularly when there seemed to be no end to the increases in the prices of food and other necessities.[40] The index of the retail cost of food in Puerto Rico increased 48 percent between

January and December 1942.[41] Also, work safety became a significant issue of contention. Between December 1941 and March 1943, 26 Puerto Ricans died in construction-related accidents overseen by the Arundel Corporation.[42]

Puerto Rico was not the only jurisdiction where U.S. contractors experienced labor conflicts. In Jamaica and British Guiana, labor protests about disparities in pay along racial lines were frequent. Since locals were paid using a lower pay scale than stateside workers, local workers went on strike. In Jamaica, the situation escalated to the point that U.S. troops had to be sent to restore peace.[43]

Bacardi Corporation established a bottling operation in Puerto Rico in 1936. Most of its production was shipped to the United States with only a small percentage sold locally. The photograph shows cases of Bacardi rum being loaded onto a cargo ship headed for the US market. Mari Aixalá Dawson, Pepín R. Argamasilla. *Bacardi: A Tale of Merchants, Family and Company* (Miami: Facundo and Amalia Bacardi Foundation, Inc, 2006), p. 65.

Rum sales boom

Before the war, British and North American whiskeys and scotch were favored by U.S consumers. However, industrial alcohol was considered a strategic war material because it was necessary for the production of tires, smokeless gunpowder, and other chemical products, and the U.S. government required that all liquor manufacturers concentrate on the production of industrial alcohol.[44] This was a boon for rum produced in the Caribbean. Rum consumption in the United States increased 169 percent from 1942 to 1943 and another 24 percent between 1943 and 1944. Puerto Rican exports increased from 2,745,322 to 5,620,713 gallons between 1942 and 1943, and Cuban exports increased from 164,922 to 4,115,665 gallons over the same time period (Table 4).[45]

What made rum exports particularly attractive to the Puerto Rican government was a law approved by the U.S. Congress on July 1, 1935, which granted that the excise taxes collected on the sale of rum be returned to the insular government. This provided the government with large unexpected proceeds that could be used to finance its economic growth programs.[46] The Federal Government returned to Puerto Rico $4 per "proof gallon" sold in the United States.[47] A "proof gallon" is a gallon of 50 percent alcohol at 60 degrees Fahrenheit.

During the first year of the law's enactment, Puerto Rico received $355,560 from rum tax rebates.[48] By 1944, this amount had increased to $65.8 million and represented 63 percent of the government's income. Unfortunately, this bonanza would be short-lived, as the percentage of income received from the rum tax decreased to 42 percent in 1946 and 26 percent in 1947 (Table 5).[49]

During the postwar years, the demand for Caribbean rum substantially shrank. Competition from North American whiskey manufacturers — particularly Seagram, Schenley, National Distillers and

TABLE 4
ORIGINS OF RUM CONSUMED IN THE UNITED STATES, 1937–47
(millions of taxable "Proof Gallons")

Year	Puerto Rico	Cuba	Virgin Islands	U.S.	French Antilles	Jamaica	Other Countries	Total
1937	718	304	164	472	10	114	81	1,864
1938	607	193	127	440	10	98	41	1,516
1939	919	176	181	611	10	118	36	2,051
1940	1,445	162	384	647	1	132	31	2,803
1941	2,586	146	642	981	1	144	46	4,545
1942	2,745	165	808	1,304	1	178	28	5,229
1943	5,621	4,116	1,726	1,348	691	442	138	14,082
1944	6,741	5,724	2,661	556	1,177	316	233	17,408
1945	2,909	453	932	527	232	152	136	5,340
1946	4,611	276	689	805	44	176	51	6,652
1947	512	52	205	326	13	71	8	1,186
Total	29,413	11,766	8,518	8,018	2,191	1,941	829	62,676
%	47%	19%	14%	13%	3%	3%	1%	100%

Sources: "Report on preliminary studies of the market for rum on the United States mainland to the Governor's Advisory Committee the Rum Industry," Arthur D. Little, Inc. Chemists-Engineers, Cambridge, Mass. Table 8-A. AFLMM, Sección IV, Presidente del Senado, Cartapacio #237, Documento #3.

Hiram Walker — intensified.[50] Puerto Rican producers lost a valuable opportunity during the war years when their competition was limited and they enjoyed strong sales. They could have positioned rum as a viable competitor to whiskey. Instead, many unscrupulous manufacturers altered the production formulas and shortened the aging process, resulting in a lower quality product. Thus, many stateside consumers saw rum as a cheap alternative to whiskey.[51] Several years after the war, on March 14, 1949, the administration of Luis Muñoz Marín, by then Governor of Puerto Rico, approved a law requiring that rum producers standardize production and aging processes. These would be closely supervised by the government, thereby breathing life to this floundering industry.[52]

TABLE 5
GOVERNMENT OF PUERTO RICO REVENUES FROM RUM, 1941–47
(millions of dollars)

Fiscal Year	Government Revenues[1]	Rum tax rebate[2]	% rum rebate
1941	$20.7	$4.6	22%
1942	37.7	13.9	37
1943	42.8	13.9	32
1944	104.1	65.8	63
1945	79.6	37.7	47
1946	82.3	34.8	42
1947	76.1	19.6	26
Total	**$443.3**	**$190.3**	**43%**

Sources:
1. Harvey S. Perloff, *Puerto Rico's Economic Future* (Chicago: The University of Chicago Press, 1950), 383.
2. Thomas Hibben & Rafael Picó, *Industrial Development of Puerto Rico and the Virgin Islands of the United States*, 208.

Impacts of the destroyers-for-bases deal

On September 2, 1940, the United States traded 50 old U.S. Navy destroyers for 99-year leases on the British bases in Antigua, the Bahamas, British Guiana, Jamaica, Saint Lucia, and Trinidad.[53] Upon hearing that an agreement had been reached, Major Sir Hubert Young, British Governor of Trinidad, felt that the United States should be willing to accept a swamp on the island off the coast of Venezuela and forgo its plan to build bases in Trinidad.[54] Washington regarded Trinidad as essential for the defense of the Panama Canal, so it was unwilling to accept Young's suggestion. He, therefore, countered that American air and naval installations should be built as far as possible from the most populated areas of the island. American military sources insisted on the desired location, and, in any case, did not need the consent of the governing colonial government regarding these matters.[55]

Naval Air Station, Trinidad, British West Indies. Commissioning ceremonies for the Naval Air Station on October 1, 1941. British and American Army and Navy officers are present. US Navy officer in center is Captain Arthur W. Radford. Note banner hanging from the building. Catalogue #: 80-G- 462774. Copyright owner: National Archives. Original Date: Wednesday, October 1, 1941. Original Medium: Black and white photograph. https://www.history.navy.mil/content/history/nhhc/our-collectionsphotography/numerical-list-of-images/nhhc-series/nh-series/80-G-463000/80-G-463774.html. Retrieved October 4, 2020.

On January 11, 1941, the British colonial government of Trinidad acquiescent, and Secretary of State Cordell Hull was able to announce that a final agreement had been reached between the United States and Great Britain. "Acceptance of the original proposals," stated Young, "[required] certain sacrifices by the people of Trinidad. The United Stated government," he added, "had given assurance of minimizing any disturbance in the normal life of the community."[56]

The historian Eric Williams describes the American presence in Trinidad as generating local resistance which helped the independence movement. According to Williams, the demands led by Governor Hubert Young included: opposition to the base site, the length of the lease, the fiscal and customs privileges, the extraterritorial rights granted, and the continuation of United States control of the area after the war.[57] Adrian Cola Rienza, a trade unionist and member of the Legislative Council of Trinidad stated that he hoped that "the Americans coming to Trinidad [would not bring] some of the objectionable practices in the Southern United States of America. I refer to 'Jim Crowism'."[58]

The base at Port of Spain was acquired from the British in 1941 when the United States leased a series of Caribbean bases for 99 years in exchange for 50 destroyers. The Navy quickly made sizeable improvements. The base was intended to supply, repair, and support the merchant fleet and Navy ships that moved freight between the United States and the Caribbean.[59] The enormous military investment of the U.S. Army and Navy helped propel the economy in Trinidad. The multiple construction projects included: docks, roads, canals, hospitals, water and electrical infrastructure, landing strips, and maintenance facilities to repair ships, among others. The Army was stationed there in order to protect the island, along with St. Lucia and Antigua, from a possible German invasion. Of the 44,899 laborers recruited for these projects, only 7,400 were continentals, the remainder were islanders. This is a considerable number as the population of Trinidad in 1941 was 492,000. Though the islanders' wages were lower than American workers, they were considerably higher than what they were previously earning. This created an economic boom as more people were employed, and additional money was flowing into the economy. The United States spent $81,913,300 in Trinidad during the construction phase from 1941 to 1944. The knowledge and skill obtained by those employed by the military would be instrumental in the postwar economic development of Trinidad.[60]

In Saint Lucia, the time when the U.S. military took over from the British is known as the 'Time of the Americans.' In March 1941, construction of the Vieux Fort airbase began. Once the war started, the U.S. military built a coastal defense at Cap Estate in the north of the island to 'keep an eye' on the developments in Vichy-French Martinique.

The U.S. Army put an enormous amount of money into circulation by Saint Lucia standards. Many remember the excesses of this period and have kept the memory alive by recalling these events with their children or grandchildren. The tales are almost of mythical proportions. There were soldiers drinking from freshly opened beer bottles and pouring the excess into the gutter. Men wiping their sweat with dollar bills. In the long run, many felt that it stigmatized the islanders, as this influx of cash and jobs was temporary, and it left the inhabitants of Saint Lucia suffering from a dependency syndrome: waiting for the return of the Americans.

According to historian Anthony Maingot, the American military presence in Jamaica was popular, with the noted exception of the local British authorities and the white aristocracy, whose power had been supplanted or at least curtailed. Various reasons account for this popularity. German submarines were sinking ships close to the Jamaican coast, a spectacle which the horrified islanders witnessed on a rather frequent basis. Many ships would burn in the vicinity, and they could watch the survivors, some severely burned, scramble towards the shore and the safety of the island. The strategy of sinking not only tankers and freighters but also the ferries which traveled between the islands exchanging food and needed supplies created a great degree of resentment against the Germans. The Jamaicans were aware the Americans were the only ones willing and able to protect them.

Jamaicans also detested the white supremacist nature of the Nazi regime. This made them more sympathetic to the moral crusade of the Allies.[60] However, some in Westminster and Kingston felt that the price for American assistance would be steep, as they would demand access to the local market of an equal footing with native business. It was feared that local business would not survive the onslaught of American capitalism. This along with Great Britain's concerns that Jamaica's bauxite and sugar were solely imperial resources added to the friction.[61]

When military and civilian populations intermingle, there is bound to be a surge in prostitution. Jamaica was no exception. According to historian Dalea Bean, during the Second World War Jamaica was a hotbed for sexual liaisons between soldiers and local women. Though prostitution was illegal, there was no vehement enforcement of these laws. Perhaps in order to shift embarrassment over the obvious spread of venereal disease, the local newspaper *Gleaner* reported in December 1942 that the spread of venereal disease was worse in Great Britain, which has seen an increase of 70 percent since the beginning of the war. Unfortunately, this did not change the perception of Jamaica as a hotspot regarding infection rates. Many ships refused to call at Jamaica on account of the crew of previous visits contracting venereal disease. With the end of the war, military personnel left Jamaica, and venereal disease rates slumped.[62]

During the war, Jamaica became a temporary haven, or holding tank, for a variety of displaced people on both sides of the conflict. There were refugees from across Europe, Germans and Italians interned in Jamaica, and German merchant seamen captured in or near Jamaica waters. While the colonial government in Kingston invited or agreed to allow these groups to come, authorities made sure that they did not mingle with the population.

The need for internment camps was considered even before the war began. By September 1940, Germans living in Jamaica, some of them Jews, were being interned. These were joined by Italian detainees and German merchant seamen brought in from Curaçao.

By the end of 1940, the number of internees was 447. By the end of 1941, there were more than 1,000 Germans internees, and by the end of 1943, there were 1,200. The most cited complaint received by the authorities was that Nazis and anti-Nazis were interned together. Newspaper accounts concur, stating that the camps interned African-born Germans, traders and planters along with prisoners of war who would likely sympathize with the Nazi regime. A more horrifying example was that of a Jewish doctor who fled Nazi Germany but was interned with ardent Nazis. Similar problems occurred in the internment camps in the United States. In October 1944, most of the internees in Jamaica were sent to Gibraltar. Others ended up in Cuba or the United States. The German POWs in Jamaica were the last to be freed. They were shipped to Germany in November 1946, though some managed to stay in Jamaica by marrying Jamaican women.[63]

Group portrait of European refugees assisted by the Emergency Rescue Committee on board the *Capitaine Paul-Lemerle*, a converted cargo ship sailing from Marseilles to Martinique. Among those pictured are: Ernst Rossmann, Karl Heidenreich, Dyno Lowenstein, Katrin Kirschmann, Emil Kirschmann, and Peter Grassmann. March 25, 1941. Photo Designation: Rescue Missions-Diplomatic Rescue-France: American Rescue Mission. Photo Credit: United States Holocaust Memorial Museum, courtesy of Dyno Lowenstein https://collections.ushmm.org/search/catalog/pa1139587. Accessed November 25, 2020.

CHAPTER VI

The Silent War with Britain, the United States and Martinique

France fell in June 1940 and signed an armistice with Germany that ceded control of the country's assets except for the French Fleet and France's African and Caribbean colonies. Over the summer of 1940, the government was forced to move its headquarters from Paris to Vichy. In the meantime, General Charles de Gaulle and his Free French Forces, which abhorred the surrender and the armistice terms, moved to London.

De Gaulle was able to win over a few of the overseas territories in French Equatorial Africa and the South Pacific to the Free French side. However, the vast majority of the colonies remained loyal to Philippe Pétain, the Word War I hero of Verdun who became the *de facto* head of the Vichy government. The local population of the colonies had little to say in the matter. Elected civil officials in the French Caribbean islands of Martinique and Guadeloupe attempted to join de Gaulle's Free French Forces, but the governor of these colonies, Admiral Georges Robert, had other plans, and he stripped the civil authorities of their power.

French warships converged on Martinique and Guadeloupe in late June 1940. Among them was the fast cruiser *Émile Bertin* which

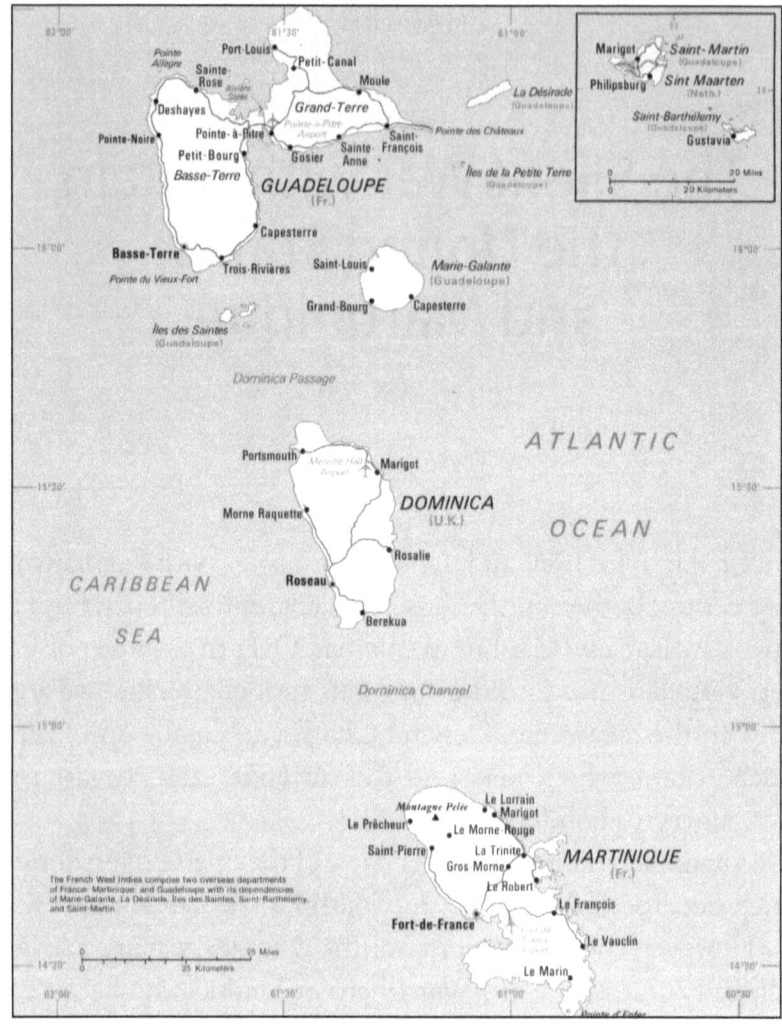

Map of Dominica, Guadeloupe, and Martinique. Contributor Names: United States: Central Intelligence Agency, 1976. Notes: Scale 1:1,100,000. "502491 1-76 (541681)." "Lambert conformal projection." Includes inset. Available also through the Library of Congress Web site as a raster image. AACR2. Medium: 1 map: col.; 22 x 17 cm. Call Number/Physical Location: G5100 1976. U5. Repository: Library of Congress Geography and Map Division Washington, D.C. 20540-4650 USA dcu. Digital Id: http://hdl.loc.gov/loc.gmd/g5100.ct002868. Library of Congress Control Number: 8069430. Language: English. Online Format: image. LCCN Permalink:https://lccn.loc.gov/80694309. Additional Metadata Formats: MARCXML Record.

carried a substantial portion of the gold from the Bank of France. It joined the aircraft carrier *Bearn* anchored in Fort-de-France. The *Jeanne d'Arc* was moored in Guadeloupe. This assemblage of naval power served to dissuade the Allies from attempting a takeover of the French islands. From 1940 to 1943, the inhabitants of Martinique and Guadeloupe would pay a steep price for the isolation and repression which marked Admiral Georges Robert's governance.[1]

The islands of Martinique and Guadeloupe were first sighted by Christopher Columbus on his second voyage in 1493 when he was on his way to the Spanish settlement at Santo Domingo. Both islands were bypassed by the Spanish, as their inhabitants, the Caribs, were known to be particularly aggressive (at least according to the Spanish). These islands were therefore used mainly as a resupply center for ships traveling to and from Europe and later for conducting slaving raids on the Caribs.

French colonization and control began in the 1630s. Martinique became an important transshipment point for slaves arriving from Africa before being sent to Saint Domingue (modern-day Haiti) for sale. By the end of the 17th century, the French established a plantation system that required the importation of slaves. By 1700, Martinique had a population of nearly 21,000 of which 15,000 were African slaves. As a byproduct of the French Revolution of 1789, slavery was abolished in the French Empire in 1794. In 1802, Napoleon Bonaparte dispatched an army to Martinique and Guadeloupe and reestablished slavery. He knew Martinique well, as it was the birthplace of his first wife Joséphine de Beauharnais. Full and immediate emancipation in the French empire was not enacted into law until April 27, 1848.

By the late 19th century, the planters of French descent, also known as the *béké*, had lost much of their sugar market share as labor costs increased, lower-cost beet sugar was produced in Europe, and new sources of cane sugar became available to consumers. Sugar production dropped from nearly 50 million tons in 1884 to 20 million in 1892. This crisis accelerated the concentration of property into the hands of a few large landlords and contributed to widening the class divisions on the island. In 1902, the volcano Mont Pelée erupted violently and destroyed the nearby city of Saint-Pierre.[2] It was estimated that around 30,000 people, 15 percent of the island's population, died as a result.[3]

Many black Martiniquais considered their citizenship fragile and subject to the powerful *béké* and the colonial administration. Admiral Georges Robert's Vichy-run government from 1940 to 1943 exacerbated the frustration and anger of Martinique's and Guadeloupe's majority black population, which were also caught between the global strategies of Britain and the United States on one hand, and Vichy France and their German oppressors on the other.[4]

Fall of France

In May 1940, Germany invaded France. President Roosevelt expressed his concern regarding the sizeable French fleet to Premier Reynaud on May 26. "If the worst comes to the worst [the defeat of France]," remarked Roosevelt, "we regard the retention of the French fleet as a force…as vital to the reconstruction of French colonies and to the ultimate control of the Atlantic and other oceans and as a vital influence towards getting less harsh terms of peace."[5] The U.S. Government was adamant that the French fleet not fall into German hands.

On June 23, 1940, the harsh terms the Germans imposed on the French were set forth in the armistice signed by both parties. France was divided into two zones, the rich northern zone with the seaports desired by the German Navy was held by the Germans while the south would be administered by the French. The army was to be demobilized and the aircraft were to remain in place at the time of the signing. From the standpoint of the Americans, the most important item was stated in Article 8 which prescribed how the French fleet was to be dealt with.

> [The French fleet] shall be demobilized and disarmed under German and Italian supervision. The German government solemnly states to the French government that it does not intend to use for its own war purposes the French fleet which will be stationed in ports under German control. Apart from that portion of the French fleet (to be determined later) which is to defend French interest in the colonial empire, all warships now away from France are to be brought back to France.[6]

The armistice brought a storm of criticism from Great Britain and the United States, though most of this criticism was directed at how the French fleet might be deployed, particularly as neither trusted the German government to abide by these terms. Admiral Jean François Darlan, the French Admiral of the Fleet made assurances that the fleet would not fall into German hands, but he too was not believed. Throughout this ordeal, the United States maintained an embassy in Vichy, just as it had one in Nazi Germany, Japan and Italy. "If I did not consent to authorize the French fleet to proceed to British ports, it was because I knew that such a decision would bring about the total occupation of metropolitan France as well as North Africa," argued Darlan.[7] In Berlin, Hitler was overjoyed with the success achieved in France and welcomed a negotiated peace, as the terms would be dictated by him and his staff. A documentary account of a meeting he held with Benito Mussolini found in the archives of the German Foreign Office after the war indicated that Hitler's chief motive in granting the armistice was to neutralize

Darlan's fleet. London concluded that it was Germany's intent to take control of the French fleet, and the military decision they shortly approved was based on this premise. It would have serious implications on the French-Anglo relations throughout the war.[8]

The United States' inner circle also expressed concerns regarding the surrender of the French fleet to the Germans. Should it be surrendered to Germany and Italy, noted General George C. Marshall, "the United States would face an extremely serious situation in the South Atlantic."[9] Meanwhile Brigadier General George V. Strong believed that Germany might strike the eastern portion of South America in the next 60 days in order to block the Panama Canal and bottle up the American naval power in the Pacific. At his urging, the Hawaiian and Panama Departments were alerted to possible sabotage or surprise attacks. Military planners also pointed out that if both Britain and France were defeated and their fleet escaped unharmed, their most likely destination would be the ports of the United States, thereby endangering its neutrality stance.[10] In the meantime, "the United States embarked on a rapid and far-reaching mobilization of its industry and manpower."[11]

After the armistice was signed, the French were left in a weakened position vis-à-vis Germany. A demarcation line was set up which divided the country in two, with a military frontier dividing the German-occupied zone from the Vichy French zone. Hundreds of thousands of French prisoners of war stayed in German prison camps and would be used as forced labor for the remainder of the war. Given the tenuous position of the Vichy regime, collaboration with Germany, in some form or other, would have to be tolerated. Vichy's only bargaining chips were its fleet and its colonies.

On July 1, 1940, London ordered Vice Admiral Sir James Somerville, commander of the powerful "Force H" in the Mediterranean, to neutralize the French fleet. On the morning of July 3, he appeared near Mers-el-Kébir in Oran, Algeria.[12] Oran, with a pre-war population of 200,000, was the capital and principal seaport of French Algeria. The city is 450 feet above the level of the Mediterranean and commands a well-protected harbor where large ships may anchor. The port was developed by the French as one of their major naval stations. The harbor at Mers-el-Kébir is five miles west of Oran and was also large and well protected. [13]

Admiral Somerville carried an ultimatum for Admiral Marcel-Bruno Gensoul, commander of the French Navy Squadron in Mers-el-Kébir. He was given several options: (1) join the British fleet; (2) sail to a British port; or (3) sail to a French port such as Martinique or to the United States and demilitarize the fleet to British satisfaction. The message gave Gensoul six hours to decide before the British fleet opened fire with the intent to sink or damage all his fleet. It was unfortunate that at that time the French were moving their headquarter from Bordeaux to Vichy, making communications quite difficult. Gensoul presumed that all the alternative's risked provoking a German invasion of the free zone. He tried to negotiate with Admiral Somerville but could not reach an agreement acceptable to London or Darlan, the head of the Vichy Navy. At six o'clock, the British warships opened fire on the French fleet. After fifteen minutes of lopsided fighting, the British had heavily damaged the French battleships *Dunkerque*, *Provence* and *Bretagne* while the battleship *Strasbourg* escaped to the French port of Toulon. Nearly 1,500 French sailors were killed in the attack.

On July 3, the British fleet under the command of Admiral Andrew Cunningham struck the French fleet in Alexandria, Egypt. A similar ultimatum was delivered to the French Admiral Rene-Émile Godfroy, though in this case, the negotiations to demobilize the French fleet at anchor succeed. Godfroy readily agreed to discharge the fuel from his ships and to remove the warheads from his torpedoes, though the British insisted that the French crews would have to be removed, an ultimatum Godfroy refused. In the meantime, Darlan ordered Godfroy to bolt from the harbor, an impossible order to obey due to the British presence blocking the entrance. Godfroy and Cunningham continued to talk and finally reached an agreement whereby the French fleet would discharge their fuel, disarm their heavy guns and torpedoes, and enter a discussion regarding a reduction of French crews. Both Admirals, on their own, averted further bloodshed and antagonizing the already deteriorated relationship between these former Allies.

The Royal Navy also began to attack all French warships at sea,[14] and two dozen French warships detained in British home ports were seized in the night by British boarding parties. The operation caused considerable bloodshed and much animosity on the part of the French toward Great Britain. The Royal Navy also tried to destroy the battleship *Richelieu*, which lay unfinished in its berth at Dakar, French West Africa. On July 8, a British squadron, including the aircraft carrier *Hermes*, attacked unsuccessfully the French fleet anchored at Dakar. It did, however, succeed in immobilizing the *Richelieu*.[15]

British fleet sets toward Martinique

As tensions grew on the European continent, President Roosevelt met with his advisors on May 16, 1940 to discuss military strategies in case of a German victory in Europe. Should France fall, they anticipated that Germany might acquire the French African colonies and strike at South America. If Great Britain also fell, Germany might acquire both fleets and launch attacks across the South Atlantic as well. In view of these possibilities, the United States engaged in conversations with the Latin American nations regarding common defensive measures. Given these extraordinary circumstances, on May 23 an American cruiser squadron, with marines aboard, set out on a 'goodwill' mission to South American ports. On the same day, Roosevelt spoke to a group of businessmen stating that the defeat of France and Britain would eliminate the buffer that protected the United States: the British fleet and the French army.[16] On May 24, President Roosevelt "discovered that it might not be long before Germany made an attempt to seize territory in the New World."[17] Admiral Harold Stark, Chief of Naval Operations, argued that the United States "should immediately and without advance publicity assert its sovereignty over these possessions and occupy them forthwith."[18] By May 25, the German land victory was certain. Three days later the Belgium Army surrendered followed by the withdrawal of the British Army from Dunkirk.[19]

As Paris was being overrun, Paul Reynaud, President of the Council of Ministers, sent an urgent message to U.S. Ambassador William C. Bullitt indicating that France's New World possessions might become the headquarters of the resistance movement. Prime Minister Winston Churchill recognized the importance of this communiqué and believed that the Allied cause could be lost if the French islands were lost to the Germans. "It seems to me," remarked Churchill, "that there must be many elements in France who will wish to continue the struggle, either in France or in the French colonies, or in both."[20]

The French New-World possessions included the tiny islands of St. Pierre and Miquelon off Newfoundland's southern coast, French Guiana in South America, and the West Indian islands of Guadeloupe and Martinique. Martinique was by far the most important of these possessions as it was the administrative center and economically the most productive.[21] On June 16, General Charles de Gaulle, as Under Secretary of State for National Defense, ordered the

French freighter *Pasteur*, loaded with a cargo of arms and ammunition and bound for Bordeaux, to change course and head for the nearest British harbor. France's only aircraft carrier, the 28,000-ton rebuilt *Bearn*, which had steamed to the United States to take on a cargo of 106 American Brewster Buffalo and Curtiss Fighter aircraft was in the mid-Atlantic.[22] These aircraft were sold by the U.S. Government to the Anglo-French Purchasing Commission, then transported to Halifax, Canada, and in June 1940, just as France was being invaded, loaded onto the *Bearn*.[23] The *Bearn* was originally laid down in 1914 as a battleship of the Normandie class and converted to an aircraft carrier in 1927. She was modernized in 1935. She was capable of a top speed of 21.5 knots and had a cruising range of 6,000 miles. Her armament included eight 6.1-inch and six 3.9-inch guns, eight 3-inch anti-aircraft guns, and six anti-aircraft machine guns.[24]

Darlan ordered her commander to take her to Martinique. Two days later, the French heavy cruiser *Émile Bertin* also anchored at Fort-de-France in Martinique. It had made a hasty departure from Canada after loading $384 million worth of gold bullion originally from the Bank of France but recently stored in Halifax.[25] Admiral Robert also had at his disposal the 6,000-ton light cruiser *Jeanne d'Arc*, the destroyer *Le Terrible*, and the armed merchant cruisers *Esterel*, *Barfleur*, and *Quercy* in addition to six tankers and nine freighters. Of special interest to the Allies was the *Émile Bertin*. Due to her extraordinary speed — she could travel at a formidable 40 knots — she was considered the pride of the French Navy. However, the Allies were more interested in the gold she was carrying.[26]

French Premier Paul Reynaud had originally requested that the gold reserve held by the Bank of France and that of occupied Belgium and Poland be evacuated from Bordeaux on an American warship as the United States was a neutral party in the conflict. The

The French aircraft carrier *Bearn* stationed in Martinique, 1941 (US Navy Naval Aviation News, 1963). Retrieved October 28, 2020.

speed with which things were changing in Europe did not make this possible, so the *Émile Bertin* was used instead. It was dispatched to Halifax, Canada which it reached on June 18, before the armistice was signed. The Canadian Prime Minister William Lyon Mackenzie King would shortly have to deal with the Vichy Government's request to permit the vessel to leave while Canada was at war with Germany but not technically with the Vichy Government of Pétain. Colonel James Layton Ralston, the Canadian Minister of Defense and the deputy head of the Bank of Canada urged Mackenzie King to restrain the ship by force if necessary. The British Admiralty insisted that the ship stay in Halifax. Prime Minister King and his government debated the issue for three days and finally decided to let the ship depart, disregarding British wishes. Wasting no time, the captain of the *Émile Bertin* sailed at full speed towards Martinique, trailed by the heavy cruiser *HMS Devonshire*, which did not interfere with its passage.[27]

Many felt that these prizes might lure the Germans to demand them, and the weak Vichy administration to comply. The Americans reacted by proposing the seizure of all British, French, Dutch and Danish colonies in the Atlantic while the British offered Admiral Robert the "opportunity" to place his islands, the Vichy fleet, and the gold under British protection. Not surprisingly, Admiral Robert rejected this proposal. As discussed later, many residents of these islands opposed the armistice and Robert's administration. However, Robert possessed the firepower and the marines to make his decisions stick.[28]

The amount of firepower assembled in Martinique during this time did not go unnoticed either by the British, the Axis, or the United States. The aircraft carrier *Bearn* was carrying 106 American aircraft to France at the time of the armistice. Accompany this powerful ensemble were two French cruisers, one faster than anything in the U.S. arsenal, as well as other naval and merchant vessels. This fleet, the gold, and all of France's possessions would be commanded by Admiral Georges Robert, the High Commissioner for France's New World Possessions, having been confirmed in 1939. To the sorrow of the Free French Forces under Charles de Gaulle, Admiral Robert would pledge his undying loyalty to the Vichy regime of Marshal Philippe Pétain.

Blockade

Attuned to the fact that Nazi Germany might have a foothold in the Caribbean, well within the U.S. Monroe Doctrine's sphere of influence, and the British fears that its oil and bauxite shipments might be disrupted, a plan to deal with this threat was concocted.

Britain was also motivated to move against Martinique with the intent that the gold, the naval vessels, and the airplanes not be seized by the Germans. The British initiated a blockade of Martinique.[29] On June 26, the light cruisers *Dundee* and *Fiji* were anchored to effectively block the departure of any ship attempting to leave Fort-de-France. Over the next few days, tensions mounted, though there were no incidents even though British sailors went ashore on Fort-de-France. In the meantime, Admiral Robert had the gold removed from the *Émile Bertin* and had it stored in one of the old colonial forts.[30] Fearing what Robert called "the eventuality of ulterior transport," he ordered the colony "under duress" as he noted in his *Memoirs*, to build 8,000 crates to store the "precious cargo" in uniform weights of 35 kilograms (77 pounds) each. Once this task was completed, the crates were stored in the rock caverns of Fort Desaix.[31]

The blockade had an immediate and detrimental impact on the island's inhabitants. Commercial establishments had no goods to sell and food inventories declined, with the foreseeable impact of rising prices. Tensions mounted along with impending disorder. On July 1, U.S. Under Secretary Sumner Welles warned British Ambassador Philip Henry Kerr (Lord Lothian) that the United Stated would not allow Britain to occupy Martinique and Guadeloupe.[32] That same day Secretary of State Cordell Hull sent a communiqué to the German Minister of Foreign Affairs in which he expressed his concern regarding a violation of the Monroe Doctrine as the possibility of Germany occupying the New World colonies of France and the Netherlands was considered real. Germany acted "surprised" at this insinuation stating that unlike France and England, they had no colonies "in the American continent." The German Minister of Foreign Affairs added that the United States was applying the Monroe Doctrine selectively as this would amount to "conferring the right to possess territories in the Western Hemisphere and not to other European countries" [like, for instance, Germany], an interpretation that Germany considered "untenable." The German note added that "if the American Republics expected to obtain respect for the Monroe Doctrine on non-interference in the affairs of the Western Hemisphere, these same republics should refrain from interference in the affairs of Europe."[33]

On July 2, the British naval forces enforcing the blockade increased to five, and on July 4, two more British cruisers were dispatched to Fort-de-France. Given the previous attacks on the French fleet at Mers-el-Kébir and the harsh terms imposed on the one anchored in Alexandria, it seemed likely that the British would shell the French warships in Martinique as well. On July 3, when the British issued an ultimatum to the French naval commanders stationed in Martinique, they refrained from delivering it to Admiral Robert. On July 5, Secretary of State Cordell Hull protested this incursion, telling Lord Lothian that should the British attempt to seize Martinique or the French naval vessels anchored in Fort-de-France, it would "involve real trouble between your government and mine."[34] In the meantime, Lothian denied that the British were trying to seize the islands by force or attempting to sink the French fleet. They were merely "observing the situation."[35] However, in the news conference the following day, Hull did not share this information with the press. He limited his remarks to indicating that the United States "was checking on reports of the blockade" and that the situation in Martinique was unclear. When asked, he declined to comment further.[36]

On July 5, General George C. Marshall and Admiral Harold R. Stark directed a joint Planning Committee to prepare for the eventuality that the United States would be required to occupy Martinique and Guadeloupe in order that they did not fall to Germany. The plan contemplated that an expeditionary force from New York would take over the islands on or about July 15.[37] An invasion of

Martinique posed serious potential pitfalls for the Americans. First, there was a question of the 106 new aircraft aboard the *Bearn* being used against an invading force. The beaches in Martinique were also unsuitable for off-loading heavy equipment. Military planners, therefore, hoped that the French would acquiesce peacefully to American occupation, particularly when presented with formidable air and naval forces just outside the harbor at Fort-de-France. If this failed to dissuade the French military, then a landing would ensue, and once Martinique was secure, the United States would go on to invade Guadeloupe. To complicate matters more, on July 5, France severed diplomatic relations with Great Britain as a result of the attack on the French fleet at Mers-el-Kébir, which according to the first reports coming out of Algiers, killed more than 1,000 French sailors. This was perceived in London as an indication that the Pétain Government was totally dependent on Germany.[38] The French, however, denounced the attack on its fleet as "treachery" and said that France was ready to defend itself by sea and air against any further attacks by the British.[39] "Mr. Churchill is guilty of an act of aggression which is without precedent in the history of the world" argued, French Foreign Minister Paul Baudouin, "because the French warships at Oran [Mers-el-Kébir] were demobilized and without steam to maneuver for battle." He added that France, with Germany's and Italy's consent, would defend herself by sea or air against further British attacks, but would not take further reprisals for the time being.[40]

Washington sources claimed that the Caribbean had become "a potential theater of conflict between the British and French naval units." The French naval forces were reported to have been expecting a British ultimatum. French sources said that when and if the demands were delivered, it would be up to the French naval forces to fight or surrender. However, as some submarines and a number of smaller craft were in Martinique, it was unlikely that the British cruisers would enter the submarine-infested waters.[41] On July 6, President Roosevelt ordered the Navy to send a cruiser and six destroyers to Martinique to watch the British force "observing" the French squadron.[42] They departed from the recently built Isla Grande Naval Base at San Juan. It was Roosevelt's contention that no European power may acquire another European power's holding in the Western World, including Britain. This resulted in the unusual circumstances where two Allies were guarding each other.[43] Sources in Washington stated that if a naval battle ensued between the British and French forces, the United States "would be forced to take action, either to assume a protectorate of the island or to force the British to abandon any effort to seize it."[44] However, official sources stated emphatically that "American warships would not participate in any naval action" but would merely standby to advise Washington and to warn shipping away from the "danger belt."[45]

The State Department issued a communiqué stating that it expected that "the situation produced by British unwillingness to allow the two French naval vessels reported to be in [Fort-de-France] to proceed to French ports can be resolved peacefully. This is unless some hot-headed naval official should get out of control and provoke a serious incident."[46] On the diplomatic front, the United States "fired a double-barreled rebuke at Germany after the Berlin government rejected the hands-off-the Western Hemisphere warning as being without object and directed at the wrong country." Germany reiterated that if the United States expected European nations to respect the Monroe Doctrine, it must keep out of European affairs. This exchange put a severe strain on United States-Germany diplomatic relations.[47] On July 7, Roosevelt proposed that any western hemisphere claims of a victorious Germany should be handled in consultation with all the Latin American and Caribbean nations and be based on democratic principles. He rejected Germany's slogan of Europe for the Europeans as actually meaning Europe for the Germans since other nations would not have an equal voice with Germany in post-war issues. White House Secretary Stephen T. Early's statement to the press noted that it was obvious Roosevelt was standing his ground by claiming "that not one inch of Western hemisphere territory shall go to Germany as a result of the European catastrophe."[48]

The following day Great Britain "assured the United States that she [was] not maintaining a blockade of Martinique against the French cruiser *Jeanne d'Arc* and the aircraft carrier *Bearn*."[49] The Americans added a heavy cruiser, reported to be the *Phoenix*, to the already stationed six destroyers. Their orders were to observe only, in the hope that no unfortunate incident takes place. In the meantime, the French government had withdrawn a cruiser and the marine police they had sent to protect the oil refinery in Aruba from German attacks and sent them to Martinique. Unofficial sources stated that should the French fleet head for a port in the United States, they would not be interfered with. However, if they headed for Europe, they would surely be stopped by the British navy once outside the 300-mile safety zone drawn around the American Hemisphere. Other sources claimed that a solution to this conundrum might be to give Canada possession of Martinique. This "solution" was discounted by Washington as Canada is a representative of the British Empire and not of the Americas, a clear violation of the much-discussed Monroe Doctrine. Another solution that was being considered was a declaration by the United States or by one or more Latin American republics in which they assumed the responsibility for the maintenance of the *status quo* until a definite peace settlement was reached. This idea had a precedent. In 1915, when a Haitian mob opened the entrance of the French Legation and killed

Vilbrum Guillaume Sam, president of Haiti, where he had taken refuge, French forces were put ashore. They withdrew when the United States assumed responsibility for restoring order.[50] President Woodrow Wilson sent the U.S. Marines into Haiti both to restore order and maintain political and economic stability in the region. They were withdrawn in 1934 as part of Roosevelt's Good Neighbor Policy.[51]

By mid-July, an outer fleet of the American Navy was guarding an inner British fleet who was in turn guarding a Vichy-French fleet in the harbor.[52] The results of the blockade were felt by the inhabitants of the island. According to an article published in the *New York Times* on July 4, 99 percent of the island's exports, consisting of sugar, rum, bananas and tinned pineapples, ceased. Merchants ships were blocked by the British, and if they got through, their merchandise could be seized by them or the Germans. After a contraband control examination, the British would let provisional laden ships enter Martinique and Guadeloupe, though their numbers dwindled on account of the warships. Traffic from the Dominican Republic had been reduced to 600-ton freighters traveling every two weeks. The communications with Puerto Rico was limited to the weekly flights of the "Baby Clippers" of Pan American Airways. Sea travel from Charlotte Amalia, Saint Thomas, and the West Indies Islands of Anguilla, St. Martin (half French and half Dutch), Guadeloupe, St. Lucia, St. Vincent, Barbados, the Grenadines and Tobago had come to an almost complete standstill.[53] Imports from the United States in the form of flour, salt, meats, and tinned goods could not be supplied. Food inventories were therefore depressed, creating a situation likely to promote an uprising or a rebellion.[54]

A temporary compromise was achieved during July and August as French Ambassador Count de Saint-Quentin sought to deescalate the situation. Saint-Quentin hinted that "French honor" had been offended by the British proposals, ironic given the humiliating French capitulation and the signing of the harsh terms of the armistice. The Americans stated emphatically that the British would sink the French fleet as they had already done at Mers-el-Kébir at the slightest provocation. The French countered with a proposition allowing the vessels to remain in Martinique under the supervision of the U.S. Naval Commission.[55] On July 16, "Hull remarked that the United States was disappointed with Vichy's procrastination and warned that if it continued, the British and this country would presumably take their own respective courses."[56] Both Hull and Lothian agreed that this delay was probably due to the fact that the Vichy administration was taking orders from the German Government. In the meantime Ambassador Saint-Quentin informed U.S. Under Secretary Sumner Welles that his government was asking Germany to waive "certain terms of the armistice in order to assure the United States that war vessels in Martinique would not leave French territorial waters."[57] He also stated that Vichy had instructed Robert to accept an American naval officer and that he would be given the "fullest facilities" to assure that the terms of the agreement are complied with.

This proposal was "totally unsatisfactory" according to Welles, as all the decisions would be contingent upon German approval. Welles explained that the United States could not tolerate German control over Martinique and Guadeloupe. Furthermore, the U.S. Naval Observer, was just that, an observer, with no real power to effect change should that be required. The United States was also interested in obtaining the airplanes in Martinique for use by themselves or to send them to Britain, which at the time was fighting the Luftwaffe raids over London with limited aircraft. This would be a continued point of contention during the long and difficult negotiations with Vichy and Robert. On July 24, the United States accepted the original proposal. The French fleet would not leave port except for the performance of administrative duties and the Naval Observer would be allowed the freedom to communicate by radio with the San Juan Naval Station. The matter of the airplanes remained unresolved. During these discussions, it became apparent to Welles that regarding the French New World Colonies, it was the High Commissioner Robert and not Marshall Pétain who dictated the final terms of this agreement.[58] Admiral Robert resisted British and American attempts to pressure him into releasing the gold and the airplanes or backing de Gaulle's Free French Forces, but he did acquiesce to a meeting to discuss the matter with an American naval representative.[59]

United States takes an aggressive posture

On August 4, 1940, Rear Admiral John W. Greenslade was instructed to fly to Fort-de-France in order to try and reach an informal agreement with Robert. It was believed that a career naval officer of equal rank would probably be better suited to negotiate with Robert than a State Department Official. The same would hold true when Roosevelt sent Admiral William D. Leahy to Vichy as its ambassador the following year. Besides negotiating with Robert, Greenslade was expected to do some "friendly" espionage of the air and naval units stationed there. Greenslade stayed in Fort-de-France for three days and repeated all of Washington's previous proposals, including the return of the aircraft. Robert agreed to all the terms regarding the fleet movements and naval observer but declined to remove the aircraft from Martinique, including the suggestion by the United States to send them to Indochina. In any case, they had been left to the elements and would require significant maintenance before they became airworthy. Even if they had been repaired, Martinique had no airfield from which they could be launched.

Robert and Greenslade reached an agreement whereby Robert would not jeopardize his neutrality by provoking in any manner the United States. He, on the other hand, pressed Greenslade for a guarantee that the United States would not actively support the Free French Forces.[60] The only promise made to him regarding this matter was that the United States "would observe the status quo and supply the islands with food, fuel and other essentials."[61] These developments, of course, upset the Free French Forces as the United States had *de facto* recognized Vichy's control of this section of the French Empire. During this time, de Gaulle's force had been fomenting a rebellion in French Guiana. When the State Department learned of this, they quickly made their displeasure known. The United States would not allow anything that would disrupt the status quo, and this was made patently clear to the Free French Forces. Though the State Department delayed de Gaulle's efforts, this would only be a temporary setback for them. In the meantime, they concealed all future operations from the Americans.[62]

The position taken by the State Department was a marked contrast with the wishes of the people of Martinique. According to a wireless communiqué published in the *New York Herald*, the citizens of Martinique planned "to hold a plebiscite in order to decide whether to continue under the Vichy government of Marshal Pétain or to join the cause of General Charles de Gaulle." An American businessman who returned from St. Thomas and a Martinique fisherman were both of the opinions that most of the inhabitants favored de Gaulle, and they were "certain that such a decision would win American approval." Guadeloupe also intended to hold a similar plebiscite.[63]

On October 22, 1940, Hitler's train stopped at the railway station in Montoire, France in order to meet with Vichy French Prime Minister Pierre Laval. The Montoire station was close to the main railway between Paris and the Spanish border. This was convenient as he was to meet General Francisco Franco with the intent of getting him to approve using Spain as a conduit for a planned invasion of Gibraltar. The station was also close to a long railway tunnel which could give the train protection in case of an Allied bombardment. Two days after the visit, Marshal Pétain announced that his government would assist Hitler's campaign against England. As Washington could not foretell the degree of collaboration, it once again set forth the plan to invade Martinique. Secretary of the Navy Frank Knox went a step further stating that Martinique and Guadeloupe should "be invaded immediately in order to head off any ruse on the part of Vichy."[64]

The United States reacted sharply to Pétain's pronouncement, warning Vichy that this alliance would wreck the traditional friendship between the Americans and the French and implied the use of force on the French colonies in the Western World. Though this message offended the French, it probably helped to dampen the enthusiasm they had for the Germans. The strong reaction on the part of the United States had to do with the possibility that the French might permit their Navy in Martinique and Dakar to fight alongside the Axis against the British. The United States even offered to purchase two French unfinished battleships, one in Dakar and the other in Casablanca, in order to keep them out of German hands, but the offer was rejected.

Despite the preference for keeping the status quo negotiated with Admiral Robert in August, Roosevelt was preparing an alternate plan in case things went awry. In October, he directed the Navy to draft an emergency operation to be executed on three days' notice, which would entail the invasion of Martinique and Guadeloupe. The Navy's plan called for an assault by a strong naval force (including two battleships and two aircraft carriers) with a landing force of

2,800 marines. The Navy requested that the Army support this operation with two reinforced regiments totaling 6,800 men. These should be scheduled to arrive five days after the assault had begun. The Navy's plan assumed that they would face only token resistance, an assumption the Army disagreed with. Admiral Robert had at his disposal between 7,000 to 8,000 French soldiers and sailors. Fort-de-France had strong defenses and was well supplied with ammunition. They, therefore, argued that the invasion would require a force of 25,000 men, trained and equipped. Army planners reflected on what impact a loss would have on the efforts of the United States to create a common block in Latin America to deflect the Nazis. They preferred to starve the island by effecting a naval blockade.

On November 2, 1940, General Marshall ordered a revised plan which made use of an overwhelming force in order to ensure quick success. Fortunately, another way was also explored,[65] as "the United States had neither the men nor the materials to guarantee success."[66]

The Navy sent Admiral Greenslade to reach an understanding with Admiral Robert which would guarantee the maintenance of the *status quo*. It must have been obvious to Robert that by now the Americans were planning a military response in case an agreement was not reached. In any case, he relied on the United States for food, fuel, and necessities, so it was in the interest of both to reach an accommodating settlement.[67] Realizing that his options were limited, Admiral Robert reached a "gentleman's agreement" with Greenslade whereby he promised not to move any of the French naval vessels except on two days' notice, as well as the immobilization of the airplanes and the gold. In return, the Americans promised to continue supplying the island's needs.[68]

Knowing his position was secure, Robert orchestrated a "quiet naval coup" against the wishes of the democratically elected officials of the colony. In Guadeloupe, "Councilor Paul Valentine had previously delivered an impassionate plea for liberty" at an extraordinary session of the general council. There he contended that he belonged to a race loathed by Nazism and Hitler and that German tyranny would "wipe non-Aryans from its soil. A misery greater than what we experienced prior to 1789 waits us," clearly implying a return to authoritarian racism and slavery. "However eloquent, Valentino's voice failed to carry the day."[69] Felix Eboue, the black former Governor of Guadeloupe estimated that a plebiscite would show that 97 percent of French West Indians favored de Gaulle's Free French. He added that Robert had implemented a police state in Martinique and Guadeloupe and had systematically jailed opponents and interned them at Balata internment camp or Fort Napoleon in Les Saintes.[70] In fact, he had set up an espionage network to keep under constant surveillance any citizen or public official who might harbor anti-Vichy sentiments.

This fear of arrest and imprisonment kept the local populace from overtly causing Robert's administration any trouble. However, much of the resentment particularly among the business class was directed against the United States for its policy of maintaining military vessels off Fort-de-France, the daily visit of a naval patrol plane, and the delays in securing oil supplies.[71] During this period of accommodation, trade continued along the Marseille-Casablanca-Fort-de-France route and the local ones from Pointe-a-Pitre and Fort-de-France to New York. The Dominican Republic and Brazil also helped provide at least some of the needed supplies and food for the local population.[72] What might have upset them even more were Rear Admiral Willian D. Leahy's remarks upon being named Ambassador to France when he declared that Martinique "would make a perfectly splendid base if we had it." When questioned by the press, he did not elaborate further.[73]

Émile Bertin (French light cruiser, 1933-1959) photographed in drydock, possibly at Martinique, French West Indies, when this ship was immobilized (and "Demilitarized") there. Catalog #: NH 88988. Copyright Owner: Naval History and Heritage Command. After this Year: 1939. Before this Year: 1945. Original Medium: BW Photo https://www.history.navy.mil/content/history/nhhc/our-collections/photography/numerical-list-of-images/nhhc-series/nh-series/NH-88000/NH-88988.html. Retrieved October 4, 2020.

The year 1940 would end with continued discussion of the Martinique crisis and the role the United States should play in it. Retired Rear Admiral Yates Stirling, Jr. believed that there was a large fifth column of Germans stationed there. He argued that German pilots could conceivably be smuggled into Martinique, man the planes parked there and "commit havoc" on the Panama Canal. Martinique was also an ideal base for the German U-boats. "The time for the United States to act is immediately, right now," he added, "by demanding the surrender of the French fleet."[74] Peter C. Rhodes, after a thorough inspection of Martinique's defenses and fighter planes, came to a different conclusion regarding the threat to, for instance, the Panama Canal. Rhodes was permitted to visit the fortifications, the naval forces, and the fighter planes, so he came to his conclusion based on firsthand information.

The American-made planes brought to Martinique aboard the aircraft carrier *Bearn* were parked in a fenced field at Pointe des Sables and had their vital instruments and guns removed. Rhodes observed that the planes were in relatively good condition but were not airworthy. The naval forces had been reduced to just the *Bearn*, the light cruiser *Émile Bertin* and the armed auxiliary *Barfleur*. The former auxiliary vessels *Quercy* and *Esterel* were disarmed and had left for Casablanca to be converted into banana transports. Rhodes added that he could not find evidence of coastal batteries. Fort de Seix and Fort St. Louis appeared to be the only fortifications guarding Fort-de-France. They were equipped with heavy guns whereas the other forts on the island had none. "The coastal road, of vital importance to the island's defenses, was completely washed out and made impossible by recent tropical rains."[75]

Winnipeg affair

The following year, tension initially eased, but only for a few months. In April and May 1941, the United States "brought an abrupt end to the Marseille-Casablanca-Fort-de-France shipping line, which had theretofore transported passengers, mail and goods from France to the Caribbean."[76] Initially, it simply cut off oil shipments, but then the Allies seized two French commercial vessels on the high seas which were bound for Martinique, the S. S. *Winnipeg* on May 26 and the *Arica* on June 1.[77]

With the passengers and crew celebrating with champagne their expected arrival at Martinique, the 8,379-ton French passenger liner *Winnipeg* was intercepted at sea by a British cruiser. The French steamer had a notable history as it had saved 2,200 Spanish immigrants fleeing the Spanish Civil War (1936-1939) where they would have most likely ended up in prison or worse. That voyage ended happily in Valparaiso, Chile on September 3, 1939. However, the trip to Martinique would not end in a similar fashion. A radio broadcast by the National Broadcasting Company reported that the *Winnipeg* was first intercepted by the Netherlands training boat, the 1,700-ton *HNLMS Van Kinsbergen* which then proceed to notify its location to the British naval forces. Two American-born women informed the press how scores of Germans bound for Martinique "threw hundreds of letters and other papers into the ocean after the cruiser had fired a shot across the *Winnipeg's* bow and escorted her to Trinidad."[78]

Of the 751 passengers aboard, 210 were Germans, 76 were Austrians, and another 70 were unclassified. All were interned pending an investigation, while the other passengers were examined onboard. Martha Seale of Dallas, Texas and Mrs. Marcel Lowenstein from Stamford, Connecticut were traveling with their French husbands.

When interviewed, they told the "dramatic story of the 26-day voyage from Marseilles to Trinidad by way of Oran, Algeria and Casablanca, French Morocco in a vessel they said was intended to carry only a small fraction of the 751" passengers. "Food was running low," they added, "but the champagne flowed freely Monday night in celebration of the expected docking on Tuesday in Martinique. Suddenly, at 2:30 a.m., a shot came across the *Winnipeg*'s bow."[79] While the Germans were interned, passengers with genuine American visas could continue their journey to the United States. At the time, British sources would not comment on the future of the vessel. In Fort-de-France, radio communiqué denied reports that the German passengers were planning to install a Nazi regime in Martinique. The communiqué added that all foreign passengers were emigrants in transit through Martinique. They remained in Trinidad provisionally while being "segregated from the rest of the population."[80]

Before the ship's arrival, the police at Martinique arranged what was called a "welcoming committee", but it was anything but welcoming. Many refugees were interned at the Balata camp or the Lazaret camp and, as if that were not enough, they were required to pay a hefty sum to cover their own internment. A Martinique resident who witnessed these events recalled the following:

> In the camps, the first Martiniquais political dissidents joined the Polish, Yugoslav and German Jewish refugees brought by the *Winnipeg* and other vessels, and who were interned [at the Lazaret camp]. These families, chased from their homelands by the German invaders, had hoped to find refuge in Martinique. Very quickly, the camp conditions revealed themselves to be inadequate, driving many of them to leave for the neighboring islands of the USA.[81]

In many ways, these camps were reminiscent of those the migrants had left behind in France. The Lazaret camp was described as a concentration camp in Martinique under the very eyes of the USA [and the] French gendarmes who acted like Nazis.... Our baggage was systematically searched. The search concerns only publications and letters; books and other publications authorized and printed in France are banned. Letters are examined from all angles, if one is in an envelope it is usually confiscated. Cameras are naturally confiscated.... We learn from authorities that we will stay here until a French boat sets sail from here to either New York or South America. How long might that take? No one knows. Only the next day, when the U.S. Consul comes to see if our visas are in order, do the authorities consent in his presence to give us courteous replies, and they end up promising that we will be allowed rotating visits [into Fort-de-France].[82]

On June 14, 238 European refugees who had escaped France on the *Winnipeg* arrived in New York aboard the *Evangeline*. According to the *New York Herald Tribune*, many of the refugees had brought with them large amounts of American and French money. When interviewed by the authorities, they claimed that about 90 percent of the passengers slept on the open decks of the *Winnipeg* as a result of the heat and congestion in the unhygienic hold of the ship. Scores of passengers suffered from food poisoning as a result of the horrible food that was served. Even worse, the amount of food available was not enough to feed the passages and crew, so by the end of the voyage, many were almost to the point of starvation.

Some of the refugees "vehemently contradicted reports that several hundred German-born refugees being held by the British in Trinidad" were actually Nazi agents. "They suggested that the British would have far more reason to suspect the pro-German French officers, crew and at least 50 French army officers and soldiers, most of whom openly said they were pro-Nazi."[83] There were so many Nazi sympathizers among the French crew and among the French soldiers that the passengers, many of them Jewish, were terrified of going to

Martinique. Many expressed relief when rescued. Others described the transatlantic voyage as horrible. "All food was served on one plate. It was inedible. One woman went crazy from illness, the heat, and the taunts from pro-Nazi French crew who kept" [telling the passengers] they would be held in concentration camps in Martinique. One of the passengers, Hermann Thorn, a lawyer and Jewish refuge whom the British named president of the German-Austrian refugee camp in Trinidad, stated that members of the crew and French army officers boasted of belonging to the New French Nazi party. "We had been told repeatedly in France," added Mr. and Mrs. Thorn, "that the Gestapo had gained control of Martinique."[84] Also, it became known among the passengers that the Vichy government did not engage non-Nazi sympathizers as officers and crew aboard ships bound for Martinique "for fear that they would join de Gaulle's forces." The *Winnipeg* was later confiscated by the British Government and sold to the Canadian Pacific Steamships. She was renamed the *Winnipeg II*. While en route to Saint John, New Brunswick, she was torpedoed and sunk on October 22, 1942 by U-443. All aboard were rescued by the Canadian corvette HMCS *Morden*.[85]

After the incident with the *Winnipeg*, "all maritime, commercial and even surface postal inks between the French Caribbean and the metropole were severed. The Marseille-Fort-de-France route ceased to exist, and with it, the exodus of refugees to the French Caribbean."[86] However, "between unrelenting U.S. pressure on Vichy to identify all refugees and to come clean on alleged shady traffic, Vichy's resulting May 21 telegram suspending the refugee flow, and the intercepting of the *Winnipeg*," it is hard to ascribe a single responsibility for the closure of the maritime route.[87]

Racism was not confined to American society or the U.S. Armed Forces, it was also prevalent in Martinique, France, and the French Armed Forces, particularly its Navy, as was anti-Semitism. Germaine

Krull, a French refugee interned in the Lazaret camp complained that "we whites are now being guarded by negroes."[88] Jewish refugees arriving in Martinique faced the peril of being sent back to Europe to face certain death. "Fitzroy Baptiste has suggested that the enigmatic Comte de Cerezy was a least partly responsible for pressuring Admiral Robert into sending select Jewish refugees back. In any event, in several instances, Vichy's authorities actually carried this out."[89] Restrictions imposed by Vichy's Colonial Ministry and naval officers also placed an undue burden on the Jewish French nationals seeking safety in the Americas. French officials in the Caribbean constantly complained that Martinique was becoming a "dumping" ground for refugees. In his April 11, 1942 report, Emile Devouton, Vichy's inspector to the colonies, wrote that:

> The influx to the French Antilles of numerous migrants, the majority of them foreigners, represents an undeniable danger. Admiral [Robert] has ordered that the governors take measures to ensure that these foreigners did not extend their stay (expulsion of those who do not obtain entry visas in countries of the Western Hemisphere, house arrest for migrants deemed suspicious, surveillance of others). In order to reduce the length of their stay as much as possible, it is important that in the future, migrants leaving Europe for the French Antilles do so only once they have received the visa necessary to enter a foreign country.[90]

Famed French historian Marc Bloch, who wished to emigrate to New York via Martinique along with his family, was one of the many Jewish immigrants that got caught put in this quagmire. At his request, on April 2, 1941 the Service des Oeuvres reached out to the Colonial Ministry via Admiral Darlan. It was explained that Bloch was conducting research on behalf of the Ministry of Education and desiring travel arrangements for him and his family. Colonial Minister Charles Platon responded by granting passage to Bloch,

USS Blakeley (DD-150) in passage from Martinique to St. Lucia, May 27, 1942, after being torpedoed two days previously. Note missing bow and lifeboat being towed astern. Also note that she is still wearing Measure One camouflage at this late date. Catalog #: NH 88042. Copyright Owner: Naval History and Heritage Command. Original Date: Wednesday, May 27, 1942. After this Year: 1939. Before this Year: 1945. Original Medium: BW Photo. https://www.history.navy.mil/content/history/nhhc/our collections/photography/numerical-list-of-images/nhhc-series/nh-series/NH-02000/NH-2210.html. Retrieved October 8, 2020.

but "due to strict orders from the admiralty," his family was not allowed to travel with him. Bloch refused to leave his family behind, so instead stayed in France. He joined the resistance, was arrested by the Nazis in March 1944, and executed three months later.[91]

United States enters the war

Tensions between the United States and Japan had been brewing for some time and started to reach a boiling point after July 1941.

On July 26, President Roosevelt announced a freeze of Japanese assets, coupled with a freeze on Chinese assets and a military order placing the Philippines armed forces under American command. This embargo cut off Japan's ability to purchase petroleum from the United States. This embargo seemed to stun Tokyo, as its war machine consumed an estimated 12,000 tons of oil each day and Japan had no source of its own. "I am a bit worried over the Japanese situation," Roosevelt told King George VI in one of his meetings with the King and Churchill, "the Emperor is for peace, I think, but the Jingoes are trying to force his hand." To Churchill he said, "the Jap situation is definitely worse, and I think they are headed north. However, in spite of this, you and I have two months of respite in the Far East."[92] He was right. On the afternoon of November 5, 1941, the Japanese privy council in the presence of the Emperor, decided to attack the United States. At the same time, the Joint Board of the Army and Navy — a precursor of the Joint Chief of Staff — advised the President to try to avoid war with Japan as this would weaken the efforts to defeat Germany.

On November 20, 1941, the Japanese presented their final offer of consolidation to the United States. The proposal was for a six-month cooling-off period that would allow both sides to reassess the situation, which was a return to the status quo before the embargo. In return, Japan would agree to no further territorial expansion and would withdraw from southern Indochina. A deadline was set for November 29.[93] As Washington did not respond, the die was cast. Roosevelt told his cabinet that "we are likely to be attacked perhaps as soon as next Monday because the Japanese are notorious for attacking without warning. The question is how to maneuver them into firing the first shot without too much danger to ourselves."[94] A few days before that meeting, on November 27, Admiral Harold Rainsford Stark, Chief of Naval Operations, had alerted Rear

Admiral Husband E. Kimmel, commander in chief of the U.S. Pacific Fleet and Admiral Thomas C. Hart, commander of the Asiatic Fleet, to be on guard. "This dispatch is to be considered a war warning. Negotiations with Japan looking toward stabilization of conditions in the Pacific have ceased and an aggressive move is expected within the next few days. The number and equipment of Japanese troops and the organization of naval task forces indicate an amphibious expedition against either the Philippines, Thai or Kra [Malay] peninsula or possibly Borneo."

The Army's warning to the commanders in the Pacific was also strongly worded:

> Negotiations with Japan appear to be terminated for all practical purposes, with only the barest possibilities that the Japanese Government might come back and offer to continue. Japanese future action unpredictable but hostile action possible at any moment. If hostilities cannot, repeat cannot, be avoided the United States decided that Japan commit the first overt act. This policy should not be construed as restricting you to a course of action that might jeopardize your defense.[95]

At 6:10 a.m. on December 7, 1941, the attack on the naval base at Pearl Harbor began. The first wave of fighters consisted of 183 and the second wave of 350. Despite widespread knowledge of the deteriorating political situation and explicit war warnings, the U.S. military in Hawaii was caught off guard. The attack lasted a little more than two hours. In that short time, the Japanese damaged or sunk 18 warships, including 8 battleships, 175 aircraft were destroyed and 159 were crippled.[96] Japanese losses amounted to 29 planes. On December 8, the United States declared war on Japan. Germany and Italy in turn declared war on the United States on December 11 in response to the United States' declaration of war. As discussed previously, the East Coast of the United States and the Caribbean would soon feel the wrath of the German U-boats.

On December 18, the United States and the French authorities on Martinique reached an agreement whereby the Vichy government stated its intentions of remaining neutral. Given this stance, the United States would continue to permit trade with the French colony in return for pledges that the French fleet anchored at Fort-de-France take no action detrimental to the United States or its American interests. As the talks were unfolding, President Roosevelt asserted that if the colony remained neutral, then its sovereignty would not be affected. Roosevelt's intent was to maintain cordial relations with France based on a mutual "understanding of the problems of both nations." According to the *New York Times* journalist and author Frank L. Kluckhohn, it was no secret that there was fear among the top military echelon in Washington "that Martinique might be used as a base for attacks on the United States by Axis forces if Vichy-Berlin cooperation became closer. The French aircraft carrier *Bearn* [is] in the harbor at Martinique and about 250 American built planes in transit to France were caught when Franco capitulated to Germany [in June 1940]."[97] Kluckhohn added that "neither on Martinique nor in Washington was there any indication of what guarantees the French commander on the spot [referring to Admiral Georges Robert] had given to Washington. Neither was it indicated whether [Robert] acted with the approval of the Pétain government or without it." He noted that "there was an attitude of close-mouthed reticence about the matter in the American capital."[98]

Martinique aids U-156

In the early hours of February 16, 1942, 32-year-old Kapitänleutnant Werner Hartenstein in *U-156* eased into the mouth of San Nicolaas, the harbor of Aruba, and sank the 2,400-ton British *Oranjestad* and severely damaged another two. Even though the Allies were aware of his presence, Hartenstein directed his crew to man the 4.1-inch deck gun and shoot at the Standard Oil refinery and the tank farm. The gunners forgot to remove the tampion from the muzzle of the gun, and the first round exploded inside the barrel killing the gunner and severely wounding the gunnery officer, Dietrich-Alfred von dem Borne. He was the son of a high-ranking Kriegsmarine officer. The U-boats medic attempted to repair Borne's shattered leg — a ghastly ordeal for both doctor and patient — but the medic's inexperience in these matters and the lack of medical equipment aboard the U-boat made it imperative to find other solutions to save the man's life. Hartenstein then requested permission from Admiral Doenitz to put Borne ashore in the Vichy controlled island of Martinique. After receiving clearance from Berlin, Doenitz authorized the landing, even though the French in Martinique knew the Americans would not be pleased.[99]

Shortly before 8:00 p.m. on February 20, *U-156* surfaced off the coast of Martinique. Hartenstein had ordered his crew to battle stations since he was not fully certain that he could trust the French colonial authorities.[100] Also, Martinique was under surveillance by both the British and American forces in order to prevent the "escape" of the aircraft carrier *Bearn* and other warships which could destroy the refineries of Aruba and Curaçao or attack the Panama Canal. For this reason, Hartenstein approached Fort-de-France with extreme caution.[101] For security reasons he ordered the U-boat's emblem covered and the new experimental FuMO 29 radar detector to be stowed below deck. *U-156* approached the coast at half speed. Due to the enforced blackout, the lights in the harbor had been extinguished and all shipping buoys removed. Hartenstein ordered the running lights to be turned on and set up lanterns to light up the battle flag raised on the extended periscope. At 9:00 p.m. he signaled French shore authorities in his best high-school French "German vessel. Please dispatch a boat for a wounded man." Despite their reluctance to this plan, French naval officers sent out a launch to bring Borne ashore. The captain spoke no German, so this craft left the vicinity. At 10:30 p.m. a patrol boat approached the *U-156*. Hartenstein could make out three officers and six black sailors, all dressed in crisp white uniforms and caps. The officers, according to Hartenstein, were very cordial. One of them spoke German, so communications between them were eased. The French brought along a medical doctor to evaluate the conditions of the wounded crewmember. In order to maintain the blackouts, the French requested that Hartenstein turn off his lanterns while the transfer was taking place. The medic aboard the *U-156* had stopped the bleeding but Borne's fever was out of control. He was brought on deck and handed over to the French sailors. Once this was accomplished, an undertaking that lasted less than three hours, *U-156* left at flank speed.[102] The French doctors were able to save Borne's life but not his leg. He eventually recovered and returned to Germany.[103]

It took about a month, but the Americans were finally informed of the assistance the French forces in Martinique rendered *U-156* after it had attacked the refineries in Aruba. By this time Washington knew that a German submarine (sources could not identify which) entered Fort-de-France on February 21 and sent ashore a wounded member of its crew. It was promptly established that the submarine "took on no supplies and did not attempt to open communication with anyone on the island."[104] Given the seriousness of this incident, a communiqué was urgently sent to Ambassador William D. Leahy at Vichy with a warning that the United States would not permit the use of French colonies by Axis warships or planes. The communiqué made it clear "that unless the United

States received categorical assurances that the French government would not again allow any Axis submarine or warplane to visit any French Western Hemisphere possession, the United States would find itself completed to take action as would protect its own interest."[105] Though what action would be taken was not spelled out, it became increasingly clear to the Vichy high officials that the United States intended to take over the island. After several diplomatic exchanges, the Vichy government gave assurances "that no Axis vessels or planes henceforth would be permitted to enter French ports or territorial waters in the Western Hemisphere under any pretext."[106]

The French, however, defended their action by saying that Germany had informed them in advance of *U-156*'s intentions and that they persisted despite their protests. Furthermore, Robert had informed the American Consul stationed in Martinique of these events prior to the date the U-boat was to encounter the French naval authorities at Fort-de-France. As noted by Ambassador Leahy in his memoirs titled *I Was There*, "it was difficult to see how France could agree to refuse to the Axis entry into French ports such as was permitted under old international law, except assuming that France still was in the status of a belligerent and therefore not neutral."[107] The American communiqué "worried" the Vichy government. In order to return to the status quo, Admiral Darlan informed Leahy that he would receive in writing a formal guarantee that similar incidents of that nature would not be repeated. Regarding the unofficial rumors that Martinique was preparing to receive and resupply the U-boats hunting in the Caribbean, Darlan reiterated the legitimacy of the incident and denied that Germany intended to use the French colonies as their base. "Vichy would not authorize under any circumstances," argued Darlan, "the utilization of French possessions in the Western Hemisphere by any of the belligerents as a base of operations."[108] This reply, noted Leahy, fell far short of that stipulated by Under Secretary Welles, which demanded categorical assurances.

During this back and forth, Vichy reiterated that the submarine received no supplies whatsoever, an account confirmed by the American naval observer. Welles also noted that Vichy had blocked the reopening of the American Consulate in Cayenne, French Guiana. "Persistent rumors related to the presence of German submarines in the territorial waters of French Guiana, the strengthening of a military garrison there and increased supplies of gasoline suggested the colony was being turned into a haven for German submarines," added Welles.[109]

Admiral William D. Leahy greeted by Marshal of France Philippe Pétain. April 27, 1942. Admiral William D. Leahy Collection. Catalog #: NH 124450. Copyright Owner: Naval History and Heritage Command. Original Date: Monday, April 27, 1942. After this Year: 1940. Before this Year: 1949. Original Medium: BW Photo. https://www.history.navy.mil/content/history/nhhc/our-collections/photography/numerical-list-of-images/nhhc-series/nh-series/NH-124000/NH-124450.html. Retrieved October 4, 2020.

Leahy leaves Vichy and tensions continue to rise in Martinique

During the first few months of 1942, major changes in the leadership of the Vichy government would alter the course of its relationship with Germany and the United States. In his New Year's address, Marshal Pétain protested German occupation policies and pressures while his Minister of Finance denounced the stiff occupation costs. Admiral Darlan had refused to encourage the emigration of skilled

French workers to Germany. Pétain had stood up against German demands for railway equipment, protested the loss of French territory, and had the electric power servicing the aluminum factories in Germany shut off. Darlan also argued against the new anti-Jewish measures which the Germans wanted imposed in France. According to Hermann Göring, the relationship between France and Germany was so bad that he recommended that people stay clear of politics until the end of the war, which he obviously thought would be in Germany's favor. By the middle of March, Hitler himself told Pétain through an emissary that "it was necessary for good relations between the two nations that [Pierre] Laval return to the French government."[110] According to Göring, Laval, who had been previously removed from the government by Pétain because of his close collaboration with Germany, was now seen as essential for the restoration of "German confidence in Vichy."

Laval warned Pétain that Germany would adopt a more repressive posture toward France as a result of his New Year's address. True to these warnings, Germany moved France's subordination under the German Army to the Schutzstaffel (SS). It seemed to Leahy and others that Darlan was to be replaced with Laval. Washington's response was that they could only view the return of Laval to a position of power and authority as a clear indication that "the French people [could] no longer look to the French government at Vichy to carry out their own desire to maintain relationships of friendship and understanding with the United States and the American people. Pierre Laval was so notoriously and completely identified with a policy of supine subservience to Germany and so obviously intent upon collaboration with the Nazis that the United States could not have confidence in the Vichy regime."[111] On April 15, Leahy was informed that he should report to Washington for "consultations." Two days later the French government announced that Admiral Darlan had resigned, leaving the *de facto* leadership of the government in Laval's hands.[112]

By April 17, 1942, the American press published the news of Leahy's recall from Vichy France. According to the *New York Tribune*, President Roosevelt recalled Ambassador Leahy due to his "displeasure at the formation of the new French government dominated by Pierre Laval, the leading exponent of collaboration with Germany."[113] A few days before, Under Secretary Welles angrily commented on this turn of events, stating that the French collaborationists had "prostituted their country" to the Nazi regime which was "bent upon nothing less than the permanent enslavement of France."[114] He added that though Leahy's departure did not constitute an open break with the Vichy regime, should Laval pursue a policy of collaboration with the Axis, this could very well happen. The Vichy reorganization demoted Admiral Darlan, previously Vice-Premier, to overseer of the Army, Navy and Air Force. He would report to Pétain.

In a press conference on April 17, Welles repeated emphatically "that all shipments to France and northern Africa would be held up indefinitely."[115] He was referring to the recent agreement between both countries whereby the United States approved the shipment of two freighters loaded with foodstuff and another Red Cross relief ship with medical supplies. Regarding Martinique, American naval and military personnel were ordered to maintain extreme vigilance over the island as well as the islands of St. Pierre and Miquelon, seized by de Gaulle's Free French Forces in December 1941.[116] Welles decided to continue the practice of sending a naval representative to meet with Robert on a regular basis. For this first meeting, Hull and Roosevelt intervened, working out the exact manner Robert should be approached and the demands which would be made. By this time things had changed at Vichy, as Pierre Laval was openly espousing a strict collaborationist doctrine. This changed the position in which Martinique found itself. Despite the fact that Robert had respected previous agreements with the United States, Hull believed that orders from Laval coupled with Robert's vow to remain loyal to Pétain amounted to a "potential enemy force inside the American defensive area."[117] Hull wanted to explore all possible peaceful solutions but did not rule out a military response if Robert did not agree "at once" to the demands made by the United States.

Tense negotiations and the final break with Vichy

Admiral John H. Hoover, Commander of the Caribbean Sea Frontier, was named to head the delegation which was to meet with Admiral Robert. He was to inform Robert that provided certain conditions were met, the United States would consider him to be the governing authority of the colonies. The American conditions — or demands — were extensive. They included: (1) immobilization of the French warships, (2) control of all communication, including radio and mail, by a U.S. official, (3) supervision of inter-island traffic, travel and immigration, (4) immobilization of military personnel, with arrangements to evacuate all or part of them to French Africa, (5) making French commercial vessels available to the United States, and (6) stationing American personnel in the colonies to oversee fulfillment of these concessions. Should these demands be fulfilled, the United States was prepared to purchase the principal exports of the colonies. Hoover added that Robert would have to comply with the demands made by the United States either peacefully or by economic or military pressure. The United States had thus turned a triangular negotiation with Vichy, Washington and Fort-de-France into a bilateral arrangement that excluded Vichy. In case these negotiations failed, Roosevelt approved a plan by the Navy to occupy the island.

On May 8, the United States requested the French Embassy to inform Robert that Hoover and his delegates would arrive the following day.[118] As Laval's government became aware of the United States' demands on the military forces stationed in Martinique, they decided to send a note to Washington and another copy to Robert. They agreed to the immobilization of the three French warships but rejected the demand to deliver the tankers and other merchant vessels to the United States. Meanwhile, Secretary of State Cordell Hull indicated that the American government would not accept any intervention by Laval's government. Hull suspected that Robert presented the demands made upon him to Laval, whom in turn dictated the communiqué to Washington. Even with the pressure exerted on Robert to distance himself from Vichy, these correspondences were proof that the policy of excluding Laval from the negotiations was doomed to fail. German sources implied that pressure was being exerted on Robert to scuttle the tankers and freighters in order to avoid having them fall into American hands. This, according to Hull, "would be regarded as a hostile act and dealt with accordingly."[119] In any case, the French were claiming incorrectly that the French warships stationed at Martinique — the aircraft carrier *Bearn*, the cruiser *Émile Bertin*, the training ship *Jeanne d'Arc* and the cruiser *Barfleur* — were immobilized after the fall of France as part of a previous arrangement.[120]

On May 13, Laval's government informed Washington that it would not hand over the tankers and merchant ships requested by the United States. They claimed that turning over the 140,000 tons of vessels would violate the French commitments stated in the armistice of 1940. The German-controlled Paris newspaper *Le Matin* claimed that the ships would be scuttled if the United States tried to take them by force. "It was only by pledging never to hand over or ceded shipping to any foreign power either in France or the colonies that France was allowed by the armistice convention to keep her merchant fleet," added the newspaper article. Meanwhile, Washington continued to ignore both Vichy and the German-controlled media, however inconceivable that position was to maintain.[121] On May 15, Representative Stephen M. Young, Democrat of Ohio, added fire to this seemingly unresolvable situation by claiming in a speech transcribed for broadcast that America's armed forces would "surely take possession of Martinique."[122] "Without doubt," he added, "tankers from Martinique have fueled German submarines raiding our Atlantic and Gulf ports, and I know you who are listening in will applaud our action in taking over this French naval base."[123] President Roosevelt meanwhile decried what he called the "loose talk on war" claiming that there was "more loose talk in Washington than in the rest of the country put together."[124] However, not all talk of war came from Washington. Captain Paul Perigord, representative of the Free French in Southern California, suggested that "the United States act forcefully in obtaining [the] airplane bases or other necessary concessions in Martinique or any French possessions in the Caribbean."[125] Perigord, a captain in the French army who served in World War I and then a professor of French at the University of California at Los Angeles (UCLA), argued that "the French people [will] ultimately resent our weakness if we approach [this] problem with timidity." He added that "the State Department need not worry about appeasing France. No matter how Laval and the Nazis may distort the situation, no matter what public demonstrations may be staged, the people of France want victory for the Allies."[126]

Vichy answered the American demands in a formal note addressed to Washington instead of through Robert, as Hull and Welles had demanded. Vichy was therefore ignoring Washington's announced intention of negotiating an agreement with Robert without regard for the government of Vichy. Vichy added that there was an accord in place regarding the military forces in Martinique and that changing it was not justifiable simply because of the change in leadership in France. Laval added that "France will never take the initiative to provoke a rupture with the United States."[127] On May 16, Laval stressed that Admiral Robert was acting under direct orders from his government "despite Washington's efforts to bypass Vichy in the negotiations."[128] He added, with a "wistful smile," that he was fully aware that his leadership in the Vichy regime did not "exactly appear to inspire the entire confidence of the Washington government."[129] Laval "bluntly rejected what he described as Washington's interference in French internal affairs, including demands that Martinique and other French West Indies possessions break away from the Vichy government and act independently."[130]

Despite the tense exchanges between the leaders of both nations, American naval officers and French authorities proceeded to immobilize the French naval vessels and to negotiate the food import needs of Martinique, which was entirely dependent on the United States for its food supply.[131] The demobilization called for the removal of the breechblocks of the guns and essential parts of the ships' machines. According to Marcel E. Malige, the American Consul stationed in Martinique, this equipment was stored under "lock and key" in the offices of the American Consulate in Fort-de-France. The agreement stipulated that French crews manning the warships would continue to maintain the vessel in order to prevent its deterioration. The land forts on the island were not to be dismantled. The planes were by then considered obsolete and having been left to the elements had suffered considerable damage. However, the disposition of the French gold held in Martinique remained unresolved for now.[132]

The major obstacle to finalizing the agreement was the transfer of the French merchant ships to the United States. Neither Vichy nor Robert was willing to test German resolve, as they feared the likely repercussions that would result if they complied with Washington's demand. Hull stepped up the pressure while Robert insisted he was attempting to secure authorization from Vichy but was unsuccessful in his endeavor. Laval was convinced that Berlin would not consent to this arrangement, even if the merchant ships were chartered to some neutral South American country. Hull retorted that Japan had seized French ships in Indochina without any protest from the French authorities and was operating them with French personnel. Of course, Hull forgot to mention that at the time, Japan and Germany were allies, so therefore, Berlin would not have reason to object to this seizure. Meanwhile, Robert did not appear intimidated by Hull's threat of military action or economic sanctions, and he outright refused to negotiate independent of Vichy. The United States finally relented on their demand for the tankers and freighters anchored in Fort-de-France and allowed the sale of Martinique produce in order to provide some economic relief to the island.[133]

In another matter, Vichy issued a statement regarding the status of her now impoverished fleet. Since the 1940 armistice, the French claimed to have lost half of her pre-war 3,000,000-ton merchant fleet. During the war, 250,000 tons were sunk. The British confiscated 630,000 tons at the time of the armistice and had seized or sunk an additional 36,000 tons. Fifty thousand tons were lost to storms and 175,000 tons were blockaded in foreign ports. This is exclusive of the liner *Normandie* which burned in New York under mysterious circumstances after being requisitioned and the *Marechal Joffre*, confiscated by the Americans at Manila.[134]

For the moment, the United States dropped its insistence on obtaining the French tankers and freighters and allowed them to be used in the trade between itself and Martinique. This had the added benefit of reducing the burden of using the Americans' limited number of vessels in this capacity. Robert's obstinance was a direct result of the instructions he received from Vichy, as the United States had failed to convince him to act independently of Laval's government or of joining the Free French Forces of de Gaulle. He continued to defer to Marshal Pétain in virtually every matter, and Pétain answered directly to Berlin. Therefore, both understood that "the price of German permission would mean further French concessions to them."[135] Washington was by this time resigned that they could not come between Robert and Pétain. But a clear break in the relations between Vichy and the United States was short in coming.

Operation Torch, the landing of American troops in French North Africa began on the night of November 7-8, 1942.[136] Just before dawn on the morning of the eighth, more than 100,000 Allied troops landed on selected beaches along the African coast, concentrating their forces at Algiers, Oran and Casablanca. When Admiral Darlan, who found himself in Algiers at the time of the invasion, realized the significance of what was transpiring, he sighted that this "would probably provoke a German invasion of the free zone of France."[137] On the evening of November 8, 1942, Pierre Laval[138] summoned Pinkney Tuck, the American chargé d'affaires at Vichy, and informed him of the decision of the government of France to terminate diplomatic relations with the United States. However, neither country moved immediately to declare war as a result of the American Army campaign in French North Africa. President Roosevelt expressed regret that Laval had taken the initiative to break off relations, adding that it was evident that he was "speaking the language prescribed by Hitler."[139] "We have not broken relations with the French," contended Roosevelt, "We never will. This government will continue as heretofore to devote its thought, its sympathy, and its aid to the rescue of the 45,000,000 people of France from enslavement and from a permanent loss of their liberties and free institutions."[140]

The United States, however, took measures to protect itself and its citizens from a now pro-Axis government. Hull directed Federal Bureau of Investigation (FBI) agents and police to surround the French Embassy "barring all those from leaving and visitors from entering, and halting communications, including telephonic."[141] The Coast Guard took custody of all Vichy ships in American harbors. Communications and commerce were restricted with both the occupied and unoccupied portions of France, as dictated by the "trading-with-the-enemy" act. All official French accounts in the United States were frozen, though at the time it had not been decided what to do with the private accounts. When Secretary Hull was asked if this situation would impact the United States' relationship with Martinique, he responded that it would not. He noted that previous emphasis was placed on conducting negotiations with Robert bypassing Vichy. Though at the time that strategy failed, Hull was optimistic that given this new set of circumstances, both sides would reach an understanding of mutual benefit. He added that the "trading-with-the-enemy" act would not be enforced on the French colonies of the Western Hemisphere, thereby giving them an economic respite.[142]

On November 11, 1942, the Germans overran the free unoccupied zone of France. In order to prevent the French fleet from falling into German hands, on November 27 Admiral Jean de Laborde, commanding officer of the Vichy French Navy High Seas Fleet, issued orders for it to be scuttled.[143] French Secretary of the Navy Gabriel Auphan had tried to persuade de Laborde to take the fleet to North Africa to join the Allies, but he refused, claiming he needed written orders from Vichy. In scuttling, the French destroyed

77 ships, including 3 battleships, 7 cruisers, 15 destroyers, and 13 torpedo boats.[144] Robert was caught in the dynamics of an ever-changing world, and the changes around him were not favorable to his military or economic position as High Commissioner of the Western French Colonies. He had neither the military might nor the economic power to sustain a blockade by the United States. The noose was tightening around his negotiating possibilities. He, therefore, asked Washington if the prior arrangement negotiated before the diplomatic break was still valid, as it was imperative for economic reasons that he maintain harmonious relations with the United States.[145]

While the Germans deployed open hostility toward France following the invasion of the French North African colonies, the French associations based in the United States were ecstatic. Frederick R. Coudert, president of the France-America Society of New York issued a statement acknowledging that its members were heartened by the aggressive military posture of the United States. He added that it would give "the oppressed French people a long-desired opportunity to join with the United States in the fight for freedom and to preserve the traditional and unique friendship between the French and American peoples."[146] Mrs. Henry R. Caraway, while addressing the School of Politics of the Women's National Republican Club, was also emphatic in her defense for President Roosevelt's African incursion, "as it represented many months of the most careful planning and long-range coordination.... We at home must stop criticizing the High Command, and must realize that the 'armchair strategists' cannot conduct wars. During the ensuing weeks we must exercise patience and faith and do our work as well as we possibly can, no matter how small or important it seems."[147] By this time, the French Embassy had been closed by the FBI, and Council General Jacques d'Aumale and his staff were put under guard at their homes

The French Admiral Georges Robert is received in San Juan by Rear Admiral John H. Hoover, Commander of the Tenth Naval District, and other US officials, 1943. (Private archive of Jorge Rodríguez Beruff)

until the State Department determined a final course of action. Meanwhile, France Forever, which represented Charles de Gaulle's Free French Forces in the United States, was convening a mass meeting at Hunter College Assembly Hall, New York, for a show of support for President Roosevelt and the U.S. military.[148]

Robert's governance nears its end

Despite the rapidly changing environment around him, Robert did not display any change in his attitude. He insisted on maintaining communication with Vichy while denying the American argument that Marshal Pétain no longer directed a functioning government. The additional pressure exerted by the United States coupled with the absence of a functioning Vichy Government and the multiple desertions towards the Free French Forces was making Robert's position untenable. Following the German takeover of the Vichy Free Zone, Robert was given the responsibility of trustee on behalf of France for all the French colonies. He was hopeful that as a neutral, the Germans would let his ship travel without the threat of being sunk, but this was not to be.

After the success of *Operation Torch*, Admiral Jean François Darlan shifted his alliance from Pétain to the Allies. Many others followed suit. These desertions greatly worried Robert, as he feared that some of the military personnel in Martinique might also join Darlan in shifting alliance. Both Darlan and Robert's former Chief of Staff, Admiral Robert M. J. Battet, tried to convince Robert of the hopelessness of his situation, but he defiantly told him he would remain loyal to Pétain. On January 25, 1943, with Washington's approval, the Free French Committee of General Henri Giraud planned to send Admiral Battet to Fort-de-France to persuade Robert to join him. Robert seemed perturbed by this, and though Robert allowed him to land in Martinique, he did not meet with Battet. Despite prolonged inactivity, many of the crews of the warships remained loyal to Robert and Pétain. When Battet defected, the crew of the *Émile Bertin* tore down his picture in disgust. This visit coincided with dwindling food supplies and fears that the Allies might invade French Guiana. On February 6 Robert reacted, rejecting the American contentions that the situation in France had changed. However, things continued to deteriorate for Robert.

On February 10, the captain, crew and officers of the French freighter *Guadeloupe* mutinied while taking on a cargo of food in New Orleans. They declared that they would not return to Martinique until Robert abandoned his stance on neutrality. Since no supplies had reached the island since November 8, the economy was in a critical state. Robert requested that the United States allow a French crew to be flown from Martinique, but the United States rejected that request. The food crisis would get worse before it got better. On February 25, Robert informed Vichy that it was urgent that he accept many if not all of the demands made by the United States, as the tense climate on the island kept getting worse due to the American *de facto* embargo on all imports. The turning over of the tankers and the freighters to the United States was the key issue that remained to be resolved. Robert, on the one hand, had to contend with civil unrest, and, on the other, the fact that many in the naval contingent remained loyal to Pétain. And, he also had to contend with the Americans and the Free French. On March 2, Admiral Battet sent him a communiqué stating that he was now considered an enemy of both. And if that was not enough, in March 1943, the German U-boats started their final assault in the Caribbean. This prompted an increased antisubmarine activity and reinforced Washington's decision to adopt a harder policy on Robert's regime, beginning with a propaganda offensive.[149]

On March 5, the Free French Committee began a radio barrage broadcasting how the tide of the war was changing, and that Vichy's days were numbered. It was hoped that this information would add to the catalyst already in place that would convince Robert and his staff that their days were numbered. The government's rationing policy instituted as a result of the food shortage was being assailed as favoring the military and the béké. This brought about the resignation of the mayor of Fort-de-France. Local dissidents expressed their rage in open petitions. It was becoming more apparent with each passing day that Robert would face an armed rebellion. However, despite these events, Robert only showed indignation and the propaganda broadcasts only served to harden his inflexibility. He ordered gunfire practice on the *Émile Bertin*, the fort in the city, and those approaching the bay of Fort-de-France.[150]

About March 20, the State Department learned that a freighter with a cargo of foodstuff from Newfoundland was scheduled to depart to Martinique. Secretary Hull surmised that the arrival of this cargo would provide Robert with some unwanted maneuvering room thereby postposing a change in his position. Hull asked the Canadian authorities to block that shipment in order to increase the economic pressure on the island. The Canadian government agreed, and the ship was not allowed to leave. In the crucial winter of 1942-1943, the Allies were in critical need of the warships, tankers and freighters anchored at Fort-de-France. Robert's refusal to hand them over to the Allies was the principal cause of the American Navy blockading the island. And to add insult to injury, the United States requisitioned the French freighter *Guadeloupe* still at anchor in New Orleans and allowed the captain to sail her loaded with critical supplies and foodstuff to Cayenne, French Guiana, now joined with the Allies. Such action caused a stir in Martinique while Robert hailed this action as "most unfriendly."

Even more important was the tension that had been building up between the majority black population of Martinique and the white naval and governmental French personnel. In 1941, Robert replaced 25 of the 31 democratically elected mayors. A popular black mayor was replaced with a white man chosen by the minority béké or white planter class. The following year the mayor of Fort-de-France joined the opposition at the time when Robert's program of food distribution proved inequitable. The crux of this problem lay in the noticeable favoritism displayed towards the military and the planter elite.[151] As noted by the Mayor of Fort-de-France, "once the Army, Navy and public establishments were supplied, only two and one-half tons of vegetables remained daily to satisfy the minimum needs of twenty tons."[152] Given that these circumstances showed no signs of relief, the Municipal Council followed the mayors' footsteps and also resigned. This put Robert in the difficult situation of either enacting martial law or making concessions to the majority black population. He chose the latter. This decision encouraged more dissension among the population.

Despite the growing crisis, Robert still reflected no change in his attitude, even though Brazil, Venezuela, and the Dominican Republic were also complying with the blockade established by the United States. On April 26, Washington informed Robert that it would no longer recognize his authority or continue negotiations with him. By this time Robert was the sole authority of the French Empire claiming alliance to Pétain. This break, however, accelerated plans for an invasion of the island to be undertaken by both American and Free French troops.[153] Meanwhile, in North Africa, "the reaction of most French leaders was that the United States [was not taking] a strong stance with Admiral Robert. The feeling seemed to be that it was odd for America to become so disturbed over the political complexion of the French in North Africa when both Guadeloupe and Martinique were permitted to remain pro-Vichy."[154]

Football matches provided a relief from the suffocating environment imposed by Robert's regime and a unique opportunity for the attendants to express their displeasure with the current situation. On May 2, in Basse-Terre, Guadeloupe, a crowd gathered in the streets chanting "Vive le goal," a subtle reference to "Vive de Gaulle." The authorities opened fire on the crowd, killing Serge Balguy, a 17-year-old fan of the Cygne Noir football club. The incident triggered outrage that ended with the resignation of Basse-Terre's mayor and its municipal council. Football had provided an outlet for large gatherings, but it had been banned by Robert's government. Unfortunately, incidents like these were not unique.[155] During this time Paul Valentino, who once held the post of President of the Executive Delegation of the General Council of Guadeloupe and suffered a coup on July 1, 1940 at the hands of Robert's naval forces, returned to Guadeloupe with the intent to displace the current military governor, Constant Sorin.[156]

On May 4, 1943, as food shortages reached critical levels, government authorities purchased a hundred head of cattle from the Dutch half of St. Martin for immediate delivery. The situation on the island became so dire that privately owned livestock was requisitioned for public distribution. Local farmers angrily protested this incursion "arguing that the beasts were vital for farm work, and in many cases, requisition attempts got bogged down in interminable negotiations."[157] On May 30, several thousand fans gathered at the Bellevue Stadium in Martinique and cheered as an American aircraft flew over the stadium, many chanting "Long live America."[158]

On June 24, the citizens of Fort-de-France called for a demonstration, which the authorities forbade. It occurred anyway. Several thousand demonstrators broke through police lines and paraded through the capital shouting "Vive America" and "Vive de Gaulle." This was the last straw for Robert. Six days later, on June 30, he asked the U.S. Naval Observer to inform Admiral Hoover in San Juan that, "in order to avoid bloodshed…I will be able to fix the method of changing authority on the issue of which, having fulfilled all my duties, I have decided to retire."[159] On July 1, the Puerto Rican local newspaper *El Mundo* published a headline that read that Robert was relinquishing his hold on Martinique. The article stated that radio Martinique transmitted Robert's statement saying he was willing to leave the island.[160]

The French Committee appointed Henri Hoppenot to oversee the peaceful transfer. In a subsequent telegram, Robert requested that the United States resume its food shipments, that the gold remains intact, that the French merchantmen fly the tricolor, and that no reprisal be taken towards those persons who supported this regime. Washington countered that he should fear no reprisals from the Free French, but no guarantees were made regarding the food shipments, the ships or the future administration. De Gaulle protested about the way the negotiations were taking place, as he claimed that it was destructive to French sovereignty but chose not to prolong the transfer.

On July 14, 1943, Bastille Day, Henri Hoppenot arrived in Fort-de-France to assume authority over the French West Indies. Hoppenot gave those allied with Pétain the option to change allegiance to the National Committee of Free France or to be repatriated to France or a neutral country. He encountered some resistance from the pro-Robert and pro-Pétain groups, but these quickly subsided. Hoppenot revived the pre-armistice *Conseil General* and encountered a brief opposition from the planter class as it was filled mostly with members of the majority black population.[161] He justified his actions to the *béké* by claiming that he had no choice in the matter "since the exodus of whites forced him to fill vacancies with negroes."[162] He added that he was expecting that the "black mayor" he selected would serve as a moderating influence on the blacks.[163] The resumption of food imports from the United States had, however, removed any threat of internal discord.

Regarding the French fleet at Fort-de-France, the machinery removed from these vessels was sent to Casablanca in May 1942. After *Operation Torch*, this territory was controlled by the Allies. Therefore, once Robert had departed from Martinique, it was possible to retrieve this machinery and partially refit the fleet. It was then taken to the United Stated for final repairs and shortly thereafter, joined the fight against Germany.[164]

Robert's interlude in Puerto Rico

Hoppenot had to contend with the departure of Robert and his entourage. He informed Robert that he could go to the United States or to another country, "in which case he would have to make his own arrangements."[165] Or he could travel to Africa where the French would coordinate his travel arrangements. However, the North Africa Committee had no desire to see Robert and, in any case, he would have to answers for his actions to the administrative or judicial authorities. This incensed the Americans as they had guaranteed Robert that there would no reprisals against him or his staff. "Consequently, Washington allowed the Swiss legation in San Juan to assume control of the Admiral's repatriation."[166]

On July 2, Vice Admiral Hoover, commander of the Caribbean, met with Admiral Robert at his suggestion in order to discuss the details of the transfer of power.[167] Hoover returned to Puerto Rico two days later and when asked by the press of his impressions, he summarized his thoughts with one word: "favorable." His comments inspired confidence that Robert would agree to withdraw with honor "and leave Martinique to Allied control under a French representative."[168] Meanwhile, the French Committee of National Liberation held a three-hour meeting presided over by General Charles de Gaulle which concluded by demanding that there be no strings attached to the transfer of power of the French colonies "and that any future commitments be arranged directly with Algiers."[169]

On July 16, Robert and his entourage arrived in San Juan. Among those accompanying Robert were Captain Constantin of the cruiser *Émile Bertin*, the captains of the *Le Tesson* and *Bearn*, Constant Sorin, the Governor of Guadeloupe, and eleven other military and governmental personnel. Robert disembarked from his ship *Le Terrible* as an honor guard saluted him for the last time as an Admiral of the French Navy. Robert was emotional throughout this formal but brief ceremony. His entourage was considered civilians and was, therefore, required to submit to the mandatory medical exams and immigration procedures. As a courtesy, Robert was not subjected to these requirements.

Robert's stay was coordinated by the Navy. While in Puerto Rico they would be treated as guests and housed in the recently built and luxurious Hotel Normandie, named after the famed French liner that mysteriously succumbed to fire in the harbor of New York in 1942. On his arrival, Robert released a statement indicating that French history would vindicate his policy. He added that Admiral Hoover's handling of the situation had given him confidence in the American representatives.[170]

The American Navy made sure that Robert and his staff were treated as VIPs. The Navy provided them with $10,000 for lodging upon their arrival to Puerto Rico. The State Department paid Robert $2,240 monthly, equivalent to the salary and stipends he had as High Commissioner. It was hoped this sum would provide for his needs in San Juan and for his repatriation travels. His second in command, Lieutenant Vaisseau P. De Boutiny, received $1,220.[171] Hoover also assisted Robert when he fell ill. He ordered that he be treated at the hospital at the naval base in San Juan where he was operated on following a "slight intestinal distress." He was expected to remain in the hospital for about three weeks.[172]

On December 24, Robert arrived by plane in Madrid from Lisbon, Portugal.[173] From there he made his way to France where Marshal Pétain appointed him General Secretary on February 4, 1944. Robert stressed that he was "the sailor-diplomat who managed to win American goodwill for himself and American tolerance for the policy he had to follow and that he [would] be able to repeat the achievement when American troops land in France."[174] According to unidentified sources, this was the only reason Pétain appointed him to that position.[175] However, things changed quickly in France after the invasion of Normandy by the Allies on June 6, 1944. On September 20, Paris radio broadcasted the news that arrest warrants had been issued for five admirals in a purge of collaborationists with the Nazis. One of these admirals was Georges Robert.[176] On March 15, 1947, 72-year-old Robert was sentenced to 10 years of hard labor on "charges that he brought dishonor to France through his close ties with Vichy while commander of the French West Indies squadron at Martinique."[177] Given his long record of service to France, the Court recommended a suspended sentence to which President Vincent Auriol, the first president of the Fourth French Republic, consented. Robert's "indictment said [that] he was innocent of collaboration but was guilty of dishonor through maintaining absolute neutrality when he was High Commissioner of the Antilles."[178] Robert died in 1965 at the age of 90.

Normandie Hotel, San Juan, Puerto Rico. Circa 1942. Image 18,458. (Collection Caleb Frants, Archivo Histórico Fundación Luis Muñoz Marín)

Captured German U-Boat U-505. June 4, 1944. Halftone reproduction of a photograph taken soon after the submarine's capture, copied from the *USS Guadalcanal* (CVE-60) Memory Log, page 28. Note the United States flag flying above the German Navy ensign. U-505 was the first enemy warship captured on the high seas by the U.S. Navy since 1815. Courtesy of the Naval Historical Foundation, Washington, DC. U.S. Naval History and Heritage Command Photograph. Since 1954, the U-505 has been showcased in the Chicago Museum of Science and Industry.

EPILOGUE

The post-war period saw rapid and dramatic changes in the Caribbean. The French and Dutch colonies strengthened their alliance with France and the Netherlands. Puerto Rico remained a colony of the United States. As a result of the Cold War, the area was militarized. The United States invaded the Dominican Republic in 1965, assisted the Cuban exiles in the invasion of the Bay of Pigs which turned into a fiasco and had the world in suspense in October 1962 with the Cuban Missile Crisis. Most of the World War II bases, with the notable exception of the naval base at Guantanamo and a few other minor ones, were closed and sold or transferred at no cost to the local government.

The independence of India, Pakistan and Sri Lanka (then Ceylon) in 1947 from Great Britain gave way for the independence of the British Caribbean colonies during the following decades. Given the Caribbean islands' close proximity to the United States and the triumph of Fidel Castro's revolution in Cuba, there was concern among the upper echelons in Washington that no other republic favor a leftist regime. In the meantime, Great Britain was trying to forge a British Commonwealth which would unite all its Caribbean colonies. This effort proved fruitless as the movement for independence had grown more forceful during the war years.

On September 19, 1961, Jamaica held a referendum in which the majority of its inhabitants voted for independence. This promoted Trinidad and Tobago to follow suit. The government of British Prime Minister Harold Macmillan granted the independence of Jamaica and Trinidad and Tobago in 1962. The Kennedy administration also provided its consent, though with reservations. In 1966, British Guiana and Barbados joined this group. The following year, St. Kitts,

Antigua, Dominica, St. Lucia, St. Vincent and Grenada, except for Montserrat, formed an apolitical association with Great Britain as a prelude to independence. They obtained their independence during the following two decades: Granada (1974), Dominica (1978), St. Lucia and San Vincent (1979), Antigua (1981) and St. Kitts (1983). Meanwhile, the Bahamas was granted independence in 1973. The Crown retained sovereignty over the British Virgin Islands, Antigua, Monserrate, Turks and Caicos, Caymans and Bermuda. The negotiations regarding independence were conditioned on economic accords which tied many economies to Washington and London, in a way, maintaining a certain degree of dependence from the "mother country."[1]

Puerto Rico continues to be an American colony. Since 1917, Puerto Ricans were entitled to American citizenship. They have one representative in the House of Representatives with no voting power, none in the Senate, and have no say in the presidential elections. On March 19, 1946, Martinique and Guadeloupe acquired the status of a French department with four deputies and two senators to represent them. In 1986, Aruba seceded from the Netherlands Antilles and became a separate autonomous member of the Kingdom of the Netherlands under the Dutch crown. The movement towards independence was halted in 1990. Curaçao and St. Maarten became countries within the Kingdom of the Netherlands on October 10, 2010.

The U.S. military started to reduce its considerable number of Caribbean bases during the 1960s. The naval base at Chaguaramas in Trinidad was transferred to the government of Eric Williams in 1968. In Puerto Rico, starting in 1947, the armed forces began to retrench. In 1973, they closed the important Ramey Air Force Base of the Strategic Air Command. In 1975, the Navy abandoned the firing range on the island of Culebra, giving way to the numerous

World War II era naval bases in Puerto Rico continued to be in use after 1945 as a result of the incipient Cold War. A US Navy aircraft carrier sits alongside the destroyer escort *USS Ottterstetter* (DER-244) and other destroyer escorts docked at the Isla Grande Naval Base in San Juan. Circa 1950. (Collection Swartgendruber, (Archivo Histórico Fundación Luis Muñoz Marín)

local protests regarding its presence. Fort Buchanan in San Juan reduced its activity during this period. In 1979, the St. Lucy base in Barbados was closed. As a result of the Torrijos-Carter agreement in 1977, the United States committed to gradually dismantling all its bases in Panamá.[2] On September 7, 1977, President Carter signed a historic treaty that would transfer control of the Panama Canal to Panamá by the end of the century. Representing Panamá was General Omar Torrijos, military ruler of the country. During the ceremony, Carter said that the signed treaty marked "the commitment of the United States to the belief that fairness, not force, should lie at the heart of our dealings with the nations of the world."[3] After much local opposition, particularly regarding the live bombings on the island of Vieques and the fatality incurred there, in 2000, Puerto Rico Governor Pedro Rosselló signed a pact with President

William J. Clinton agreeing that the Navy would cease its military exercises in Vieques on May 1, 2003. That year the United States closed the naval bases of Roosevelt Roads and Vieques.[4]

As a result of the Cold War, the United States poured a significant amount of money and resources to shore up the Latin American and Caribbean republics against what they perceived to be the communist threat. Between 1950 and 1968, the Military Assistance Program dispersed $687 million among these nations. Less was forthcoming to the Caribbean nations. However, Cuba received $10.8 million, the Dominican Republic $18.3 million, Haiti $3.2 million, and Jamaica $1.1 million. The United States also served as a training center for many military officers of these recipient nations.

As a consequence of the wars of liberations fought in Malaya, Vietnam and Algeria as well as the 1959 Cuban Revolution and Central Intelligence sponsored invasion of Cuba in the Bay of Pigs in April 1961, the Kennedy administration introduced changes in its global military strategies and specifically, in Latin American. The Alliance for Progress spearheaded by Puerto Rican Teodoro Moscoso, architect of Puerto Rico's manufacturing bonanza, was one of the political and ideological offensives sponsored by this administration. They also abandoned alliances with the military dictatorships previously supported by the United States, such as those of Rafael Leónidas Trujillo in the Dominican Republic and François Duvalier in Haiti. However, the negotiations with the Soviet Union to deescalate the tensions brought about by the October 1962 missile crisis would severely curtail any military action or initiative of other sorts that would topple the Castro regime in Cuba.

Under the doctrine adopted by President Lyndon B. Johnson, no country under the sphere of influence of the United States would be permitted to fall under a communist regime.[5] Therefore, on April 25, 1965, during the height of the Cold War, and concerned about the communist influence in the Dominican Republic, the United States invaded this country. U.S. Ambassador W. Tapley Bennett, Jr. witnessed the election of Donald Reid y Cabral by what he called communist-inspired groups of armed civilians. "I recommend that serious thought be given to armed intervention to restore order beyond a mere protection of lives. If the present loyalist efforts fail," continued Bennett, "the power will go to groups whose aims are identified with the Communist Party."[6] The Johnson administration succeeded in placing a "friendlier administration" in the country and one responsive to the interest of the United States.[7] The last military intervention of the United States in the Caribbean was on October 25, 1983 under the presidency of Ronald Reagan. Nearly 2,000 U.S. Marines invaded the small island of Grenada to counter perceived threats to the nearly 1,000 U.S. citizens living or studying there. The Marxist regime backed militarily by Cuban forces was replaced, after some fierce fighting, by a democratically elected government.[8] Slowly, the United States' interest in the Caribbean faded. Current events dictate that the strategic policies of the United States' are concentrated in areas such as Asia and the Middle East.

NOTES

Introduction

1. John Terraine, The U-Boat Wars 1916-1945 (New York: Henry Holt and Company, 1989), 768. According to the Appendix D, page, 768, 2,116 allied ships were sunk between January 1942 and July 1943.
2. David J. Bercuson, Holger H. Herwig, *Long Night of the Tankers* (Calgary, University of Calgary Press, 2014), 275.
3. Stetson Conn, Rose C. Engelman, Byron Fairchild, *The Western Hemisphere: Guarding the United States and its Outposts*, (Washington, D.C., Center of Military History, 2000), 431.
4. Conn, Engelman, Fairchild, The Western Hemisphere, 429.

Chapter I

1. Rexford Guy Tugwell, *The Stricken Land: The Story of Puerto Rico* (Garden City, New York, Doubleday & Company, Inc., 1947), 304-305.
2. David J. Bercuson, Holger H. Herwig, *Long Night of the Tankers* (Calgary, University of Calgary Press, 2014), 275.
3. Bercuson and Herwig, *Long Night*, 275.
4. Bercuson and Herwig, *Long Night*, 277.
5. Bercuson and Herwig, *Long Night*, 277.
6. Bercuson and Herwig, *Long Night*, 275. According to these authors, the number of ships sunk was 397. Stetson Conn, Rose C. Engelman, and Byron Fairchild in the book *The Western Hemisphere: Guarding the United States and its Outposts*, (Washington, D.C., Center of Military History, 2000), Table 5, p431 claim that the number of ships sunk was 374.
7. Paul Schubert, "U-Boat Warfare," *Washington Post*, July 5, 1943, 8.
8. Paul Schubert, "U-Boat Warfare," *Washington Post*, July 5, 1943, 8.
9. "The News of the Week in Review: The First Nine Days of Europe's...," *New York Times*, September 10, 1939, E1.
10. "The News of the Week in Review: The First Nine Days of Europe's..., *New York Times*, September 10, 1939, E1.
11. Harold L. Ickes, *The Secret Diary of Harold L. Ickes, Volume II: The Lowering Clouds 1939-1941* (New York: Simon and Schuster, 1955), 48.
12. Harold L. Ickes, *The Secret Diary of Harold L. Ickes, Volume II: The Lowering Clouds 1939-1941* (New York: Simon and Schuster, 1955), 57.
13. "Dominican cutter seen as war victim," *New York Times*, October 3, 1939, 5.
14. "Dominican cutter seen as war victim," *New York Times*, October 3, 1939, 5.
15. "Dominican cutter seen as war victim," *New York Times*, October 3, 1939, 5.
16. Eric Paul Roorda, *The Dictator Next Door. The Good Neighbor Policy and the Trujillo Regime in the Dominican Republic, 1930-1945* (Durham: Duke University Press, 1998), 205-205.
17. "Roosevelt Issues Stern Warning Against Smuggling Aid to U-boats," *The Atlanta Constitution*, October 4, 1939, 7.

18. "Roosevelt Issues Stern Warning Against Smuggling Aid to U-boats," *The Atlanta Constitution*, October 4, 1939, 7.
19. Bernardo Vega, "La Isla y la Segunda Guerra Mundial," *Puerto Rico en la Segunda Guerra Mundial: El Escenario Regional*, Jorge Rodríguez Beruff, José L. Bolívar Fresneda, Ed. (San Juan: Ediciones Callejón, 2015), 127-129.
20. "Old Rum Runners Said to Aid U-Boats," *New York Times*, October 12, 1939, 6.
21. "French Deny Sinking Craft in Caribbean," *New York Amsterdam*, October 4, 1939, 5.
22. "French Deny Sinking Craft in Caribbean," *New York Amsterdam*, October 4, 1939, 5.
23. Calvin Warner Hines, *United States Diplomacy in the Caribbean during World War II*, PhD diss. (Austin: The University of Texas at Austin, 1968), 74.
24. Calvin Warner Hines, *United States Diplomacy in the Caribbean during World War II*, PhD diss. (Austin: The University of Texas at Austin, 1968), 74-75.
25. "Aid to Nazi Craft Hinted in Mexico," *New York Times*, October 15, 1939, 39.
26. In relative terms, this ship had a gross tonnage of almost twice that of the RMS Titanic, which had a gross tonnage of 46,000.
27. "Aid to Nazi Craft Hinted in Mexico," *New York Times*, October 15, 1939, 39.
28. "Aid to Nazi Craft Hinted in Mexico," *New York Times*, October 15, 1939, 39.
29. "Aid to Nazi Craft Hinted in Mexico," *New York Times*, October 15, 1939, 39.
30. "Aid to Nazi Craft Hinted in Mexico," *New York Times*, October 15, 1939, 39.
31. "U.S. Destroyer in Caribbean," *New York Amsterdam News*, October 28, 1939, 8.
32. "U.S. Destroyer in Caribbean," *New York Amsterdam News*, October 28, 1939, 8.
33. "U-Boats Reported Stalking Caribbean Shipping Routes," *Washington Post*, January 26, 1940, 1.
34. Jorge Rodríguez Beruff, "Rediscovering Puerto Rico and the Caribbean: United States Strategic Debate and War Planning on the eve of the Second World War," Jorge Rodríguez Beruff, José L. Bolivar Fresneda, Ed., *Island at War. Puerto Rico in the Crucible of the Second World War*, (Jackson: University Press of Mississippi, 2015), 5-6.
35. Jorge Rodríguez Beruff, editor, *Las Memorias de Leahy: Los relatos del almirante William D. Leahy sobre su gobernación de Puerto Rico (1939-1940)*, (San Juan: Fundación Luis Muñoz Marín, 2012), 58-59, 86-87.
36. "Marines Intensify West Indies Drill," *New York Times*, January 29, 1940, 4.
37. Cornelis Ch. Goslinga, *A Short History of the Netherlands Antilles and Surinam*, (The Hague: Martinus Nijhoff Publishers, 1979), 1.
38. https://www.curacaohistory.com/1634-the-conquest-of-curacao. Retrieved July 18, 2020.
39. https://www.britannica.com/event/Eighty-Years-War. Retrieved July 18, 2020.
40. https://www.aruba.com/us/our-island/history-and-culture/history. Retrieved July 18, 2020.
41. The Navy Department Library, *Building the Navy's Bases in World War II, Volume II (Part III), Chapter XVIII, Bases in South America and the Caribbean area, including Bermuda*, 1-21.
42. Gerhard L. Weinberg, *A World at Arms: A Global History of World War II* (Cambridge: Cambridge University Press, 1994), 241.
43. The Navy Department Library, *Building the Navy's Bases in World War II, Volume II (Part III), Chapter XVIII, Bases in South America and the Caribbean area, including Bermuda*, 22-23.
44. Humberto García Muñiz, *La estrategia de Estados Unidos y la militarización del Caribe* (Río Piedras, PR: Instituto de Estudios del Caribe, University of Puerto Rico, 1988), 50, 53.

45. The Navy Department Library, *Building the Navy's Bases in World War II, Volume II (Part III), Chapter XVIII, Bases in South America and the Caribbean area, including Bermuda,* 22-35.
46. Jean Edward Smith, *FDR* (New York: Random House Publishing Group, 2008), 489; "Lend Lease Bill," January 10, 1941, NARA, RG 233, Record of the House of Representatives, HR 77A-D13.
47. Jean Edward Smith, *FDR* (New York: Random House Publishing Group, 2008), 490-491.
48. Jorge Rodríguez Beruff, *Strategy as Politics: Puerto Rico on the Eve of the Second World War* (San Juan: La Editorial de la Universidad de Puerto Rico, 2007), 351-352.
49. "Waters of West Indies Troubled by War Storms," *Chicago Daily Tribune*, March 9, 1942, 8.
50. Jorge Rodríguez Beruff, *Strategy as Politics: Puerto Rico on the Eve of the Second World War* (San Juan: La Editorial de la Universidad de Puerto Rico, 2007), 351-352.
51. Jorge Rodríguez Beruff, *Strategy as Politics: Puerto Rico on the Eve of the Second World War* (San Juan: La Editorial de la Universidad de Puerto Rico, 2007), 351-353.
52. Harold L. Ickes, *The Secret Diary of Harold L. Ickes, Volume II: The Lowering Clouds 1939-1941* (New York: Simon and Schuster, 1955), 216.
53. Jorge Rodríguez Beruff, *Strategy as Politics: Puerto Rico on the Eve of the Second World War* (San Juan: La Editorial de la Universidad de Puerto Rico, 2007), 351-353.
54. In 1961, Leicester published *My Brother, Ernest Hemingway*, which brought him recognition and significant financial rewards. By the time of this trip, his brother was an accomplished writer, having published A *Farewell to Arms* and *For Whom the Bells Tolls*, which would be nominated for the Pulitzer Prize.
55. Leicester Hemingway, Anthony Jenkinson, "Nazi fueling bases for U-boats and raiders set up in Caribbean," *New York Times*, August 21, 1940, 8.
56. Leicester Hemingway, Anthony Jenkinson, "Oil is Stored by Pro-Nazis in Caribbean: Investigating Writers Get Offer to Help 'Run' Fuel Supply," *The Atlanta Constitution*, August 26, 1940, 5.
57. Rafael Simón Arce, "Volverán Banderas Victoriosas…" Falange en Puerto Rico 1937-1941, *Puerto Rico en la Segunda Guerra Mundial: El Escenario Regional*, Jorge Rodríguez Beruff, José L. Bolívar Fresneda, Ed. (San Juan: Ediciones Callejón, 2015), 212.
58. www.pdr.uscourts.gov/robert-archer-cooper-1934-1947-0. Accessed on March 26, 2020 in Guaynabo, Puerto Rico.
59. "Sacaron al "Colorado" del caño de San Antonio," El Mundo, May 4, 1941; "Denegada la moción de tripulantes del "Colorado," *El Mundo*, June 26, 1941; "Trasladan pronto tripulantes del "Colorado," *El Mundo*, June 26, 1941.
60. Calvin Warner Hines, *United States Diplomacy in the Caribbean during World War II*, PhD diss., (Austin, Texas: University of Texas at Austin, 1968), VII.
61. Stetson Conn, Rose C. Engelman, Byron Fairchild, *The Western Hemisphere: Guarding the United States and its Outposts*, (Washington, D.C., Center of Military History, 2000), 331.
62. Stetson Conn, Rose C. Engelman, Byron Fairchild, *The Western Hemisphere: Guarding the United States and its Outposts*, (Washington, D.C., Center of Military History, 2000), 331.
63. Calvin Warner Hines, *United States Diplomacy in the Caribbean during World War II*, PhD diss., (Austin, Texas: University of Texas at Austin, 1968), 237.
64. Calvin Warner Hines, *United States Diplomacy in the Caribbean during World War II*, PhD diss., (Austin, Texas: University of Texas at Austin, 1968), 237.
65. Calvin Warner Hines, *United States Diplomacy in the Caribbean during World War II*, PhD diss., (Austin, Texas: University of Texas at Austin, 1968), 238-240.

66. Calvin Warner Hines, *United States Diplomacy in the Caribbean during World War II*, PhD diss., (Austin, Texas: University of Texas at Austin, 1968), 244.
67. David J. Bercuson, Holger H. Herwig, *Long Night of the Tankers* (Calgary, University of Calgary Press, 2014), 275-276.
68. Gaylor T. M. Kelshall, *The U-Boat War in the Caribbean*, (Port-of-Spain, Trinidad: Paria Publishing Company Limited, 1988), 27-28.
69. Gaylor T. M. Kelshall, *The U-Boat War in the Caribbean*, (Port-of-Spain, Trinidad: Paria Publishing Company Limited, 1988), 32-41.
70. C. H. Calhoun, "Aruba is Shelled. Nazis Attack Refinery 700 Miles from Canal. Near U.S. Bases," *New York Times*, February 17, 1942, 1.
71. C. H. Calhoun, "Aruba is Shelled. Nazis Attack Refinery 700 Miles from Canal. Near U.S. Bases," *New York Times*, February 17, 1942, 1.
72. "U-boats Lair Hunter in Caribbean Area," *New York Times*, February 18, 1942, 2.
73. "U-boats Lair Hunter in Caribbean Area," *New York Times*, February 18, 1942, 2.
74. Stetson Conn, Rose C. Engelman, Byron Fairchild, *The Western Hemisphere: Guarding the United States and its Outposts*, (Washington, D.C., Center of Military History, 2000), 331.
75. General George C. Marshall would be remembered for formulating the "Marshall Plan" program to reconstruct Europe after the War. He held the positions of Secretary of State and Secretary of War. He received the Nobel Prize for Peace in 1953. https://www.nobelprize.org/prizes/peace/1953/marshall/biographical/. Retrieved on April 28, 2020 at Guaynabo, Puerto Rico.
76. Stetson Conn, Rose C. Engelman, Byron Fairchild, *The Western Hemisphere: Guarding the United States and its Outposts*, (Washington, D.C., Center of Military History, 2000), 331.
77. "Berlin Claims 3 Tankers," *New York Times*, February 18, 1942, 2.
78. United Press, "Sub Sinks 32nd East Coast Ship," *Los Angeles Times*, February 18, 1942, 1.
79. Andrew Robert Lefebvre, "Forgotten by History: The Panama Canal in World War Two," PhD diss. (Calgary, Alberta: University of Calgary, 2009), iii, 2.
80. 'U-boats Still Lurking in West Indies Waters," *Los Angeles Times*, February 19, 1942, 3.
81. "Brazilian Aviation to Aid Ship Convoys: belief Held in Rio that Vichy is Helping," *Wireless to the New York Times*, February 20, 1942, 4.
82. "U-boat Raids Aruba Again: Shells fall to Fire Refinery as Submarine Attacked by Bombers," *Los Angeles Times*, February 20, 1942, A.
83. "U-boat Raids Aruba Again: Shells fall to Fire Refinery as Submarine Attacked by Bombers," *Los Angeles Times*, February 20, 1942, A.
84. "German U-boats Shell West Indies Island." *New York Amsterdam Star News*, February 21, 1942, 1.
85. "German U-boats Shell West Indies Island." *New York Amsterdam Star News*, February 21, 1942, 1.
86. Rexford G. Tugwell, *The Stricken Land: The Story of Puerto Rico*, (Garden City, New York: Doubleday & Company, Inc.,1947), 240.
87. "Nazi Thread to Puerto Rico Recalled by Raid on Aruba," *New York Times*, February 17, 1942, 3.
88. "Nazi Thread to Puerto Rico Recalled by Raid on Aruba," *New York Times*, February 17, 1942, 3.
89. Rexford G. Tugwell, *The Stricken Land: The Story of Puerto Rico*, (Garden City, New York: Doubleday & Company, Inc., 1947), 240.

90. Gaylor T. M. Kelshall, *The U-Boat War in the Caribbean*, (Port-of-Spain, Trinidad: Paria Publishing Company Limited, 1988), 67-71.
91. Gaylor T. M. Kelshall, *The U-Boat War in the Caribbean*, (Port-of-Spain, Trinidad: Paria Publishing Company Limited, 1988), 71.

Chapter II

1. Stetson Conn, Rose C. Engelman, Byron Fairchild, *The Western Hemisphere: Guarding the United States and its Outposts*, (Washington, D.C., Center of Military History, 2000), 429.
2. Stetson Conn, Rose C. Engelman, Byron Fairchild, *The Western Hemisphere: Guarding the United States and its Outposts*, (Washington, D.C., Center of Military History, 2000), 429.
3. Clay Blair, *Hitler's U-Boat War. The Hunters, 1939-1942* (New York: Modern Library, 1996), 493.
4. Stetson Conn, Rose C. Engelman, Byron Fairchild, *The Western Hemisphere: Guarding the United States and its Outposts*, (Washington, D.C., Center of Military History, 2000), 430.
5. George Fielding Eliot, "Anxiety of Enemy Believed Growing," *Los Angeles Times*, February 26, 1942, 4.
6. Jordan Vause, *U-Boat Ace. The story of Wolfgang Luth* (Annapolis: United States Naval Institute Press, 1990), 88-89.
7. Jordan Vause, *U-Boat Ace. The story of Wolfgang Luth* (Annapolis: United States Naval Institute Press, 1990), 88-90.
8. "4 More Sinkings in the Caribbean Region Revealed," *Chicago Daily Tribune*, March 13, 1942, 4.
9. www.uboat.net/allies/merchants/ship/1389.html. Accessed on April 1, 2020 in Guaynabo, Puerto Rico.
10. "Puerto Rican Isle Shelled by Enemy," *New York Times*, March 4, 1942, 3.
11. www.uboat.net/allies/merchants/ship/1403.html. Accessed April 2, 2020 in Guaynabo, Puerto Rico.
12. "U-Boats Destroy Five More Ships," *New York Times*, March 15, 1942, 1.
13. "U-Boats Destroy Five More Ships," *New York Times*, March 15, 1942, 1.
14. John G. Norris, "Navy Pilot Lands in Rough Sea to Rescue 17 Adrift on Raft," *Washington Post*, April 15, 1942, 1.
15. www.uboat.net/allies/merchants/1402.html. Accessed March 30, 2020 in Guaynabo, Puerto Rico.
16. John G. Norris, "Navy Pilot Lands in Rough Sea to Rescue 17 Adrift on Raft," *Washington Post*, April 15, 1942, 1.
17. John G. Norris, "Navy Pilot Lands in Rough Sea to Rescue 17 Adrift on Raft," *Washington Post*, April 15, 1942, 1.
18. John G. Norris, "Navy Pilot Lands in Rough Sea to Rescue 17 Adrift on Raft," *Washington Post*, April 15, 1942, 1.
19. John G. Norris, "Navy Pilot Lands in Rough Sea to Rescue 17 Adrift on Raft," *Washington Post*, April 15, 1942, 1.
20. www.uboat.net/allies/merchants/1402.html. Accessed March 30, 2020 in Guaynabo, Puerto Rico.
21. "U-Boats Destroy Five More Ships," *New York Times*, March 15, 1942, 1.
22. www.uboat.net/allies/merchants/ship/1427.html. Accessed April 2, 2020 in Guaynabo, Puerto Rico.

23. "U-Boats Destroy Five More Ships," *New York Times*, March 15, 1942, 1.
24. "6 More Ships Hit by U-Boat," *Chicago Daily Tribune*, March 15, 1942, 1.
25. www.uboat.net/allies/merchants/ship/1427.html. Accessed April 2, 2020 in Guaynabo, Puerto Rico.
26. Tugwell, *Stricken Land*, 286-287.
27. Tugwell, *Stricken Land*, 287.
28. www.uboat.net/men/achilles.htm. Accessed March 31, 2020 in Guaynabo, Puerto Rico.
29. www.uboat.net/allies/merchants/ship/1418.html. Accessed March 31, 2020 in Guaynabo, Puerto Rico.
30. www.uboat.net/men/achilles.htm. Accessed March 31, 2020 in Guaynabo, Puerto Rico.
31. "Axis Sub in St. Laurence," *Chicago Daily Tribune*, May 13, 1942, 1.
32. "Axis Sub in St. Laurence," *Chicago Daily Tribune*, May 13, 1942, 1.
33. Karl Doenitz, *Memoirs. Ten Years and Twenty Days* (Annapolis: Naval Institute Press, 1990), 218-219.
34. Karl Doenitz, *Memoirs. Ten Years and Twenty Days* (Annapolis: Naval Institute Press, 1990), 219.
35. Karl Doenitz, *Memoirs. Ten Years and Twenty Days* (Annapolis: Naval Institute Press, 1990), 219.
36. Karl Doenitz, *Memoirs. Ten Years and Twenty Days* (Annapolis: Naval Institute Press, 1990), 219; John Terraine, *The U-Boat Wars 1916-1945* (New York: Henry Holt and Company, Inc., 1989), 420; Stetson Conn, Rose C. Engelman, Byron Fairchild, *The Western Hemisphere: Guarding the United States and its Outposts*, (Washington, D.C., Center of Military History, 2000), 431.
37. Karl Doenitz, *Memoirs. Ten Years and Twenty Days* (Annapolis: Naval Institute Press, 1990), 219.
38. Karl Doenitz, *Memoirs. Ten Years and Twenty Days* (Annapolis: Naval Institute Press, 1990), 219.
39. Karl Doenitz, *Memoirs. Ten Years and Twenty Days* (Annapolis: Naval Institute Press, 1990), 221.
40. Clay Blair, *Hitler's U-Boat War. The Hunters, 1939-1942* (New York: Modern Library, 2000), 591-592.
41. www.uboat.net/allies/merchants/ship/1569.html. Accessed April 3, 2020 in Guaynabo, Puerto Rico; "Axis subs bag More Vessels," *Los Angeles Times*, June 7, 1942, 7.
42. www.uboat.net/allies/merchants/ship/1569.html. Accessed April 3, 2020 in Guaynabo, Puerto Rico; "Axis subs bag More Vessels," *Los Angeles Times*, June 7, 1942, 7.
43. "Axis subs bag More Vessels," *Los Angeles Times*, June 7, 1942, 7.
44. www.uboat.net/boats/u106.html. Accessed April 3, 2020 in Guaynabo, Puerto Rico.
45. "Dissatisfaction with union delegate in New Orleans. Crew and officers urge that the man be removed, or they will quit the Association," National Archives and Records Administration (NARA-New York), Record Group (RG) 181, Naval Districts and Shore Establishments, 10Th Naval District General Correspondence, 1940-1952, A 6-5 to A8, Box 45.
46. National Archives and Records Administration (NARA-New York), Record Group (RG) 181, Naval Districts and Shore Establishments, 10Th Naval District General Correspondence, 1940-1952, A 6-5 to A8, Box 45.
47. National Archives and Records Administration (NARA-New York), Record Group (RG) 181, Naval Districts and Shore Establishments, 10Th Naval District General Correspondence, 1940-1952, A 6-5 to A8, Box 45.

48. National Archives and Records Administration (NARA-New York), Record Group (RG) 181, Naval Districts and Shore Establishments, 10Th Naval District General Correspondence, 1940-1952, A 6-5 to A8, Box 45.
49. https://www.uboat.net/allies/merchants/ship/3493.html. Accessed April 19, 2020 at Guaynabo, Puerto Rico.
50. César de Windt Lavandier, *La Segunda Guerra Mundial y los submarinos alemanes en el Mar Caribe* (Santo Domingo: Amigo del Hogar, 1997), 233-239.
51. https://www.uboat.net/boats/u125.htm. Retrieve on April 20, 2020 at Guaynabo, Puerto Rico.
52. César de Windt Lavandier, *La Segunda Guerra Mundial y los submarinos alemanes en el Mar Caribe* (Santo Domingo: Amigo del Hogar, 1997), 245-251.
53. "U-Boats sink 2 more vessels in waters off U.S.," *Chicago Daily Tribune*, June 8, 1942, 5.
54. www.uboat.net/allies/merchants/ship.html?=shipid=1799. www.uboat.net/allies/merchants/ship/1633.html. Accessed April 3, 2020 at Guaynabo, Puerto Rico.
55. www.uboat.net/allies/warships/ship/9243.html. Accessed April 4, 2020 in Guaynabo, Puerto Rico.
56. "4 days aboard U-boat told by U.S. seaman," *The Atlanta Constitution*, July 27, 1942, 7.
57. "4 days aboard U-boat told by U.S. seaman," *The Atlanta Constitution*, July 27, 1942, 7.
58. "4 days aboard U-boat told by U.S. seaman," *The Atlanta Constitution*, July 27, 1942, 7.
59. https://www.uboat.net/boats/u172.htm. Accessed April 4, 2020 at Guaynabo, Puerto Rico.
60. Peter Padfield, *War Beneath the Sea*, (Canada: John Wiley & Sons, Inc., 1998), 283.
61. Peter Padfield, *War Beneath the Sea*, (Canada: John Wiley & Sons, Inc., 1998), 283.
62. Jordan Vause, *U-Boat Ace. The story of Wolfgang Luth*, (Annapolis: United States Naval Institute Press, 1990), 118.
63. Jordan Vause, *U-Boat Ace: The story of Wolfgang Luth*, (Annapolis: United States Naval Institute Press, 1990), 119.
64. "3 more vessels sunk by subs in U.S. waters," *Chicago Daily Tribune*, June 16, 1942, 1.
65. "3 more vessels sunk by subs in U.S. waters," *Chicago Daily Tribune*, June 16, 1942, 1.
66. www.uboat.net/allies/merchants/ship/1726.html. Accessed April 4, 2020 at Guaynabo, Puerto Rico.
67. www.uboat.net/allies/merchants/ship/1729.html. Accessed April 4, 2020 at Guaynabo, Puerto Rico.
68. www.georgisrncyclopedia.org/articles/goverment-politics/car;-vinson-1883-1981. Accessed April 3, 2020 at Guaynabo, Puerto Rico.
69. "U.S. is winning war on U-boats asserts Vinson," *Chicago Daily Tribune*, June 8, 1942, 5; "War on submarine gains, says, Vinson," *New York Times*, June 8, 1942, 8.
70. "U.S. is winning war on U-boats asserts Vinson," *Chicago Daily Tribune*, June 8, 1942, 5; "War on submarine gains, says, Vinson," *New York Times*, June 8, 1942, 8.
71. "U.S. is winning war on U-boats asserts Vinson," *Chicago Daily Tribune*, June 8, 1942, 5; "War on submarine gains, says, Vinson," *New York Times*, June 8, 1942, 8.
72. Associated Press, "House Report Praises Navy's Fight on Subs," *Washington Post*, June 8, 1942, 1.
73. Associated Press, "House Report Praises Navy's Fight on Subs," *Washington Post*, June 8, 1942, 1.
74. Associated Press, "House Report Praises Navy's Fight on Subs," *Washington Post*, June 8, 1942, 1.

75. Arthur Herman, *Freedom's Forge. How American Business Produced Victory in World War II* (New York: Random House, 2012), 216-217.
76. Arthur Herman, *Freedom's Forge. How American Business Produced Victory in World War II* (New York: Random House, 2012), 249.
77. Arthur Herman, *Freedom's Forge. How American Business Produced Victory in World War II* (New York: Random House, 2012), 248.
78. Arthur Herman, *Freedom's Forge. How American Business Produced Victory in World War II* (New York: Random House, 2012), 335-336.
79. United Press, "Young deck crew destroys U-Boat," *New York Times*, June 12, 1942, 1; "Three U-Boats reported destroyed in Caribbean," *Los Angeles Times*, June 12, 1942, 6.
80. United Press, "Young deck crew destroys U-Boat," *New York Times*, June 12, 1942, 1; "Three U-Boats reported destroyed in Caribbean," *Los Angeles Times*, June 12, 1942, 6.
81. United Press, "Young deck crew destroys U-Boat," *New York Times*, June 12, 1942, 1; "Three U-Boats reported destroyed in Caribbean," *Los Angeles Times*, June 12, 1942, 6.
82. United Press, "Young deck crew destroys U-Boat," *New York Times*, June 12, 1942, 1; "Three U-Boats reported destroyed in Caribbean," *Los Angeles Times*, June 12, 1942, 6.
83. United Press, "Young deck crew destroys U-Boat," *New York Times*, June 12, 1942, 1; "Three U-Boats reported destroyed in Caribbean," *Los Angeles Times*, June 12, 1942, 6.
84. www.uboat.net/boats/u157.html. Accessed April 4, 2020 at Guaynabo, Puerto Rico.
85. www.uboat.net/allies/merchants/ship/1786.html. Accessed April 4, 2020 at Guaynabo, Puerto Rico.
86. Karl Doenitz, *Memoirs. Ten Years and Twenty Days* (Annapolis: Naval Institute Press, 1990), 221. John Terraine, *The U-Boat Wars 1916-1945* (New York: Henry Holt and Company, Inc., 1989), 422-423.
87. "Merchantmen being convoyed off East Coast, Navy reveals," *Los Angeles Times*, June 23, 1942, 4.
88. "Merchantmen being convoyed off East Coast, Navy reveals," *Los Angeles Times*, June 23, 1942, 4.
89. "13 ships sunk in Caribbean," *Los Angeles Times*, June 24, 1942, 1.
90. "13 ships sunk in Caribbean," *Los Angeles Times*, June 24, 1942, 1.
91. "Axis gets 15 ships; dead, missing: Army men among 86 feared lost...," *New York Times*, June 24, 1942, 1.
92. www.uboat.net/allies/merchants/ship/1548.html. Accessed April 6, 2020 in Guaynabo, Puerto Rico.
93. www.uboat.net/allies/merchants/ship/1828.html. Accessed April 6, 2020 at Guaynabo, Puerto Rico.
94. "Two more sinkings listed," *New York Times*, July 4, 1942, 1.
95. "Two more sinkings listed," *New York Times*, July 4, 1942, 1.
96. "Enemy mines U.S. Waters," *Los Angeles Times*, June 21, 1942, 7.
97. Stetson Conn, Rose C. Engelman, Byron Fairchild, *The Western Hemisphere: Guarding the United States and its Outposts*, (Washington, D.C., Center of Military History, 2000), 431.
98. John Terraine, *The U-Boat Wars 1916-1945* (New York: Henry Holt and Company, Inc., 1989), 423-424.
99. "Army Officer Hero: Work leads to arrest of ship line head, Cabaret...," *New York Times*, July 3, 1942, 1.

100. "Army Officer Hero: Work leads to arrest of ship line head, Cabaret…," *New York Times*, July 3, 1942, 1.
101. "Army Officer Hero: Work leads to arrest of ship line head, Cabaret…," *New York Times*, July 3, 1942, 1.
102. "Briton's Oil Feb U-Boats," *Los Angeles Times*, July 5, 1942, 8.
103. "Army Officer Hero: Work leads to arrest of ship line head, Cabaret…," *New York Times*, July 3, 1942, 1.
104. "Army Officer Hero: Work leads to arrest of ship line head, Cabaret…," *New York Times*, July 3, 1942, 1.
105. "Army Officer Hero: Work leads to arrest of ship line head, Cabaret…," *New York Times*, July 3, 1942, 1.
106. "Saboteurs to face 7-general court; 20 arrested for refueling axis submarines," *The Atlanta Constitution*, July 3, 1942, 1.
107. www.historynet.com/world-war-ii-german-saboteurs-invade-america-in-1942.htm. Accessed April 7, 2020 at Guaynabo, Puerto Rico.
108. Anthony P. Maingot, *Estados Unidos y el Caribe: retraso de una relación asimétrica* (Río Piedras, La Editorial de la Universidad de Puerto Rico, 2005), 80.
109. Thomas D. Schoonover, *Hitler's Man in Havana* (Louisville: University Press of Kentucky, 2008), description.
110. www.thecubanhistory.com/2012/04/nazi-spy-executed-in-cuba/. Accessed April 7, 2020 at Guaynabo, Puerto Rico.
111. Nelson Rockefeller, "Fighting the traitors within: Mr. Rockefeller gives a first-hand…," *New York Times*, January 3, 1943, SM 6.
112. Nelson Rockefeller, "Fighting the traitors within: Mr. Rockefeller gives a first-hand…," *New York Times*, January 3, 1943, SM 6.
113. Gaylor T. M. Kelshall, *The U-Boat War in the Caribbean*, (Port-of-Spain, Trinidad: Paria Publishing Company Limited, 1988), 265.
114. Gaylor T. M. Kelshall, *The U-Boat War in the Caribbean*, (Port-of-Spain, Trinidad: Paria Publishing Company Limited, 1988), 241.
115. "Nazi aide in Detroit convicted; one of few U.S. Treason Cases," *New York Times*, July 3, 1942, 1.
116. www.mythicdetroit.org/index.php?n=Main.NaziUndergroundRailroad. Accessed April 7, 2020 at Guaynabo, Puerto Rico.
117. "Fighting the traitors within: Mr. Rockefeller gives a first-hand…," *New York Times*, January 3, 1943, SM 6.

Chapter III

1. Karl Doenitz, *Memoirs. Ten Years and Twenty Days* (Annapolis: Naval Institute Press, 1990), 251.
2. "23 trapped in hold in bold harbor raid," *Washington Post*, July 4, 1942, 1.
3. www.uboat.net/allies/merchants/ship/1881.html. Accessed April 8, 2020 in Guaynabo, Puerto Rico.
4. "23 trapped in hold in bold harbor raid," *Washington Post*, July 4, 1942, 1. d
5. www.uboat.net/allies/merchants/ship/1881.html. Accessed April 8, 2020 in Guaynabo, Puerto Rico.
6. "Cuba cuts power use," *New York Times*, July 14, 1942, 13
7. "Pledges Puerto Rico food despite U-boats," *New York Times*, June 10, 1942.
8. Mayra Rosario Urrutia, "The Anglo-American Caribbean Commission: A Socioeconomic Strategy Designated for Military Security, 1942-1946," Jorge Rodríguez Beruff,

José L. Bolívar Fresneda, Editors, *Islands at War. Puerto Rico in the Crucible of the Second World War* (Jackson: University Press of Mississippi, 2015), 188, 201.
9. Mayra Rosario Urutia, "The Anglo-American Caribbean Commission: A Socioeconomic Strategy Designated for Military Security, 1942-1946," Jorge Rodriguez Beruff, José L. Bolívar Fresneda, Editors, *Islands at War. Puerto Rico in the Crucible of the Second World War* (Jackson: University Press of Mississippi, 2015), 208-209.
10. Ernest Lindley, "Back to sailing," *New York Times*, July 15, 1942, 11.
11. "372 saved from torpedoed ship, one of 4 more sunk by U-boats," *New York Times*, July 16, 1942, 1.
12. www.uboat.net/allies/merchants/ship/1879.html. Accessed April 9, 2020 at Guaynabo, Puerto Rico.
13. "372 saved from torpedoed ship, one of 4 more sunk by U-boats," *New York Times*, July 16, 1942, 1.
14. www.uboat.net/allies/merchants/ship/1672.html. Accessed April 9, 2020 at Guaynabo, Puerto Rico.
15. "372 saved from torpedoed ship, one of 4 more sunk by U-boats," *New York Times*, July 16, 1942, 1.
16. Walter Trohan, "Ship losses halts second front; Agitation dwindles in Britain," *Chicago Daily Tribune*, July 17, 1942, 4.
17. Gaylor T. M. Kelshall, *The U-Boat War in the Caribbean*, (Port-of-Spain, Trinidad: Paria Publishing Company Limited, 1988), 119-120.
18. www.uboat.net/boats/u153.htm. Accessed April 9, 2020 at Guaynabo, Puerto Rico.
19. "Georgian cited for blasting German U-boat," *The Atlanta Constitution*, March 27, 1943, 2.
20. "Caribbean U-boats foiled by convoys," *New York Time*, July 29, 1942, 4; E.V. W. Jones, "Blaze Safety Trail," *Chicago Daily Tribune*, July 29, 1942, 6.
21. "Caribbean U-boats foiled by convoys," *New York Time*, July 29, 1942, 4; E.V. W. Jones, "Blaze Safety Trail," *Chicago Daily Tribune*, July 29, 1942, 6.
22. John Terraine, *The U-Boat Wars 1916-1945* (New York: Henry Holt and Company, Inc., 1989), 431.
23. Stetson Conn, Rose C. Engelman, Byron Fairchild, *The Western Hemisphere: Guarding the United States and its Outposts*, (Washington, D.C., Center of Military History, 2000), 431.
24. "Anti-Sub measures called effective," *The Atlanta Constitution*, July 18, 1942, 8.
25. Naval Correspondent, "The Convoy System," *The Observer*, July 19, 1942, 8.
26. "Caribbean U-boats foiled by convoys," *New York Time*, July 29, 1942, 4; E.V. W. Jones, "Blaze Safety Trail," *Chicago Daily Tribune*, July 29, 1942, 6.
27. "Caribbean U-boats foiled by convoys," *New York Time*, July 29, 1942, 4; E.V. W. Jones, "Blaze Safety Trail," *Chicago Daily Tribune*, July 29, 1942, 6.
28. "Caribbean U-boats foiled by convoys," *New York Time*, July 29, 1942, 4; "Blaze Safety Trail," *Chicago Daily Tribune*, July 29, 1942, 6.
29. 'Caribbean held safer for ships," *Los Angeles Times*, August 4, 1942, 2.
30. "London sees curb on U-boats off U.S.," *New York Times*, August 6, 1942, 8.
31. "U-boat attack upon convoys is feared soon," *Washington Post*, August 6, 1942, 7.
32. Rexford G. Tugwell, *The Stricken Land: The Story of Puerto Rico*, (Garden City, New York: Doubleday & Company, Inc.,1947), 360-361.
33. Rexford G. Tugwell, *The Stricken Land: The Story of Puerto Rico*, (Garden City, New York: Doubleday & Company, Inc.,1947), 360.
34. Karl Doenitz, *Memoirs. Ten Years and Twenty Days* (Annapolis: Naval Institute Press, 1990), 251-252.

35. Gaylor T. M. Kelshall, *The U-Boat War in the Caribbean*, (Port-of-Spain, Trinidad: Paria Publishing Company Limited, 1988), 119-120.
36. Memorandum. From: The Commanding Offices, To: The Commandant, July 24, 1942, NARA, NYC, RG #181, Blackouts and Air Raids, A16-3(2), Box 14; www.uboat.net. Accessed May 16, 2020.
37. Memorandum To: The chief of the Bureau of Medicine and Surgery, Washington, From: Lieutenant Stephen J. Donovan, July 23, 1942, NARA, NYC, RG #181, Blackouts and Air Raids, A16-3(2), Box 14.
38. Memorandum To: The chief of the Bureau of Medicine and Surgery, Washington, From: Lieutenant Stephen J. Donovan, July 23, 1942, NARA, NYC, RG #181, Blackouts and Air Raids, A16-3(2), Box 14.
39. Memorandum To: The chief of the Bureau of Medicine and Surgery, Washington, From: Lieutenant Stephen J. Donovan, July 23, 1942, NARA, NYC, RG #181, Blackouts and Air Raids, A16-3(2), Box 14.
40. Associated Press, "Allied War on U-boats slashes Atlantic sinkings," *Los Angeles Times*, August 17, 1942, 5.
41. https://uboat.net/allies/merchants/ship/1992.html. Accessed April 9, 2020 at Guaynabo, Puerto Rico.
42. "Britain says Allied shipping losses lower during July," *Los Angeles Times*, August 14, 1942, 5.
43. "3 more ships are torpedoes in West Atlantic," *The Atlanta Constitution*, August 15, 1942, 12.
44. Gustavo Placer Cervera, "Los marinos cubanos en la Segunda Guerra Mundial," *Puerto Rico en la Segunda Guerra Mundial: El Escenario Regional*, Jorge Rodríguez Beruff, José L. Bolívar Fresneda, Ed. (San Juan: Ediciones Callejón, 2015), 144.
45. https://uboat.net/allies/merchants/ship/2044.html. Accessed April 11, 1942 at Guaynabo, Puerto Rico.
46. "U-boats getting aid in Caribbean," *Washington Post*, August 15, 1942, 3.
47. https://uboat.net/allies/merchants/ship/2057.html. Accessed on April 12, 2020 at Guaynabo, Puerto
48. "30 persons perish in new sinkings," *New York Times*, August 28, 1942, 3. This article stated that the third ship sunk was Latvian while the site uboat.net, using post war records, identified it as Egyptian.
49. "30 persons perish in new sinkings," *New York Times*, August 28, 1942, 3.
50. "30 persons perish in new sinkings," *New York Times*, August 28, 1942, 3.
51. https://uboat.net/allies/merchants/ship/2080.html. Accessed on April 12, 2020 at Guaynabo, Puerto Rico; United Press, "Sub get two ships in Gulf," *Los Angeles Times*, August 27, 1942, 4.
52. https://uboat.net/boats/u94.htm. Accessed on April 12, 1942 in Guaynabo, Puerto Rico.
53. Gaylor T. M. Kelshall, *The U-Boat War in the Caribbean*, (Port-of-Spain, Trinidad: Paria Publishing Company Limited, 1988), 174.
54. Gaylor T. M. Kelshall, *The U-Boat War in the Caribbean*, (Port-of-Spain, Trinidad: Paria Publishing Company Limited, 1988), 166-167.
55. https://uboat.net/allies/technical/asdic.htm. Accessed on April 15, 2020 at Guaynabo, Puerto Rico.
56. Gaylor T. M. Kelshall, *The U-Boat War in the Caribbean*, (Port-of-Spain, Trinidad: Paria Publishing Company Limited, 1988), 167-173.
57. Karl Doenitz, *Memoirs. Ten Years and Twenty Days* (Annapolis: Naval Institute Press, 1990), 252-253.

58. Karl Doenitz, *Memoirs. Ten Years and Twenty Days* (Annapolis: Naval Institute Press, 1990), 256.
59. Karl Doenitz, *Memoirs. Ten Years and Twenty Days* (Annapolis: Naval Institute Press, 1990), 256.
60. Peter Padfield, *War Beneath the Sea*, (Canada: John Wiley & Sons, Inc., 1998), 295.
61. Karl Doenitz, *Memoirs. Ten Years and Twenty Days* (Annapolis: Naval Institute Press, 1990), 259.
62. Karl Doenitz, *Memoirs. Ten Years and Twenty Days* (Annapolis: Naval Institute Press, 1990), 263.
63. John Terraine, *The U-Boat Wars 1916-1945* (New York: Henry Holt and Company, Inc., 1989), 767-768.
64. Stetson Conn, Rose C. Engelman, Byron Fairchild, *The Western Hemisphere: Guarding the United States and its Outposts*, (Washington, D.C., Center of Military History, 2000), 431.
65. https://uboat.net/fates/losses/1942.htm. Accessed April 16, 2020 at Guaynabo, Puerto Rico.
66. Robert D. Billinger, Jr, *Hitler's Soldiers in the Sunshine State. German POWs in Florida* (Gainesville: University Press of Florida, 2000), 217.
67. Robert D. Billinger, Jr, *Hitler's Soldiers in the Sunshine State. German POWs in Florida* (Gainesville: University Press of Florida, 2000), 47-50.
68. Robert D. Billinger, Jr, *Hitler's Soldiers in the Sunshine State. German POWs in Florida* (Gainesville: University Press of Florida, 2000), XIII, 14-15.
69. "A Report on the U.S. Navy's repair, conversions overhaul of United Nations vessels under the Lend-Lease Program, November 5, 1943." NARA, RG 181 Naval District Shore Establishments, 10Th Naval District General Correspondence, A6-A8, Box 18.
70. "Lend-Lease: Cuba receives American vessels for war on U-Boats," *New York Times*, March 23, 1943, 7.
71. "Lend-Lease: Cuba receives American vessels for war on U-Boats," *New York Times*, March 23, 1943, 7.
72. "Lend-Lease: Cuba receives American vessels for war on U-Boats," *New York Times*, March 23, 1943, 7.
73. Eric Paul Roorda, *The Dictator Next Door. The Good Neighbor Policy and the Trujillo Regime in the Dominican Republic, 1930-1945* (Durham: Duke University Press, 1998), 219-220.
74. Gustavo Placer Carrera, "Los marinos cubanos en la Segunda Guerra Mundial," *Puerto Rico en la Segunda Guerra Mundial: El Escenario Regional*, Jorge Rodríguez Beruff, José L. Bolívar Fresneda, Ed. (San Juan: Ediciones Callejón, 2015), 144.
75. Anthony August Hoffman, *Panic Emigration: Jewish Agricultural settlements in Bolivar and the Dominican Republic, 1935-1960*, Master's Thesis (Los Angeles: University of California at Los Angeles, 2016), 3-4.
76. Jorge Rodriguez Beruff, *Política miliar y dominación. Puerto Rico en el contexto latinoamericano* (San Juan: Ediciones Huracán, 1988), 152-153.
77. "Ship limps 1,600 miles; 40-foot hole in her side," *The Atlanta Constitution*, January 10, 1943, 10A.
78. "Ship limps 1,600 miles; 40-foot hole in her side," *The Atlanta Constitution*, January 10, 1943, 10A.
79. "U.S. Cargo ship sunk by Axis in Caribbean," *New York Times*, March 23, 1942, 6.
80. Associated Press, Seamen from U.S. Cargo Vessel, torpedoed in the Atlantic, tell how escort ship battles with ten U-boats," *New York Times*, March 24, 1943, 3.

81. Associated Press, Seamen from U.S. Cargo Vessel, torpedoed in the Atlantic, tell how escort ship battles with ten U-boats," *New York Times*, March 24, 1943, 3.
82. https://uboat.net/allies/merchants/ship/2777.html. Accessed on April 23, 2020 at Guaynabo, Puerto Rico.
83. "Cargo ship fights U-boat to finish," *New York Times*, March 28, 1943, 11.
84. "Cargo ship fights U-boat to finish," *New York Times*, March 28, 1943, 11.
85. "Cargo ship fights U-boat to finish," *New York Times*, March 28, 1943, 11.
86. https://uboat.net/boats/u68.htm. Accessed on April 23, 2020 at Guaynabo, Puerto Rico.
87. Stetson Conn, Rose C. Engelman, Byron Fairchild, *The Western Hemisphere: Guarding the United States and its Outposts*, (Washington, D.C., Center of Military History, 2000), 431.
88. Karl Doenitz, *Memoirs. Ten Years and Twenty Days* (Annapolis: Naval Institute Press, 1990), 218-219; John Terraine, *The U-Boat Wars 1916-1945* (New York: Henry Holt and Company, Inc., 1989), 335.
89. "Flyer's attack cripples U-boat; saves convoy," *Chicago Daily Tribune*, May 24, 1943, 9; "U-boat sunk in Caribbean," *Los Angeles Times*, May 24, 1943, 5; "Virginian decorated for sinking U-boat," *The Atlanta Constitution*, May 24, 1943, 5.
90. "German submarine sunk in Caribbean," *New York Times*, May 24, 1943, 3; "U-boat sunk in Caribbean," *Los Angeles Times*, May 24, 1943, 5; "Virginian decorated for sinking U-boat," *The Atlanta Constitution*, May 24, 1943, 5.
91. "Flyer's attack cripples U-boat; saves convoy," *Chicago Daily Tribune*, May 24, 1943, 9; "U-boat sunk in Caribbean," *Los Angeles Times*, May 24, 1943, 5; "Virginian decorated for sinking U-boat," *The Atlanta Constitution*, May 24, 1943, 5.
92. Gustavo Placer Cervera, "Los marinos cubanos en la Segunda Guerra Mundial," Jorge Rodríguez Beruff, José L. Bolívar Fresneda, *Puerto Rico en la Segunda Guerra Mundial: El Escenario Regional*, Ed (San Juan: Ediciones Callejón, 2015), 146-149.
93. Gustavo Placer Cervera, "Los marinos cubanos en la Segunda Guerra Mundial," Jorge Rodríguez Beruff, José L. Bolívar Fresneda, *Puerto Rico en la Segunda Guerra Mundial: El Escenario Regional*, Editors (San Juan: Ediciones Callejón, 2015), 146-149.
94. César de Windt Lavandier, *La Segunda Guerra Mundial y los submarinos alemanes en el Mar Caribe* (Santo Domingo: Amigo del Hogar, 1997), 183-187.
95. Gustavo Placer Cervera, "Los marinos cubanos en la Segunda Guerra Mundial," Jorge Rodríguez Beruff, José L. Bolivar Fresneda, *Puerto Rico en la Segunda Guerra Mundial: El Escenario Regional*, Ed (San Juan: Ediciones Callejón, 2015), 146-149.
96. https://uboat.net/boats/u176.htm. Accessed April 4, 2020 at Guaynabo, Puerto Rico.
97. Stetson Conn, Rose C. Engelman, Byron Fairchild, *The Western Hemisphere: Guarding the United States and its Outposts*, (Washington, D.C., Center of Military History, 2000), 437; www.uboat.net. Accessed April 25, 2020 at Guaynabo, Puerto Rico.
99. https://uboat.net/boats/u359.htm; https://uboat.net/boats/u159.htm; https://uboat.net/boats/u759.htm. Accessed April 25, 2020 at Guaynabo, Puerto Rico.
99. John G. Norris, "Nazi sub sunk by U.S. planes after 10-hour Caribbean battle," *New York Times*, November 21, 1943, M1; "U-boat destroyed in 10-hour battle," *New York Times*, November 21, 1943, 36; "U.S. planes lick U-boat in 10 hours," *Chicago Daily Tribune*, November 21, 1943, 1.
100. John G. Norris, "Nazi sub sunk by U.S. planes after 10-hour Caribbean battle," *New York Times*, November 21, 1943, M1; "U-boat destroyed in 10-hour battle," *New York Times*, November 21, 1943, 36; "U.S. planes lick U-boat in 10 hours," *Chicago Daily Tribune*, November 21, 1943, 1.
101. John G. Norris, "Nazi sub sunk by U.S. planes after 10-hour Caribbean battle," *New*

York Times, November 21, 1943, M1; "U-boat destroyed in 10-hour battle," *New York Times*, November 21, 1943, 36; "U.S. planes lick U-boat in 10 hours," *Chicago Daily Tribune*, November 21, 1943, 1.
102. Stetson Conn, Rose C. Engelman, Byron Fairchild, *The Western Hemisphere: Guarding the United States and its Outposts*, (Washington, D.C., Center of Military History, 2000), 431.

Chapter IV

1. Rafael Pico, *The Geographic Regions of Puerto Rico* (Rio Piedras: University of Puerto Rico Press, 1950), 200-205.
2. Santiago Caraballo, "Guerra, reforma y colonialismo: Luis Muñoz Marín, las reformas del P.D.P. y su vinculación con la militarización de Puerto Rico en el contexto de la Segunda Guerra Mundial." PhD diss., (Rio Piedras: University of Puerto Rico, 2005), 59.
3. Rodríguez Beruff, *Strategy as Politics*, 355.
4. César J. Ayala Casás; José L. Bolívar Fresneda, *Battleship Vieques: Puerto Rico from World War II to the Korean War* (Princeton, NJ: Markus Wiener, 2011), 21.
5. Rodríguez Beruff, *Strategy as Politics*, 355.
6. Rodríguez Beruff, *Strategy as Politics*, 355-356.
7. Private Archive of the Arundel Corporation (hereafter PAAC), Minutes of the Board of Directors, November 29, 1939, 16. The Consolidated Engineering Company, established in 1867, was responsible for designing, constructing, and maintaining the shore facilities needed to support the U.S. Navy around the world.
8. PAAC, Minutes of the Board of Directors, November 29, 1939, 16.
9. "Sgt. Claude A. Swanson, Departamento de la Marina al Secretario de lo Interior," December 29, 1934, Archivo General de Puerto Rico (hereafter AGPR), Fondo: Obras Públicas, Ser. Asuntos Varios, Leg. no. 398, Caja no. 240; and "Armando Morales Caños, jefe de la División de Terrenos Públicos al Comisionado Interino," January 8, 1941, AGPR, Fondo: Obras Públicas, Ser. Asuntos Varios, Leg. no. 98, Caja no. 241.
10. "Commander H.W. Johnson a José E. Colom, Commissioner," May 22, 1940, AGPR, Fondo: Asuntos Varios, Leg. # 398, Car. # 240.
11. "Interior sacó ayer a subasta varias obras importantes," *El Mundo* (San Juan), January 14, 1939, 1.
12. "Interior proyecta construir ocho modernos aeropuertos," *El Mundo* (San Juan), January 21, 1939, 1.
13. "Se realizan obras en los túneles," *El Mundo* (San Juan), March 23, 1939, 1.
14. Luis E. González Vales, "Puerto Rico: baluarte defensivo en el Caribe," Luis E. González Vales and María Dolores Luque, editors, *Historia de Puerto Rico, Volumen IV* (Río Piedras: Ediciones Doce Calles, 2010), 300-302.
15. "Se realizan obras en los túneles," *El Mundo* (San Juan), March 23, 1939, 1.
16. "Obras de ingeniería de la "PRRA," *El Mundo* (San Juan), November 14, 1939, p. 6.
17. Samuel E. Badillo, "Toman las huellas digitales a miles de empleados. En las obras que se realizan en Isla Grande y Punta Santiago, a solicitud de la FBI," *El Mundo* (San Juan), December 2, 1939, 1.
18. Centro de Investigación Histórica de la Universidad de Puerto Rico (CIH), Memorandum, To: Assistant Chief of Staff, War Department General Staff, Washington, DC, From: Lieutenant Colonel C. S. Ferrin, Caja #20, Cart # 10, Número 4.
19. Centro de Investigación Histórica de la Universidad de Puerto Rico (CIH), Memo-

randum, To: Assistant Chief of Staff, War Department General Staff, Washington, DC, From: Lieutenant Colonel C. S. Ferrin, Caja #20, Cart # 10, Número 4.
20. PAAC, Minutes of the Board of Directors, February 25, 1941, 234.
21. PAAC, Minutes of the Board of Directors, March 17, 1941.
22. "Comenzara pronto construcción base Juana Díaz," *El Mundo* (San Juan), October 26, 1940, 1.
23. "Memorandum To: The Honorable Governor of Puerto Rico. From: Sergio Cuevas," January 8, 1942, AGPR, Fondo: Obras Públicas, Ser. Asuntos Varios, Leg. # 253A, Car.: # 198, 1–3.
24. "De: Sergio Cuevas. A: Jorge Luis Córdova," March 20, 1942, AGPR, Fondo: Obras Públicas, Ser. Asuntos Varios, Leg. # 253A, Car.: # 197.
25. "De: Sergio Cuevas. A: Jorge Luis Córdova," March 20, 1942, AGPR, Fondo: Obras Públicas, Ser. Asuntos Varios, Leg. # 253A, Car.: # 197.
26. "De: Sergio Cuevas. A: Rafael del Valle Zeno," March 18, 1942, AGPR, Fondo: Obras Públicas, Ser. Asuntos Varios, Leg. # 253A, Car.: # 197.
27. "De: Sergio Cuevas. A: Rafael del Valle Zeno," March 18, 1942, AGPR, Fondo: Obras Públicas, Ser. Asuntos Varios, Leg. # 253A, Car.: # 197.
28. "De: Sergio Cuevas. A: Dr. Carlos F. Muñoz MacCormick," July 16, 1943, AGPR, Fondo: Obras Públicas, Ser. Asuntos Varios, Leg. # 253A, Car.: # 197.
29. Rodríguez Beruff, *Strategy as Politics*, 358-359.
30. José Bolívar Fresneda, *Guerra, banca y desarrollo, El Banco de Fomento y la Industrialización de Puerto Rico*, 37.
31. Rodríguez Beruff, *Strategy as Politics*, 358-359.
32. Carlos M. González Morales, "Borinquen Field y Aguadilla: Un municipio en la guerra," *Puerto Rico en la Segunda Guerra Mundial: Baluarte del Caribe*, Jorge Rodríguez Beruff and José L. Bolívar Fresneda, Editors, 271-272.
33. Rodríguez Beruff, *Strategy as Politics*, 359-360.
34. Bolívar Fresneda, *Guerra, banca y desarrollo*, 36-38.
35. Rodríguez Beruff, *Strategy as Politics*, 359-360.
36. Gerardo M. Piñero Cádiz, "La base aeronaval Roosevelt Roads: El Pearl Harbor del Caribe." *Puerto Rico en la Segunda Guerra Mundial: Baluarte del Caribe*, Jorge Rodríguez Beruff and José L. Bolívar Fresneda, Editor, 298-299.
37. Tugwell, *Stricken Land*, 67-68.
38. Tugwell, *Stricken Land*, 67-68.
39. Gerardo M. Piñero Cádiz, "La base aeronaval Roosevelt Roads: El Pearl Harbor del Caribe." *Puerto Rico en la Segunda Guerra Mundial: Baluarte del Caribe*, Jorge Rodríguez Beruff and José L. Bolívar Fresneda, Editor, 302-306.
40. Bolívar Fresneda, *Guerra, banca y desarrollo*, 36-38.
41. Bibiano Torres, "La isla de Vieques," *Anuario de Estudios Americanos* (Sevilla) 12 (1955), 452.
42. Roberto Rabin, "Compendio de lecturas sobre la historia de Vieques," (Vieques: Museo Fuerte Conde de Mirasol, 1994).
43. Juan Amedée Bonnet Benítez, *Vieques en la historia de Puerto Rico* (San Juan: F. Ortiz Nieves, 1976), 126.
44. Based on the database of all property assessments in Vieques in 1940, 1945 and 1950.
45. NARA, Memorandum. To: Judge Advocate General, From: Chief of the Bureau of Yards and Docks, October 29, 1941, NYC, Record Group 181, Naval District and Shore Establishment, 10th Naval District, General Correspondence, A7-A2, Box 14.
46. Department of the Navy, *Continued use of the Atlantic Fleet Weapons Training Facility Inner Range (Vieques): Draft Environmental Impact Statement*, (Tippetts-Abbett-McCarthy-Stratton: Ecology and Environment, 1979).

47. Interview with Aurelio Tio, son of Juan Ángel Tio.
48. Bonnet Benítez, *Vieques en la historia de Puerto Rico*, 126-127; J. Pastor Ruiz, *Vieques antiguo y moderno* (Yauco: Tipografía Rodríguez Lugo, 1947), 207.
49. Proyecto Caribeño de Justicia y Paz, "Entrevista a los expropiados e Vieques, Puerto Rico," (Vieques: Archivo del Fuerte del Conde de Mirasol, 1979).
50. Department of the Navy, *Continued Use*, Vol. 1-2, 213.
51. Katherine T. McCaffrey, "Culture, Power and Struggle: Anti-military protests in Vieques, Puerto Rico," PhD. Diss, (New York: City University of New York, 1999), 77-78.
52. Department of the Navy, *Continued Use*, Vol. 1, 204.
53. Piñero Cádiz, "La base naval Roosevelt Roads," 300-302.
54. González Morales, "Borinquen Field y Aguadilla,"267.
55. González Morales, "Borinquen Field y Aguadilla,"268-270.

Chapter V

1. César J. Ayala and Laird W. Bergad, *Agrarian Puerto Rico. Reconsidering Rural Economy and Society, 1899-1940* (Oxford: Cambridge University Press, 2020), 270.
2. Véase, por ejemplo, "Puerto Rico Capital Lacks Bread," *New York Times*, May 24, 1942, 13.
3. "The Puerto Rican Economy during the War Year of 1942," June 1943, AFLMM, Sección XII, 1–6.
4. "Comercio de arroz no ha podido sustanciar petición," *El Mundo*, April 16, 1942, 1.
5. "El Gobernador proclama racionamiento arroz," *El Mundo*, June 17, 1942,1.
6. "Puerto Rico May Get Food by Air," *New York Times*, June 6, 1942, 27.
7. "Protest in Puerto Rico," New York Times, May 24, 1942, 13.
8. "Filipo de Hostos acusa a la Comisión de Alimentos," *El Mundo*, May 5, 1942,1.
9. "Comisión alimentos compra 9,000 sacos de arroz," *El Mundo*, May 12, 1942,1.
10. "Nuevos precios máximos regirán en Puerto Rico," *El Mundo*, June 26, 1,5.
11. "Henderson anuncia vasta modificación de control de precios en la Isla," *El Mundo*, June 27, 1942,1.
12. "Washington abaratara los alimentos en la Isla," *El Mundo*, September 10, 1942, 1,11.
13. "La OPA hace estudio sobre el precio de la leche," *El Mundo*, September 16, 1942, 1.
14. "La OPA fija precios máximos establecidos para varios artículos," *El Mundo*, November 13, 1942, 1.
15. Esteban A. Bird, "Report on the Sugar Industry in Relation to the Social and Economic System of Puerto Rico," San Juan, Puerto Rico Reconstruction Administration, 1937, 42.
16. "Carta de Luis Muñoz Marín a Paul Gordon, del Departamento de lo Interior," August 17, 1942, AFLMM, Sec. IV, Presidente del Senado, Car. # 7, Doc. # 1.
17. "The Puerto Rican Economy During the War Year of 1942," June 1943, AFLMM, Sección XII, 14B, 15, 18.
18. Harvey S. Perloff, *Puerto Rico's Economic Future: A study in planned development* (Chicago: The University of Chicago Press, 1950), 154.
19. Perloff, *Puerto Rico's Economic Future*, 60.
20. "Obreros para la construcción de obras militares," El *Mundo* (San Juan) (San Juan), May 31, 1940, 1.
21. "Jefe de la WPA comenta el paro de Isla Grande," *El Mundo* (San Juan), January 16, 1942, 1; "Seguía ayer el paro de obreros de Isla Grande," *El Mundo* (San Juan), January 20, 1942, 6.

22. "Base de Vieques será levantada por obreros portorriqueños," *El Mundo* (San Juan), February 27, 1941, 8; "Progresan rápidamente el entrenamiento de obreros," *El Mundo* (San Juan), April 13, 1941, 1; "Se espera otra asignación destinada a Puerto Rico," *El Mundo* (San Juan), May 24,1941, 1.
23. Morris J. McGregor, *Integration of the Armed Forces, 1940–1965* (Washington, D.C.: Center of Military History, United States Army, 1981), 72–73.
24. Ayala Casás and Bolívar Fresneda, *Battleship Vieques*, 108.
25. Mara Loveman and Jeronimo Muñiz, "How Puerto Rico became white: an analysis of racial statistics in the 1910 and 1920 Census," unpublished paper prepared for presentation at the Center for Demography and Ecology, University of Wisconsin-Madison, February 7, 2006, 4.
26. Ayala Casás and Bolívar Fresneda, *Battleship Vieques*, 117.
27. Ayala Casás and Bolívar Fresneda, *Battleship Vieques*, 117
28. Ayala Casás and Bolívar Fresneda, *Battleship Vieques*, 117.
29. CIH, "Selective Service," Caja 316, Cart. 3, Numero 3 (A-M), 1944-1946.
30. "Arundel no permite que los puertorriqueños tomen agua fría; es para los continentales," *El Imparcial* (San Juan), April 14, 1943, 5.
31. U.S.N.–S.M.A., "Technical Report and Project History Contract NOy-3680: Section 22 St. Thomas, Roosevelt Roads, San Juan, St. Lucia, Antigua, Culebra," NOy3680 Administrative Data NOy-3680: contract; Factual Survey Vol. I General Report, re: The Arundel Corporation and Consolidated Engineering Company, Incorporated, March 22, 1943, 31.
32. "How Puerto Rico became white: boundary dynamics and intercensus racial reclassification," American Sociological Review, Vol. 72, No. 6, (December 2007): 915-939.
33. Ayala Casás and Bolívar Fresneda, *Battleship Vieques*, 107.
34. Morris J. McGregor, *Integration of the Armed Forces, 1940–1965* (Washington, D.C.: Center of Military History, United States Army, 1981), 72–73.
35. César J. Ayala and Rafael Bernabe, *Puerto Rico in the American Century: A History since 1898* (Chapel Hill: The University of North Carolina Press, 2007), 136-145.
36. Juan Giusti Cordero, "La Huelga Cañera de 1942, crónica de una Huelga General," *Fundamentos*, (Río Piedras: Revisa de Estudios Generales de la Universidad de Puerto Rico, 5-6, 1997-1998), 85.
37. "Minutes of the Board of Directors," P.A.A.C., 1939-1943, 100-496.
38. Giusti Cordero, "La Huelga Cañera de 1942," 96.
39. Rafael Pico, "Committee for the Investigation of Vieques," March 18, 1943, AFLMM, Presidente del Senado, Section IV, 1941-48, Series 9, Cart. No. 506-3, 1.
40. "Electricistas de Arundel irán a la huelga si no se les aumenta su salario," *El Imparcia* (San Juan), June 1, 1943, 2.
41. "The Puerto Rican Economy During the War Year of 1942," June 1943, AFLMM, Section 12, Material de y sobre Luis Muñoz Marín, Proyecto de Recopilación de Documentos, Biblioteca Harry S. Truman Library, 18.
42. U.S.N.–S.M.A., "Technical Report and Project History Contract NOy-3680: Section 22 St. Thomas, Roosevelt Roads, San Juan, St. Lucia, Antigua, Culebra," NOy3680 Administrative Data NOy-3680: contract; Factual Survey Vol. I General Report, re: The Arundel Corporation and Consolidated Engineering Company, Incorporated, March 22, 1943, Fdr. 41 of 43.
43. García Muñiz, La estrategia de Estados Unidos, 54.
44. United Press, "Se admite que quizás se limiten las importaciones," *El Mundo* (San Juan), November 17, 1943.
45. "Report on the preliminary studies of the market for Rum on the United States to the Governor's Advisory Committee on the Rum Industry," Arthur D. Little, Inc.

Chemist-Engineers, Cambridge, MA. Table 2, AFLMM, Sección IV, Presidente del Senado, Cartapacio no.237, Documento no.3; Bolívar Fresneda, "The war economy of Puerto Rico," 124-125; Bolívar Fresneda, "Las inversiones y los programas militares: construyendo la infraestructura y los recursos humanos de la posguerra," Jorge Rodríguez Beruff and José L. Bolívar Fresneda, editors, *Puerto Rico en la Segunda Guerra Mundial: Baluarte del Caribe*, (San Juan: Ediciones Callejón, 2012), 161-163; Bolívar Fresneda, *Guerra, banca y desarrollo*, 38-46.

46. Guy J. Swope, *Forty-First Annual Report of the Governor of Puerto Rico*, 1941, p. 9.
47. "Report on the preliminary studies of the market for Rum on the United States to the Governor's Advisory Committee on the Rum Industry," Arthur D. Little, Inc. Chemist-Engineers, Cambridge, MA. Table 2, AFLMM, Sección IV, Presidente del Senado, Cartapacio no.237, Documento no.3.
48. Guy J. Swope, *Forty-First Annual Report of the Governor of Puerto Rico*, 1941, 9.
49. Thomas Hibben and Rafael Picó, *Industrial Development of Puerto Rico and the Virgin Islands of the United States, Report of the United States Section, Caribbean Commission* (Port of Spain: Caribbean Commission,1948), 208-209.
50. Peter Foster, *Family Spirits: The Bacardi Saga. Rum, Riches and Revolution* (Toronto: Macfarlane Walter & Ross, 1990), 71.
51. José A. Bolívar, interview by the author, Guaynabo, Puerto Rico, February 2008. Bolívar, an engineer by profession, is a retired vice president of the Bacardi Corporation who worked at Bacardi from 1949 to 1993 at Santiago de Cuba, San Juan, Recife, Brazil and Jacksonville, Florida.
52. Laws of Puerto Rico, no. 354, May 14, 1949, Tomo 13, Artículo 1679, 867-868.
53. "Hull announces base sits accord as Trinidad accepts U.S. selections," *New York Times*, January 12, 1941, 1.
54. Frank L. Kluckhohn, "Snag encountered on Trinidad base," *New York Times*, December 11, 1940, 1,
55. Frank L. Kluckhohn, "Snag encountered on Trinidad base," *New York Times*, December 11, 1940, 1,
56. "Hull announces base sits accord as Trinidad accepts U.S. selections," *New York Times*, January 12, 1941, 1.
57. Rita Pemberton, "War, Food and Security: feeding Trinidad and Tobago in Wartime, 1939-1945," Karen E. Eccles and Debbie McCollin, editors, *World War II and the Caribbean* (Jamaica: The University of the West Indies, 2017), Chapter 4.
58. Ronald Williams, "The Exchange: Imperialism and the Impact of World War II on Trinidad and Tobago," Karen E. Eccles and Debbie McCollin, editors, *World War II and the Caribbean* (Jamaica: The University of the West Indies, 2017), Chapter 7.
59. Robert N. Sturdevant, "Army, Navy Fight U-Boats Off Trinidad, Washington Post, January 14, 1943, 6.)
60. Anthony P. Maingot, Estados Unidos y el Caribe: retos de una relación asimétrica (Río Piedras: La Editorial de la Universidad de Puerto Rico, 2005), 82-83.
61. Anthony P. Maingot, *Estados Unidos y el Caribe: retos de una relación asimétrica* (Rio Piedras, La Editorial de la Universidad de Puerto Rico, 2005), 81-83.
62. Ken Post, *Strike the Iron. A Colony at War: Jamaica 1939-1945* (The Hague: The Institute of Social Studies, 1978), Vol 1, 418.
63. Dalea Bean, "Bodies in Conflict: Policing Sexual Lessons in Jamaica during World War II," Karen E. Eccles and Debbie McCollin, editors, *World War II and the Caribbean* (Jamaica: The University of the West Indies, 2017), Chapter 12.
64. Suzanne Francis-Brown, "Jamaica: Fixed-term Haven and Holding Tank during World War II," Karen E. Eccles and Debbie McCollin, editors, *World War II and the Caribbean* (Jamaica: The University of the West Indies, 2017), Chapter 11.

Chapter VI

1. Eric T. Jennings, "The French Caribbean in World War II. Upheavals, Repression and Resistance," Karen E. Eccles and Debbie McCollin, editors, *World War II and the Caribbean* (Jamaica: The University of the West Indies Press, 2017), Chapter 5.
2. "Martinique hit by war, Nature," *The Indianapolis*, June 1, 1941, 32.
3. https://www.britannica.com/place/Mount-Pelee. Retrieved July 15, 2020.
4. Andrew M. Daily, "Staying French: Martiniquans and Guadeloupeans Between Empire and Independence, 1946-1973," PhD Diss., (New Jersey: The State University of New Jersey, 2001), 23-52.
5. Ricard James Champoux, "Liberal Critics of the United States Policy toward the Vichy Government, 1940-1943," PhD Diss., (Bozeman: Montana State University, 1959), 5.
6. Ricard James Champoux, "Liberal Critics of the United States Policy toward the Vichy Government, 1940-1943," PhD Diss., (Bozeman, Montana: Montana State University, 1958), 7.
7. George Edward Melton, "Admiral Darlan and the Diplomacy of Vichy, 1940-1942," PhD Diss, (Chapel Hill: University of North Carolina, 1966), 22.
8. George Edward Melton, "Admiral Darlan and the Diplomacy of Vichy, 1940-1942," PhD Diss, (Chapel Hill: University of North Carolina, 1966), 22.
9. Stetson Conn and Byron Fairchild, *United States Army in World War II. The Western Hemisphere. The Framework of Hemisphere Defense* (Washington: The U.S. Army Center of Military History, 1958), loc 854.
10. Stetson Conn and Byron Fairchild, *United States Army in World War II. The Western Hemisphere. The Framework of Hemisphere Defense* (Washington: The U.S. Army Center of Military History, 1958), loc 854-868.
11. Stetson Conn and Byron Fairchild, *United States Army in World War II. The Western Hemisphere. The Framework of Hemisphere Defense* (Washington: The U.S. Army Center of Military History, 1958), loc 949.
12. Stetson Conn and Byron Fairchild, *United States Army in World War II. The Western Hemisphere. The Framework of Hemisphere Defense* (Washington: The U.S. Army Center of Military History, 1958), loc 949.
13. Navy Department Library, *Building the Navy's Bases in World War II, Volume II (Part III), Chapter XVIII, Bases in South America and the Caribbean area, including Bermuda*, 77.
14. George Edward Melton, "Admiral Darlan and the Diplomacy of Vichy, 1940-1942," PhD Diss, (Chapel Hill: University of North Carolina, 1966), 43-50.
15. George Edward Melton, "Admiral Darlan and the Diplomacy of Vichy, 1940-1942," PhD Diss, (Chapel Hill: University of North Carolina, 1966), 50-51
16. Stetson Conn and Byron Fairchild, *United States Army in World War II. The Western Hemisphere. The Framework of Hemisphere Defense* (Washington: The U.S. Army Center of Military History, 1958), loc 1097-1121.
17. Calvin Warner Hines, "United States Diplomacy in the Caribbean during World War II," PhD Diss. (Austin: The University of Texas at Austin, 1968), 162.
18. Calvin Warner Hines, "United States Diplomacy in the Caribbean during World War II," PhD Diss. (Austin: The University of Texas at Austin, 1968), 162.
19. Stetson Conn and Byron Fairchild, *United States Army in World War II. The Western Hemisphere. The Framework of Hemisphere Defense* (Washington: The U.S. Army Center of Military History, 1958), loc 1097-1121.
20. Calvin Warner Hines, "United States Diplomacy in the Caribbean during World War II," PhD Diss. (Austin: The University of Texas at Austin, 1968), 165.

21. Stetson Conn and Byron Fairchild, *United States Army in World War II. The Western Hemisphere. The Framework of Hemisphere Defense* (Washington: The U.S. Army Center of Military History, 1958), loc 1097-1121.
22. Calvin Warner Hines, "United States Diplomacy in the Caribbean during World War II," PhD Diss. (Austin: The University of Texas at Austin, 1968), 172-176.
23. David J. Bercuson and Holger H. Herwig, *Long Night of the Tankers* (Calgary: University of Calgary Press, 2015), 74-75. According to these authors, the amount of gold was as high as $300 million.
24. "Battle is Feared in Caribbean Sea," *The Philadelphia Inquirer*, July 6, 1940, 3.
25. According to Stenson Conn, Rose C. Engelman and Byron Fairchild, *Guardian The United States and its Outposts* (Washington: Center of Military History, United States Army, 2000), 328, the amount of gold was $250 million.
26. David J. Bercuson and Holger H. Herwig, *Long Night of the Tankers* (Calgary: University of Calgary Press, 2015), 74-75.
27. David J. Bercuson and Holger H. Herwig, *Long Night of the Tankers* (Calgary: University of Calgary Press, 2015), 75-76.
28. Calvin Warner Hines, "United States Diplomacy in the Caribbean during World War II," PhD Diss. (Austin: The University of Texas at Austin, 1968), 172-176.
29. Stetson Conn and Byron Fairchild, *United States Army in World War II. The Western Hemisphere. The Framework of Hemisphere Defense* (Washington: The U.S. Army Center of Military History, 1958), 50.
30. Stetson Conn and Byron Fairchild, *United States Army in World War II. The Western Hemisphere. The Framework of Hemisphere Defense* (Washington: The U.S. Army Center of Military History, 1958), 50.
31. David J. Bercuson and Holger H. Herwig, *Long Night of the Tankers* (Calgary: University of Calgary Press, 2015), 76.
32. Stetson Conn and Byron Fairchild, *United States Army in World War II. The Western Hemisphere. The Framework of Hemisphere Defense* (Washington: The U.S. Army Center of Military History, 1958), 50.
33. "Hull's Statement on German Defiance of Monroe Doctrine," *The Philadelphia Inquirer*, July 6, 1940, 3.
34. Stetson Conn and Byron Fairchild, *United States Army in World War II. The Western Hemisphere. The Framework of Hemisphere Defense* (Washington: The U.S. Army Center of Military History, 1958), 50.
35. Calvin Warner Hines, "United States Diplomacy in the Caribbean during World War II," PhD Diss. (Austin: The University of Texas at Austin, 1968), 185.
36. "Battle is Feared in Caribbean Sea," *The Philadelphia Inquirer*, July 6, 1940, 3.
37. Stetson Conn and Byron Fairchild, *United States Army in World War II. The Western Hemisphere. The Framework of Hemisphere Defense* (Washington: The U.S. Army Center of Military History, 1958), 50.
38. "Pétain severs U.K. Relations," *The Gazette*, (Montreal, Canada), July 6, 1940, 1.
39. "French Break with Britain over Seizer," *Pittsburg Post-Gazette*, July 6, 1940, 1.
40. "Britain called traitor for French Fleet Raid," *The Detroit Free Press*, July 6, 1940, 1.
41. "English Fleet Bottles French Warships off Venezuela is Reported," *Pittsburg Post-Gazette*, July 6, 1940, 1.
42. "Capital Fars Battle is Near Off West Indies," *The Detroit Free Press*, July 6, 1940, 1.
43. "Islands in Caribbean fear Nazi dictation," *New York Times*, July 4, 1940, 4.
44. "Capital Fars Battle is Near Off West Indies," *The Detroit Free Press*, July 6, 1940, 1.
45. "U.S. Ships Watching action in Martinique," *Minneapolis Star Journal*, July 7, 1940, 3.

46. "Blockade of Martinique Reported to Keep U.S. Planes from France," *The Gazette*, (Montreal, Canada), July 6, 1940, 1.
47. "Firm Hands-Off Notice is Given Reich by Hull," *Pittsburg Post-Gazette*, July 6, 1940, 1.
48. "Firm Against German Gain in New World," *Minneapolis Star Journal*, July 7, 1940, 3.
49. "British Deny Martinique Blockade, but U.S. Warships Continue Watch," *New York Times*, July 9, 1940, 6.
50. "British Deny Martinique Blockade, but U.S. Warships Continue Watch," *New York Times*, July 9, 1940, 6.
51. https://history.state.gov/milestones/1914-1920/haiti. Retrieved June 28, 2020.
52. Stetson Conn and Byron Fairchild, *United States Army in World War II. The Western Hemisphere. The Framework of Hemisphere Defense* (Washington: The U.S. Army Center of Military History, 1958), 50.
53. Carlos J. Videla, San Juan, Puerto Rico, "Specter of Nazidom Hangs Over the Lesser Antilles," *The Calgary Herald*, August 21,1940, 3.
54. "Islands in Caribbean fear Nazi dictation," *New York Times*, July 4, 1940,4.
55. Calvin Warner Hines, "United States Diplomacy in the Caribbean during World War II," PhD Diss. (Austin: The University of Texas at Austin, 1968), 186-189.
56. Calvin Warner Hines, "United States Diplomacy in the Caribbean during World War II," PhD Diss. (Austin: The University of Texas at Austin, 1968), 203.
57. Calvin Warner Hines, "United States Diplomacy in the Caribbean during World War II," PhD Diss. (Austin: The University of Texas at Austin, 1968), 204.
58. Calvin Warner Hines, "United States Diplomacy in the Caribbean during World War II," PhD Diss. (Austin: The University of Texas at Austin, 1968), 205-208.
59. Stetson Conn and Byron Fairchild, *United States Army in World War II. The Western Hemisphere. The Framework of Hemisphere Defense* (Washington: The U.S. Army Center of Military History, 1958), 50.
60. Calvin Warner Hines, "United States Diplomacy in the Caribbean during World War II," PhD Diss. (Austin: The University of Texas at Austin, 1968), 209-211.
61. Calvin Warner Hines, "United States Diplomacy in the Caribbean during World War II," PhD Diss. (Austin: The University of Texas at Austin, 1968), 211.
62. Calvin Warner Hines, "United States Diplomacy in the Caribbean during World War II," PhD Diss. (Austin: The University of Texas at Austin, 1968), 211-212.
63. "Vote on Revolt may be taken by Martinique," *New York Herald Tribune*, September 3, 1940, 3.
64. Calvin Warner Hines, "United States Diplomacy in the Caribbean during World War II," PhD Diss. (Austin: The University of Texas at Austin, 1968), 217.
65. Stetson Conn and Byron Fairchild, *United States Army in World War II. The Western Hemisphere. The Framework of Hemisphere Defense* (Washington: The U.S. Army Center of Military History, 1958), 83-86.
66. Calvin Warner Hines, "United States Diplomacy in the Caribbean during World War II," PhD Diss., (Austin: The University of Texas at Austin, 1968), 219.
67. Stetson Conn and Byron Fairchild, *United States Army in World War II. The Western Hemisphere. The Framework of Hemisphere Defense* (Washington: The U.S. Army Center of Military History, 1958), 83-86.
68. Stetson Conn and Byron Fairchild, *United States Army in World War II. The Western Hemisphere. The Framework of Hemisphere Defense* (Washington: The U.S. Army Center of Military History, 1958), 83-86.
69. Eric T. Jennings, "The French Caribbean in World War II: Upheavals, Repression and

Resistance," Karen E. Eccles and Debbie McCollin, *World War II and the Caribbean*, (Jamaica: The University of the West Indies Press, 2017), Chapter 5.
70. Eric T. Jennings, "The French Caribbean in World War II: Upheavals, Repression and Resistance," Karen E. Eccles and Debbie McCollin, *World War II and the Caribbean*, (Jamaica: The University of the West Indies Press, 2017), Chapter 5.
71. Calvin Warner Hines, "United States Diplomacy in the Caribbean during World War II," PhD Diss., (Austin: The University of Texas at Austin, 1968), 223.
72. Eric T. Jennings, "The French Caribbean in World War II: Upheavals, Repression and Resistance," Karen E. Eccles and Debbie McCollin, *World War II and the Caribbean*, (Jamaica: The University of the West Indies Press, 2017), Chapter 5.
73. "Martinique base is eyed by Leahy," *New York Times*, December 3, 1940, 14.
74. Rear Admiral Yates Stirling, Jr., "Nazi control of Island Probable," *The Courier-Journal*, Louisville, December 3, 1940, 2.
75. Peter C. Rhodes, "Tour of Martinique shows writer French not bolstering defenses," *The Courier-Journal*, Louisville, December 3, 1940, 2.
76. Eric T. Jennings, "The French Caribbean in World War II: Upheavals, Repression and Resistance," Karen E. Eccles and Debbie McCollin, *World War II and the Caribbean*, (Jamaica: The University of the West Indies Press, 2017), Chapter 5.
77. Eric T. Jennings, "The French Caribbean in World War II: Upheavals, Repression and Resistance," Karen E. Eccles and Debbie McCollin, *World War II and the Caribbean*, (Jamaica: The University of the West Indies Press, 2017), Chapter 5.
78. "210 Germans taken off Vichy ship at Trinidad," *New York Herald Tribune*, May 31, 1941, 3.
79. "210 Germans taken off Vichy ship at Trinidad," *New York Herald Tribune*, May 31, 1941, 3.
80. "210 Germans taken off Vichy ship at Trinidad," *New York Herald Tribune*, May 31, 1941, 3.
81. Eric T. Jennings, *Escape from Vichy. The Refugee Exodus to the French Caribbean* (Cambridge: Harvard University Press, 2018), 145.
82. Eric T. Jennings, *Escape from Vichy*, 145-146.
83. "French Nazis reported busy on Martinique," *New York Herald Tribune*, June 14, 1941, 3.
84. "French Nazis reported busy on Martinique," *New York Herald Tribune*, June 14, 1941, 3.
85. https://en.wikipedia.org/wiki/SS_Winnipeg. Retrieved July 7, 2020.
86. Eric T. Jennings, *Escape from Vichy*, 216.
87. Eric T. Jennings, *Escape from Vichy*, 216-217.
88. Eric T. Jennings, *Escape from Vichy*, 146.
89. Eric T. Jennings, *Escape from Vichy*, 164.
90. Eric T. Jennings, *Escape from Vichy*, 216.
91. Eric T. Jennings, *Escape from Vichy*, 214-215.
92. Jean Edward Smith, *FDR* (New York: Random House Trade Publications, 2008), 523.
93. Jean Edward Smith, *FDR* (New York: Random House Trade Publications, 2008), 523-526.
94. Jean Edward Smith, *FDR* (New York: Random House Trade Publications, 2008), 527.
95. Jean Edward Smith, *FDR* (New York: Random House Trade Publications, 2008), 529.
96. Jean Edward Smith, *FDR* (New York: Random House Trade Publications, 2008), 534-535.
97. Frank L. Kluckhohn, "U.S. and Martinique reach an accord for neutrality," *New York Times*, 1, 7.

98. Frank L. Kluckhohn, "U.S. and Martinique reach an accord for neutrality," *New York Times*, 1, 7.
99. Clay Blair, *Hitler's U-Boat War. The Hunters, 1939-1942* (New York: Modern Library, 2000), 504-505.
100. David J. Bercuson and Holger H. Herwig, *Long Nights of the Tankers* (Calgary, University of Calgary Press, 2014), 73.
101. Clay Blair, *Hitler's U-Boat War. The Hunters, 1939-1942* (New York: Modern Library, 2000), 504-505.
102. David J. Bercuson and Holger H. Herwig, *Long Nights of the Tankers* (Calgary, University of Calgary Press, 2014), 73-74.
103. Clay Blair, *Hitler's U-Boat War. The Hunters, 1939-1942* (New York: Modern Library, 2000), 504-505.
104. "U.S. Near Seizer of Martinique," *The Atlanta Constitution*, March 21, 1942, 7.
105. "U.S. Near Seizer of Martinique," *The Atlanta Constitution*, March 21, 1942, 7.
106. "U.S. Near Seizer of Martinique," *The Atlanta Constitution*, March 21, 1942, 7.
107. Calvin Warner Hines, "United States Diplomacy in the Caribbean during World War II," PhD Diss. (Austin: The University of Texas at Austin, 1968), 254-256.
108. Calvin Warner Hines, "United States Diplomacy in the Caribbean during World War II," PhD Diss. (Austin: The University of Texas at Austin, 1968), 254-256.
109. Calvin Warner Hines, "United States Diplomacy in the Caribbean during World War II," PhD Diss. (Austin: The University of Texas at Austin, 1968), 254-256.
110. James Houghton Holmes, "Admiral Leahy in Vichy France," PhD Diss. (Washington, DC: The George Washington University, 1974), 212-213.
111. James Houghton Holmes, "Admiral Leahy in Vichy France," PhD Diss. (Washington, DC: The George Washington University, 1974), 217.
112. James Houghton Holmes, "Admiral Leahy in Vichy France," PhD Diss. (Washington, DC: The George Washington University, 1974), 218-221.
113. Wilfrid Fleisher, "Leahy called from Vichy in blow to Laval," *New York Tribune/Herald Tribune*, April 18, 1942, 1.
114. Wilfrid Fleisher, "Leahy called from Vichy in blow to Laval," *New York Tribune/Herald Tribune*, April 18, 1942, 1.
115. Wilfrid Fleisher, "Leahy called from Vichy in blow to Laval," *New York Tribune/Herald Tribune*, April 18, 1942, 1.
116. Wilfrid Fleisher, "Leahy called from Vichy in blow to Laval," *New York Tribune/Herald Tribune*, April 18, 1942, 1.
117. Calvin Warner Hines, "United States Diplomacy in the Caribbean during World War II," PhD Diss., (Austin: The University of Texas at Austin, 1968), 264.
118. Calvin Warner Hines, "United States Diplomacy in the Caribbean during World War II," PhD Diss., (Austin: The University of Texas at Austin, 1968), 267-269.
119. Wilfrid Fleisher, "U.S. ignoring Laval in parley on Martinique," *New York Herald Tribune*, May 14, 1942, 2A.
120. Wilfrid Fleisher, "U.S. ignoring Laval in parley on Martinique," *New York Herald Tribune*, May 14, 1942, 2A.
121. United Press, "Vichy won't yield ships at Martinique," *New York Herald Tribune*, May 14, 1942, 1.
122. "Expects U.S. to get Martinique," *New York Times*, May 16, 1942, 4.
123. "Expects U.S. to get Martinique," *New York Times*, May 16, 1942, 4.
124. "Roosevelt decries loose talk on war," *The Philadelphia Inquirer*, May 16, 1942.
125. Associated Press, "U.S. advised to put bases on Martinique," *The Baltimore Sun*, May 16, 1942, 3.

126. Associated Press, "U.S. advised to put bases on Martinique," *The Baltimore Sun*, May 16, 1942, 3.
127. United Press, "Vichy won't yield ships at Martinique," *New York Herald Tribune*, May 14, 1942, 1.
128. Associated Press, "Laval still uses words of defiance," *The Windsor Daily Star*, Ontario, Canada, May 16, 1942, 1.
129. Associated Press, "Laval still uses words of defiance," *The Windsor Daily Star*, Ontario, Canada, May 16, 1942, 1.
130. "Laval note spurns U.S. Island plea," *Minneapolis Sunday Tribune and Star Journal*, May 17, 1942, 1
131. "U.S., Martinique study use of French cargo ships, Hull reveals," *The Philadelphia Inquirer*, May 16, 1942.
132. Wilfrid Fleisher, "U.S. will take key parts off French ships," *New York Herald Tribune*, May 16, 1942, 1.
133. Calvin Warner Hines, "United States Diplomacy in the Caribbean during World War II," PhD Diss., (Austin: The University of Texas at Austin, 1968), 277-279.
134. United Press, "Vichy won't yield ships at Martinique," *New York Herald Tribune*, May 14, 1942, 1.
135. Calvin Warner Hines, "United States Diplomacy in the Caribbean during World War II," PhD Diss., (Austin: The University of Texas at Austin, 1968), 280-281.
136. Calvin Warner Hines, "United States Diplomacy in the Caribbean during World War II," PhD Diss., (Austin: The University of Texas at Austin, 1968), 283-284.
137. George Edward Melton, "Admiral Darlan and the Diplomacy of Vichy, 1940-1942," PhD Diss., (Chapel Hill: University of North Carolina, 1966), 261-264.
138. Pierre Laval is mostly associated with the deportation of Jews. At his trial he was accused of plotting against the safety of the state and of intelligence with the enemy. His 3,000-word indictment referred to the persecution of the Jews, freemasons, Communists and resistance groups of all parties, the introduction of the Gestapo and the arrest of 22,000 people in Paris in one night. He was convicted on October 9, 1945 and executed on October 15. Alexander John Upward, "Ordinary Sailors: The French Navy, Vichy and the Second World War," PhD Diss., (Morgantown, West Virginia: West Virginia University, 2016), 259.
139. "Roosevelt rebukes Laval as diplomatic ties are cut," New York Times, November 10, 1942, 1.
140. "Roosevelt rebukes Laval as diplomatic ties are cut," New York Times, November 10, 1942, 1.
141. "Roosevelt rebukes Laval as diplomatic ties are cut," New York Times, November 10, 1942, 1.
142. "Roosevelt rebukes Laval as diplomatic ties are cut," New York Times, November 10, 1942, 1.
143. Alexander John Upward, "Ordinary Sailors: The French Navy, Vichy and the Second World War," PhD Diss. (Morgantown, West Virginia: West Virginia University, 2016), 254.
144. After the liberation of France, de Laborde was tried and convicted of treason for not attempting to save the fleet. He was found guilty and sentenced to death. This was later commuted to life imprisonment. He was granted clemency in 1947 and died in 1977 at the age of 99. https://www.thoughtco.com/world-war-ii-operation-lila-2361440. Retrieved July 14, 2020.
145. Calvin Warner Hines, "United States Diplomacy in the Caribbean during World War II," PhD Diss. (Austin: The University of Texas at Austin, 1968), 283-284.

146. "Our Vichy policy wins high praise," *New York Times*, November 11, 1942, 5.
147. "Our Vichy policy wins high praise," *New York Times*, November 11, 1942, 5.
148. "Our Vichy policy wins high praise," *New York Times*, November 11, 1942, 5.
149. Calvin Warner Hines, "United States Diplomacy in the Caribbean during World War II," PhD Diss., (Austin: The University of Texas at Austin, 1968), 285-316.
150. Calvin Warner Hines, "United States Diplomacy in the Caribbean during World War II," PhD Diss., (Austin: The University of Texas at Austin, 1968), 318-323.
151. Calvin Warner Hines, "United States Diplomacy in the Caribbean during World War II," PhD Diss. (Austin: The University of Texas at Austin, 1968), 371-373
152. Calvin Warner Hines, "United States Diplomacy in the Caribbean during World War II," PhD Diss. (Austin: The University of Texas at Austin, 1968), 373.
153. Calvin Warner Hines, "United States Diplomacy in the Caribbean during World War II," PhD Diss. (Austin: The University of Texas at Austin, 1968), 374-390.
154. Robert Sherwood, author, playwright and District Intelligence Officer for overseas operations was in North Africa after the invasion by the Allies in order to access the French thoughts regarding the Caribbean colonies. Quote is from an interview conducted by Lieutenant John C. Goodboy of the Travel Control Unit and sent to the Director of Naval Intelligence in Washington on April 19. NARA, Record Group # 181, Naval Districts and Shore Establishments, 10th Naval District, General Correspondence, Box 21, A16-AL1.
155. Eric T. Jennings, "The French Caribbean in World War II. Upheavals, Repression and Resistance," Karen E. Eccles and Debbie McCollin, editors, *World War II and the Caribbean* (Jamaica: The University of the West Indies Press, 2017), Chapter 5.
156. Jorge Rodríguez Beruff, "Puerto Rico y la crisis de Martinica (1940-1943)," Jorge Rodríguez Beruff and José L. Bolívar Fresneda, editors, *Puerto Rico en la Segunda Guerra Mundial: El Escenario Regional* (San Juan: Ediciones Callejón, 2015), 95.
157. Eric T. Jennings, "The French Caribbean in World War II. Upheavals, Repression and Resistance," Karen E. Eccles and Debbie McCollin, editors, *World War II and the Caribbean* (Jamaica: The University of the West Indies Press, 2017), Chapter 5.
158. Eric T. Jennings, "The French Caribbean in World War II. Upheavals, Repression and Resistance," Karen E. Eccles and Debbie McCollin, editors, *World War II and the Caribbean* (Jamaica: The University of the West Indies Press, 2017), Chapter 5.
159. Calvin Warner Hines, "United States Diplomacy in the Caribbean during World War II," PhD Diss. (Austin: The University of Texas at Austin, 1968), 392.
160. "Robert llama plenipotenciarios para realizar entrega del mando," *El Mundo*, July 1, 1943, 1.
161. Calvin Warner Hines, "United States Diplomacy in the Caribbean during World War II," PhD Diss. (Austin: The University of Texas at Austin, 1968), 393-400.
162. Calvin Warner Hines, "United States Diplomacy in the Caribbean during World War II," PhD Diss. (Austin: The University of Texas at Austin, 1968), 401.
163. Calvin Warner Hines, "United States Diplomacy in the Caribbean during World War II," PhD Diss. (Austin: The University of Texas at Austin, 1968), 401.
164. Calvin Warner Hines, "United States Diplomacy in the Caribbean during World War II," PhD Diss. (Austin: The University of Texas at Austin, 1968), 400.
165. Calvin Warner Hines, "United States Diplomacy in the Caribbean during World War II," PhD Diss. (Austin: The University of Texas at Austin, 1968), 402.
166. Calvin Warner Hines, "United States Diplomacy in the Caribbean during World War II," PhD Diss. (Austin: The University of Texas at Austin, 1968), 402.
167. "Martinique talks arranged by Navy," *New York Times*, July 3, 1943, 1,4.
168. "Admiral Hoover optimistic about Martinique accord," *New York Times*, July 5, 1943.

169. "French Committee firm on Martinique," *New York Times*, July 10, 1943.
170 "Robert companion 'explains' action," *New York Times*, July 18, 1943, 1.
171. Jorge Rodríguez Beruff, "Puerto Rico y la crisis de Martinica (1940-1943)," Jorge Rodríguez Beruff and José L. Bolívar Fresneda, editors, *Puerto Rico en la Segunda Guerra Mundial: El Escenario Regional* (San Juan: Ediciones Callejón, 2015), 97.
172. "Robert enters hospital," *New York Times*, August 30, 1943, 3.
173. "Admiral Robert reaches Madrid," *New York Times*, December 25, 1943, 3.
174. Pertinax, North American newspaper Alliance, "Pétain's mind fails, diplomat reports," *New York Times*, February 4, 1944, 3.
175. Pertinax, North American newspaper Alliance, "Pétain's mind fails, diplomat reports," *New York Times*, February 4, 1944, 3.
176. "French accuse admirals," *New York Times*, September 21, 1944, 4.
177. "Clemency is urged for Admiral Robert," *New York Times*, March 15, 1947, 7.
178. "Clemency is urged for Admiral Robert," *New York Times*, March 15, 1947, 7.

Epilogue

1. Rafael Cox Alomar, "La Segunda Guerra Mundial y la Deconstrucción del Imperio británico en el Caribe," *Puerto Rico en la Segunda Guerra Mundial: Baluarte del Caribe*, Jorge Rodríguez Beruff and José L. Bolívar Fresneda, Editors, 40-45.
2. Jorge Rodríguez Beruff, *Política Militar y Dominación. Puerto Rico en el Contexto Latinoamericano* (San Juan: Ediciones Huracán, 1988), 108-109.
3. John M. Goshko, "Carter, Torrijos sign Panama Canal treaties," *Washington Post*, September 8, 1977.
4. Amanda Pérez Pintado, "Así se gestó la campana para sacar a la Marina de Vieques," *El Nuevo Dia*, Abril 14, 2019.
5. Jorge Rodríguez Beruff, *Política Militar y Dominación. Puerto Rico en el Contexto Latinoamericano* (San Juan: Ediciones Huracán, 1988), 34-69.
6. https://www.army.mil/article/37660/operation_power_pack_u_s_military_intervention_in_the_dominican_republic. Retrieved July 21, 2020.
7. https://www.army.mil/article/37660/operation_power_pack_u_s_military_intervention_in_the_dominican_republic. Retrieved July 21, 2020.
8. https://www.thoughtco.com/grenada-invasion-4571025. Retrieved July 21, 2020.

BIBLIOGRAPHY

Archival Sources

National Archives and Records Administration (NARA), Washington, D.C.
Private Archive of the Arundel Corporation
Archivo General de Puerto Rico
Centro de Investigación Histórica de la Universidad de Puerto Rico
Proyecto Caribeño de Justicia y Paz, University of Puerto Rico
Archivo Fundación Luis Muñoz Marín

Printed primary sources

Picó, Rafael. "Committee for the Investigation of Vieques," March 18, 1943, AFLMM, Presidente del Senado, Section IV, 1941-48, Series 9, Cart. No. 506-3: 1.
"The Puerto Rican Economy During the War Year of 1942," June 1943. AFLMM, Section 12, Material de y sobre Luis Muñoz Marín, Proyecto de Recopilación de Documentos, Biblioteca Harry S. Truman Library: 18.
Swope, Guy J. *Forty-First Annual Report of the Governor of Puerto Rico*, 1941: 9.
Arthur D. Little, Inc. Chemist-Engineers, Cambridge, MA. "Report on the preliminary studies of the market for Rum on the United States to the Governor's Advisory Committee on the Rum Industry," Table 2.
Laws of Puerto Rico, no. 354, May 14, 1949, Tomo 13, Artículo 1679:867-868.

Printed secondary sources

BOOKS

Ayala Casás, César J. and Bolívar Fresneda, José L. *Battleship Vieques: Puerto Rico from World War II to the Korean War.* Princeton, NJ: Markus Wiener, 2011.

Ayala, César J. and Bernabe, Rafael. *Puerto Rico in the American Century: A History since 1898*. Chapel Hill: The University of North Carolina Press, 2007.

Bean, Dalea. "Bodies in Conflict: Policing Sexual Lessons in Jamaica during World War II," Karen E. Eccles and Debbie McCollin. Editors. *World War II and the Caribbean*. Jamaica: The University of the West Indies, 2017, Chapter 12.

Bercuson, David J., Herwig, Holger H., *Long Night of the Tankers*. Calgary: University of Calgary Press, 2014.

Billinger, Jr., Robert D. *Hitler's Soldiers in the Sunshine State. German POWs in Florida*. Gainesville: University Press of Florida, 2000.

Blair, Clay. *Hitler's U-Boat War. The Hunters, 1939-1942*. New York: Modern Library, 1996.

Bolívar Fresneda, José L. *Guerra, banca y desarrollo. El Banco de Fomento y la Industrialización de Puerto Rico*. San Juan: Fundación Luis Muñoz Marín and the Institute of Puerto Rican Culture, 2011.

Bolívar Fresneda, José L. "Las inversiones y los programas militares: construyendo la infraestructura y los recursos humanos de la posguerra," Jorge Rodríguez Beruff and José L. Bolívar Fresneda. Editors. *Puerto Rico en la Segunda Guerra Mundial: Baluarte del Caribe*. San Juan: Ediciones Callejón, 2012.

Bonnet Benítez, Juan Amedée. *Vieques en la historia de Puerto Rico*. San Juan: F. Ortiz Nieves, 1976.

Conn, Stetson, Engelman, Rose C. and Fairchild, Byron. *The Western Hemisphere: Guarding the United States and its Outposts*. Washington, D.C.: Center of Military History, 2000.

Cox Alomar, Rafael. "La Segunda Guerra Mundial y la Deconstrucción del Imperio británico en el Caribe," Jorge Rodríguez Beruff and José L. Bolívar Fresneda. Editors. *Puerto Rico en la Segunda Guerra Mundial: Baluarte del Caribe*, San Juan: Ediciones Callejón, 2015.

Dawson Axialá, Mari and Argamasilla, Pepín. *Bacardi: A Tale of Merchants, Family and Corporation*. Miami: Facundo y Amalia Bacardi Foundation, Inc., 2006.

Doenitz, Karl. *Memoirs. Ten Years and Twenty Days*. Annapolis: Naval Institute Press, 1990.

Foster, Peter. *Family Spirits: The Bacardi Saga. Rum, Riches and Revolution*. Toronto: Macfarlane Walter & Ross, 1990.

Francis-Brown, Suzanne. "Jamaica: Fixed-term Haven and Holding Tank during World War II," Karen E. Eccles and Debbie McCollin. Editors. *World War II and the Caribbean*. Jamaica: The University of the West Indies, 2017, Chapter 11.

García Muñiz, Humberto. *La estrategia de Estados Unidos y la militarización del Caribe*. Río Piedras, PR: Instituto de Estudios del Caribe, University of Puerto Rico, 1988.

González Morales, Carlos M. "Borinquen Field y Aguadilla: Un municipio en la guerra," Jorge Rodríguez Beruff and José L. Bolívar Fresneda. Editors. *Puerto Rico en la Segunda Guerra Mundial: Baluarte del Caribe*. San Juan: Ediciones Callejón, 2015.

González Vales, Luis E. "Puerto Rico: baluarte defensivo en el Caribe," Luis E. González Vales and María Dolores Luque. Editors. *Historia de Puerto Rico, Volumen IV*. Río Piedras: Ediciones Doce Calles, 2010.

Goslinga, Cornelis Ch. *A Short History of the Netherlands Antilles and Surinam*. The Hague: Martinus Nijhoff Publishers, 1979.

Gregory, G. H. *Posters of World War II*. New York: Gramercy, 1996.

Herman, Arthur. *Freedom's Forge. How American Business Produced Victory in World War II*. New York: Random House, 2012.

Hibben, Thomas and Picó, Rafael. *Industrial Development of Puerto Rico and the Virgin Islands of the United States, Report of the United States Section, Caribbean Commission*. Port of Spain: Caribbean Commission. 1948.

Ickes, Harold L. *The Secret Diary of Harold L. Ickes, Volume II: The Lowering Clouds 1939-1941*. New York: Simon and Schuster, 1955.

Jennings, Eric T. *Escape from Vichy. The Refugee Exodus to the French Caribbean*. Cambridge: Harvard University Press, 2018.

Jennings, Eric T. "The French Caribbean in World War II. Upheavals, Repression and Resistance," Karen E. Eccles and Debbie McCollin. Editors. *World War II and the Caribbean*. Jamaica: The University of the West Indies Press, 2017, Chapter 5.

Kelshall, Gaylor T. M. *The U-Boat War in the Caribbean*. Port-of-Spain, Trinidad: Paria Publishing Company Limited, 1988.

Lavandier, César de Windt. *La Segunda Guerra Mundial y los submarinos alemanes en el Mar Caribe*. Santo Domingo: Amigo del Hogar, 1997.

Maingot, Anthony P. *Estados Unidos y el Caribe: retraso de una relación asimétrica*. Río Piedras, La Editorial de la Universidad de Puerto Rico, 2005.

McGregor, Morris J. *Integration of the Armed Forces, 1940–1965*. Washington, D.C.: Center of Military History, United States Army, 1981.

Navy, Department Library. *Building the Navy's Bases in World War II, Volume II (Part III), Chapter XVIII, Bases in South America and the Caribbean area, including Bermuda*.

Navy, Department of. *Continued use of the Atlantic Fleet Weapons Training Facility Inner Range (Vieques): Draft Environmental Impact Statement*. Tippetts-Abbett-McCarthy-Stratton: Ecology and Environment, 1979.

Padfield, Peter. *War Beneath the Sea*. Canada: John Wiley & Sons, Inc., 1998.

Pemberton, Rita. "War, Food and Security: feeding Trinidad and Tobago in Wartime, 1939-1945," Karen E. Eccles and Debbie McCollin. Editors. *World War II and the Caribbean*. Jamaica: The University of the West Indies, 2017, Chapter 4.

Perloff, Harvey S. *Puerto Rico's Economic Future: A study in planned development*. Chicago: The University of Chicago Press, 1950.

Picó, Rafael. *The Geographic Regions of Puerto Rico*. Rio Piedras: University of Puerto Rico Press, 1950.

Piñero Cádiz, Gerardo M. "La base aeronaval Roosevelt Roads: El Pearl Harbor del Caribe." Jorge Rodríguez Beruff and José L. Bolívar Fresneda. Editors. *Puerto Rico en la Segunda Guerra Mundial: Baluarte del Caribe*. San Juan: Ediciones Callejón, 2015.

Placer Cervera, Gustavo. "Los marinos cubanos en la Segunda Guerra Mundial," *Puerto Rico en la Segunda Guerra Mundial: El Escenario Regional*, Jorge Rodríguez Beruff, José L. Bolívar Fresneda, Editors. San Juan: Ediciones Callejón, 2015.

Post, Ken. *Strike the Iron. A Colony at War: Jamaica 1939-1945, Volume I*. The Hague: The Institute of Social Studies, 1978.

Rodríguez Beruff, Jorge. *Política miliar y dominación. Puerto Rico en el contexto latinoamericano*. San Juan: Ediciones Huracán, 1988.

Rodríguez Beruff, Jorge. *Strategy as Politics: Puerto Rico on the Eve of the Second World War*. San Juan: La Editorial de la Universidad de Puerto Rico, 2007.

Rodríguez Beruff, Jorge. "Rediscovering Puerto Rico and the Caribbean: United States Strategic Debate and War Planning on the eve of the Second World War." Rodríguez Beruff, Jorge and Bolívar Fresneda, José

L. Editors. *Puerto Rico en la Segunda Guerra Mundial: El Escenario Regional*. San Juan: Ediciones Callejón, 2015.

Rodríguez Beruff, Jorge. "Puerto Rico y la crisis de Martinica (1940-1943)," Jorge Rodríguez Beruff and José L. Bolívar Fresneda. Editors. *Puerto Rico en la Segunda Guerra Mundial: El Escenario Regional*. San Juan: Ediciones Callejón, 2015.

Rodríguez Beruff, Jorge. Editor. *Las Memorias de Leahy: Los relatos del almirante William D. Leahy sobre su gobernación de Puerto Rico (1939-1940)*. San Juan: Fundación Luis Muñoz Marín, 2012.

Rodríguez Beruff, Jorge and Bolívar Fresneda, José L. Editors. *Island at War. Puerto Rico in the Crucible of the Second World War*. Jackson: University Press of Mississippi, 2015.

Roorda, Eric Paul. *The Dictator Next Door. The Good Neighbor Policy and the Trujillo Regime in the Dominican Republic, 1930-1945*. Durham: Duke University Press, 1998.

Rosario Urrutia, Mayra. "The Anglo-American Caribbean Commission: A Socioeconomic Strategy Designated for Military Security, 1942-1946," Jorge Rodríguez Beruff, and José L. Bolívar Fresneda, Editors. *Islands at War. Puerto Rico in the Crucible of the Second World War* Jackson: University Press of Mississippi, 2015.

Schoonover, Thomas D. *Hitler's Man in Havana*. Louisville: University Press of Kentucky, 2008.

Simón Arce, Rafael. " 'Volverán Banderas Victoriosas...' Falange en Puerto Rico 1937-1941." Rodríguez Beruff, Jorge and Bolívar Fresneda, José L. Editors. *Puerto Rico en la Segunda Guerra Mundial: El Escenario Regional*, San Juan: Ediciones Callejón, 2015.

Smith, Jean Edward. *FDR*. New York: Random House Publishing Group, 2008.

Terraine, John. *The U-Boat Wars 1916-1945*. New York: Henry Holt and Company, Inc., 1989.

Tugwell, Rexford G. *The Stricken Land: The Story of Puerto Rico*. Garden City, New York: Doubleday & Company, Inc., 1947.

Vause, Jordan. *U-Boat Ace. The story of Wolfgang Luth*. Annapolis: United States Naval Institute Press, 1990.

Vega, Bernardo. "La Isla Española y la Segunda Guerra Mundial." Rodríguez Beruff, Jorge and Bolívar Fresneda, José L. Editors. *Puerto Rico en* la *Segunda Guerra Mundial: El Escenario Regional*, San Juan: Ediciones Callejón, 2015.

Weinberg, Gerhard L. *A World at Arms: A Global History of World War II*. Cambridge: Cambridge University Press, 1994.

Williams, Ronald. "The Exchange: Imperialism and the Impact of World War II on Trinidad and Tobago," Karen E. Eccles and Debbie McCollin. Editors. *World War II and the Caribbean*. Jamaica: The University of the West Indies, 2017), Chapter 7.

JOURNALS

Torres, Bibliano. "La isla de Vieques," *Anuario de Estudios Americanos* (Sevilla) 12 (1955): 452.

Giusti Cordero, Juan. "La Huelga Cañera de 1942, crónica de una Huelga General," *Fundamentos*, (Río Piedras: Revisa de Estudios Generales de la Universidad de Puerto Rico, 5-6, 1997-19998): 85.

NEWSPAPERS

Washington Post
January 26, 1940
April 15, 1942
June 8, 1942
July 4, 1942
August 6, 1942
August 15, 1942
January 14, 1943
July 5, 1943
September 8, 1977

New York Times
September 10, 1939
October 3, 1939
October 12, 1939
October 15, 1939
January 29, 1940

July 4, 1940
July 9, 1940
August 21, 1940
December 3, 1940
December 11, 1940
January 12, 1941
February 17, 1942
February 18, 1942
March 4, 1942
March 15, 1942
March 23, 1942
May 16, 1942
June 10, 1942
June 12, 1942
June 24, 1942
July 3, 1942
July 4, 1942

July 14, 1942
July 15, 1942
July 16, 1942
July 29, 1942
August 6, 1942
August 28, 1942
November 10, 1942
November 11, 1942
January 3, 1943
March 23, 1943
March 24, 1943
March 28, 1943
May 24, 1943
July 3, 1943
July 5, 1943
July 10, 1943
July 18, 1943
August 30, 1943
November 21, 1943
December 25, 1943
February 4, 1944
September 21, 1944
March 15, 1947

The Atlanta Constitution
October 4, 1939
August 26, 1940
March 21, 1942
July 3, 1942
July 27, 1942
August 15, 1942
January 10, 1943
March 27, 1943

New York Amsterdam
October 4, 1939
October 28, 1939

Chicago Daily Tribune
March 9, 1942
March 13, 1942
June 8, 1942
June 16, 1942
July 17, 1942
July 29, 1942
May 24, 1943
November 21, 1943

El Mundo (San Juan)
January 14, 1939
January 21, 1939
March 23, 1939
November 14, 1939
December 2, 1939
May 31, 1940
October 26, 1940
February 27, 1941
April 13, 1941
May 4, 1941
May 24, 1941
January 16, 1942
January 20, 1942
November 17, 1943

El Imparcial (San Juan)
April 14, 1943
June 1, 1943

El Nuevo Dia (San Juan)
April 14, 2019

Los Angeles Times
February 18, 1942
February 19, 1942
February 20, 1942
February 26, 1942
June 7, 1942
June 12, 1942
June 21, 1942
July 5, 1942
August 4, 1942
August 14, 1942
August 17, 1942
August 28, 1942

New York Amsterdam Star News
February 21, 1942

The Observer
July 19, 1942

The Indianapolis
June 1, 1941

The Philadelphia Inquirer
July 6, 1940
May 16, 1942

The Gazette, (Montreal, Canada)
July 6, 1940

Pittsburg Post-Gazette
July 6, 1940

The Detroit Free Press
July 6, 1904

Minneapolis Star Journal
July 7, 1940
May 17, 1942

The Calgary Herald
August 21, 1940

New York Herald Tribune
September 3, 1940
May 31, 1941
June 14, 1941
April 18, 1942
May 14, 1942
May 16, 1942

The Courier-Journal, Louisville
December 3, 1940

The Baltimore Sun
May 16, 1942

The Windsor Daily Star,
Ontario, Canada
May 16, 1942

Unpublished dissertations

Caraballo, Santiago. "Guerra, reforma y colonialismo: Luis Muñoz Marín, las reformas del P.D.P. y su vinculación con la militarización de Puerto Rico en el contexto de la Segunda Guerra Mundial", PhD diss., Rio Piedras: University of Puerto Rico, 2005.
Champoux, Ricard James. "Liberal Critics of the United States Policy toward the Vichy Government, 1940-1943," PhD diss., Bozeman, Montana: Montana State University, 1958.
Daily, Andrew M. "Staying French: Martiniquans and Guadeloupeans Between Empire and Independence, 1946-1973," PhD diss., New Jersey: The State University of New Jersey, 2001.
Holmes, James Houghton. "Admiral Leahy in Vichy France," PhD diss., Washington, DC: The George Washington University, 1974.
Lefebvre, Andrew Robert. "Forgotten by History: The Panama Canal in World War Two." PhD diss., Calgary, Alberta: University of Calgary, 2009.
McCaffrey, Katherine T. "Culture, Power and Struggle: Anti-military protests in Vieques, Puerto Rico." PhD diss., New York: City University of New York, 1999.
Melton, George Edward. "Admiral Darlan and the Diplomacy of Vichy, 1940-1942," PhD diss., Chapel Hill: University of North Carolina, 1966.
Upward, Alexander John. "Ordinary Sailors: The French Navy, Vichy and the Second World War," PhD diss., Morgantown, West Virginia: West Virginia University, 2016.
Warner Hines, Calvin. "United States Diplomacy in the Caribbean during World War II." PhD diss., Austin: The University of Texas at Austin, 1968.

Unpublished Papers

Loveman, Mara and Muñiz, Jeronimo. "How Puerto Rico became white: an analysis of racial statistics in the 1910 and 1920 Census." Unpublished paper prepared for presentation at the Center for Demography and Ecology, University of Wisconsin-Madison, February 7, 2006
US Navy. "Technical Report and Project History Contract NOy-3680: Section 22 St. Thomas, Roosevelt Roads, San Juan, St. Lucia, Antigua,

Culebra," NOy-3680 Administrative Data NOy-3680: contract; Factual Survey Vol. I General Report, re: The Arundel Corporation and Consolidated Engineering Company, Incorporated, March 22, 1943.

Interviews

José A. Bolívar Pérez, interview with the author's father, Guaynabo, Puerto Rico, February 2008. Bolívar, an engineer and Master Brewer by profession, is a retired vice president of the Bacardi Corporation. He worked there from 1949 to 1993 in: Santiago de Cuba; San Juan, Puerto Rico; Recife, Brazil, and Jacksonville, Florida.

Internet Sources

https://www.curacaohistory.com/1634-the-conquest-of-curacao. Retrieved July 18, 2020.
https://www.britannica.com/event/Eighty-Years-War. Retrieved July 18, 2020.
https://www.aruba.com/us/our-island/history-and-culture/history. Retrieved July 18, 2020.
www.pdr.uscourts.gov/robert-archer-cooper-1934-1947-0. Retrieved March 26, 2020.
https://www.nobelprize.org/prizes/peace/1953/marshall/biographical/. Retrieved April 28, 2020.
www.uboat.net/allies/merchants/ship/1389.html. Retrieved April 1, 2020.
www.thecubanhistory.com/2012/04/nazi-spy-executed-in-cuba/. Retrieved April 7, 2020.
www.mythicdetroit.org/index.php?n=Main.NaziUndergroundRailroad. Retrieved April 7, 2020.
https://history.state.gov/milestones/1914-1920/haiti. Retrieved June 28, 2020.
https://www.thoughtco.com/world-war-ii-operation-lila-2361440. Retrieved July 14, 2020.
https://www.army.mil/article/37660/operation_power_pack_u_s_military_intervention_in_the_dominican_republic. Retrieved July 21, 2020.
https://www.thoughtco.com/grenada-invasion-4571025. Retrieved July 21, 2020.

INDEX

Alcoa Partner 53
Aleutian Islands 39
Andrews, Lieutenant General Frank 31, 87, 96
Anglo-American Caribbean Commission 82
Aruba 1, 17-18, 24-25, 27-31, 33-35, 40-41, 43, 48, 51, 103, 120, 183, 202-203, 228
Arundel Corporation 22, 124-125, 152, 157-158

Batista, President of Cuba Fulgencio 76, 95, 115-116
Bauxite 1, 2, 7, 24, 28-30, 33, 37, 53, 83, 165, 178
Benítez Rexach, Félix 125
Bercuson, David J. 1
British Guiana 1, 20, 22-24, 30, 83, 158, 161, 227
Bullitt, U.S. Ambassador William C. 175

Camp, Balata 190, 194
Camp, Lazaret 194, 197
Chaguaramas Naval Base 36, 228
Churchill, Winston 20, 24, 175
Cold War 142, 227, 229, 230
Collins, Major General James L. 27, 35
Conn, Stetson 2, 38
Convoys 2, 9, 23, 38-39, 51, 69, 79, 89-90
Cooper, Judge Robert A. 26
Curaçao 59

Darlan, Admiral Jean François 171, 217
De Gaulle, General Charles 167, 175, 187
De Hostos, Filipo L. 147
Doenitz, Grand Admiral Karl 7, 28, 30, 36, 51, 79, 88, 90-91, 95, 99-100, 102-103, 116, 202

Engelman, Rose C. 2, 38
Eliot, George Fielding 16, 40

Fairchild, Byron 2, 38
Falangistas 127
Franco, General Francisco 126-127, 188
French Guiana 3, 25, 104, 120, 175, 187, 205, 217, 219

General Electric 66
General Motors 65
Gensoul, Admiral Marcel-Bruno 173
Greenslade, Rear Admiral John W. 186
Gough, George 73
Guadeloupe 3, 25, 34, 56, 167-170, 175, 179-181, 184-185, 187-190, 217, 219-221, 223, 228
Guantanamo Naval Base 11, 18-19, 45-46, 96, 113, 227

Hemingway, Leicester 25
Herwig, Holger H. 1-2
Hoover, Admiral John H. 64, 208, 216
Hotel Normandie 125, 224-225
Hull, Secretary of State Cordell 162, 179-180, 209

Ickes, Harold 52
Isern, Dr. Antonio Fernós 146

Jenkinson, Anthony 25
Jim Crow laws 152

Knox, Secretary of the Navy, Colonel William F. 9, 88, 115, 188, 214
Krug, German POW Hans Peter 77

Laval, Vichy French Prime Minister Pierre 187
Leahy, Admiral William D. 17, 138, 186, 205
Lunning, Heinz 75
Lusitania 9

Maingot, Historian Anthony 164
Maracaibo, Gulf of 30

Marshall, Secretary of State George 40
McCormack, Representative John W. 23
Mers-el-Kébir 173, 180-181, 185
Monroe Doctrine 3, 178-180, 182-183

News Organizations:
    Associated Press 47, 53, 89, 94, 97, 111
    Chicago Daily Tribune 58, 117-118
    El Mundo 125, 139, 149, 221
    Los Angeles Times 32, 69, 95
    New York Times 11, 25, 67, 73, 89, 110, 117, 184, 201
    Prensa Libre 95
    The Atlanta Constitution 25, 95
    United Press 67, 97
    Washington Post 7, 117

Office of Price Management 147
Operation Neuland 7, 36
Operation Paukenschlag 7
Operation Torch 7, 213, 217, 222

Panama Canal 2, 16, 18-20, 27, 31-33, 73, 87, 108, 113, 121-123, 161, 172, 192, 202, 229
Pan American Airways 184
Pétain, Philippe 167, 178
Port-au-Prince, Haiti 83

Ramírez Delgado, Captain Mario 114
Reynaud, President of the Council of Ministers Paul 170, 175-176
Robert, Admiral Georges 3, 167, 169-170, 178, 201
Rodríguez Beruff, Jorge xi, 3, 138
Roosevelt, Franklin D. 12, 14, 17, 20, 23-28, 52-53, 74-77, 82, 108, 125-126, 128, 132, 156, 170, 174-175, 182-184, 186, 188, 199, 201, 207-208, 210, 213, 215-216
Royal Dutch Shell Oil Company 24

Ships, Merchants:
    Atenas 53-54
    Barbara 45-47
    Beth 84
    Cardonia 43-45
    Ceres 111, 113
    Cities Service of Missouri 111
    City of Flint 9-10
    Colabee 47
    Colorado (interned in San Juan) 26
    Crijnssen 59
    Empire Corporal 96
    Empire Mica 71
    Femern 58
    Fort la Reine 96
    Frank Seamans 53
    Hagan 68
    Hampton Roads 62-63
    Heinrich von Riedemann 48
    Karmt 48, 54
    Lady Nelson 48
    Laguna 74, 109-110
    Lebore 59-60
    Lise 58-59
    Louisiana 7, 96-97
    Maldonado 94-95
    Mambi 114, 116
    Manzanillo 76, 95, 108
    Michael Jebsen 96
    Nickeliner 114, 116
    Moena 97
    Pennsylvania Sun 57
    Presidente Trujillo 56-57, 108
    Quentin 98-99
    Raphael Semmens 70
    Rio Tercero 70
    Robert E. Lee 92
    Samir 96, 97
    Sam Houston 70, 92, 93
    San Pablo 79, 81
    San Rafael 11, 56, 108
    Santiago de Cuba 76, 83, 95, 108
    Socrates 58
    Standella 96
    Tachirá 86-87
    Tillie Lykes 70
    Victoria 69-70
    Vimy 98-99
    Warrior 84
    William Rockefeller 70
Ships, Armed Forces:
    Bearn 169, 176-178, 181, 183, 192,

201-202, 209, 223
USS *Biddle* 111-113
USS *CG-460* 70
USS *CG Thetis* 68, 86
Émile Bertin 167, 176-177, 179, 191-192, 209, 217, 219, 223,
USS *Erie* 59
USS *Guadalcanal* 113, 226
Jeanne d'Arc 169, 176, 183, 209
USS *Lansdowne* 86
USS *Leary* 113
USS *Mulberry* 44
HMCS *Oakville* 98, 109
HMS *Pathfinder* 98
HNLMS *Van Kinsbergen* 193
Somerville, Vice Admiral Sir James 172
Standard Oil Company of New Jersey 24, 30-31, 70
Stark, Admiral Harold 175, 180, 199
St. Thomas 2, 128, 155, 187
Surinam 1, 24, 28, 30

Taft, Senator Robert 23
Tio, Juan Ángel 140
Trujillo, dictator of the Dominican Republic Rafael 11-13, 56-57, 108, 125, 230
Tugwell, Governor of Puerto Rico Rexford G. 5-6, 35, 43, 48, 82, 91, 133-134, 146-147

U-66 48, 53, 98
U-68 111, 113
U-69 58
U-94 87, 98, 103-104, 109, 120
U-108 50, 96
U-110 39
U-116 51
U-125 56
U-126 43-44, 47, 84
U-129 30, 87
U-131 61
U-134 61
U-157 68, 86, 103, 116, 120
U-159 116-117, 120
U-161 30-31, 48, 79
U-162 53, 84-85, 97-99, 104-105, 120
U-172 59-61
U-176 114, 116, 120
U-332 70
U-359 116-117, 120
U-459 50-51
U-460 51
U-505 226
U-506 101
U-507 101
U-508 76
U-512 104, 120
U-571 57
U-574 61
U-598 96
U-615 117, 119, 120
U-654 98, 103-104, 120
U-701 70
U-759 117, 120

Van Hook, Rear Admiral Clifford Evans 90
Vinson, Representative Carl 64-65

Wattenberg, Captain Jürgen 85, 98-99, 104-105
Williams, Historian Eric 163
Wilson, Vice Admiral Russell 64
Works Projects Administration 125

ABOUT THE AUTHOR

José L. Bolívar Fresneda is the author of: *Guerra, banca y desarrollo: el Banco de Fomento y la industrialización de Puerto Rico*; co-author of: *Battleship Vieques: Puerto Rico from World War II to the Korean War* — named Distinguished Academic Title — and *Fundador de la República: Federico Pérez Carbó y sus combates por la independencia de Cuba (1855-1902)*; and author and co-editor of: *Island at War: Puerto Rico in the crucible of the Second World War, Puerto Rico en la Segunda Guerra Mundial: Baluarte del Caribe* and *Puerto Rico en la Segunda Guerra Mundial: El Escenario Regional*.

Bolívar Fresneda has a Doctorate in History from the University of Puerto Rico, a Master's in Business Administration from the University of Florida, and a Bachelor's in Industrial and Systems Engineering from the Georgia Institute of Technology.

He is a professor at the Centro de Estudios Avanzados de Puerto Rico y el Caribe.

His weekly columns are published in *El Nuevo Dia*. Many of his writings and lectures are available at: www.joselbolivar.com.

www.ingramcontent.com/pod-product-compliance
Lightning Source LLC
Chambersburg PA
CBHW030231170426
43201CB00006B/178